The

SUGAR KING

of

HAVANA

The

SUGAR KING

of

HAVANA

The Rise and Fall of Julio Lobo,

Cuba's Last Tycoon

JOHN PAUL RATHBONE

THE PENGUIN PRESS

New York

2010

THE PENGUIN PRESS
Published by the Penguin Group
Penguin Group (USA) Inc., 375 Hudson Street, New York, New York 10014, U.S.A. ·
Penguin Group (Canada), 90 Eglinton Avenue East, Suite 700, Toronto, Ontario,
Canada M4P 2Y3 (a division of Pearson Penguin Canada Inc.) · Penguin Books Ltd,
80 Strand, London WC2R 0RL, England · Penguin Ireland, 25 St. Stephen's Green,
Dublin 2, Ireland (a division of Penguin Books Ltd) · Penguin Books Australia Ltd,
250 Camberwell Road, Camberwell, Victoria 3124, Australia (a division of Pearson
Australia Group Pty Ltd) · Penguin Books India Pvt Ltd, 11 Community Centre,
Panchsheel Park, New Delhi – 110 017, India · Penguin Group (NZ), 67 Apollo
Drive, Rosedale, North Shore 0632, New Zealand (a division of Pearson
New Zealand Ltd) · Penguin Books (South Africa) (Pty) Ltd, 24 Sturdee Avenue,
Rosebank, Johannesburg 2196, South Africa

Penguin Books Ltd, Registered Offices:
80 Strand, London WC2R 0RL, England

First published in 2010 by The Penguin Press,
a member of Penguin Group (USA) Inc.

Excerpt from "Ogres and Pygmies" from *Collected Poems* by Robert Graves.
Used by permission of Carcanet Press Limited.

LIBRARY OF CONGRESS CATALOGING IN PUBLICATION DATA
Rathbone, John Paul.
The sugar king of Havana : the rise and fall of Julio Lobo, Cuba's last tycoon / John
Paul Rathbone.
p. cm.
Includes bibliographical references and index.
ISBN 978-1-59420-258-2
1. Lobo, Julio, 1898–   2. Sugar trade—Cuba—History—20th century.
3. Businessmen—Cuba—Biography.   4. Cuba—History—1985–   I. Title.
HD9114.C89L637   2010
338.7'63361092—dc22
[B]   2010013790

Printed in the United States of America
1   3   5   7   9   10   8   6   4   2

DESIGNED BY AMANDA DEWEY

To Lella

For Ruby and Mo

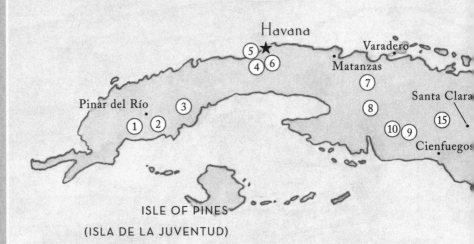

CUBA

Gulf of Mexico

Havana ★

Varadero

Matanzas

Santa Clara

Pinar del Río

③

①②

⑤
④⑥

⑦

⑧

⑩⑨

⑮

Cienfuegos

ISLE OF PINES

(ISLA DE LA JUVENTUD)

SUGAR MILLS

Lobo's Mills

(date of purchase/sale)

1. La Francia (1950)
2. San Cristobal (1944)
3. El Pilar (1951)
4. San Antonio (1958)
5. Hershey (1958)
6. Rosario (1958)
7. Tinguaro (1944)
8. Araújo (1953)

9. Perseverancia (1950)
10. El Parque Alto (1951)
11. Agabama, aka Escambray (1926)
12. Tánamo (1951)
13. Niquero (1948)
14. Pilón, aka Cabo Cruz (1943)
15. Caracas (1946/53)
16. Unión (1945/53)

Sanchez Family Mill

17. Senado

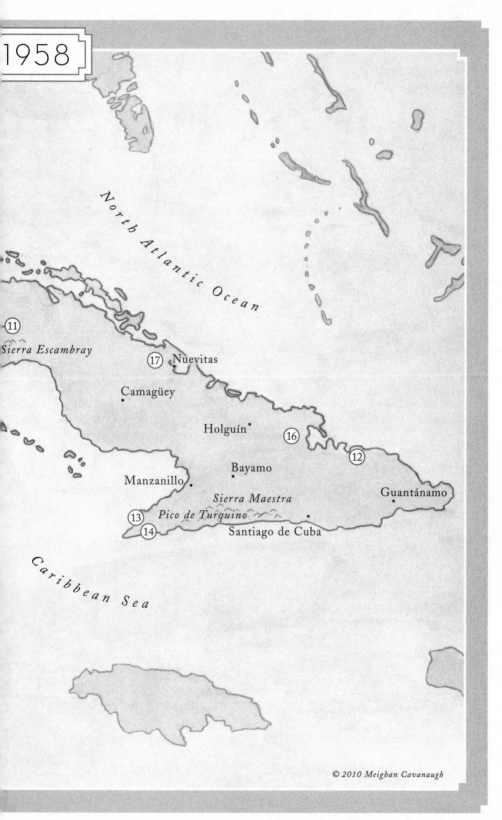

1958

North Atlantic Ocean

⑪
Sierra Escambray

⑰ Nuevitas

Camagüey

Holguín

⑯

⑫

Bayamo

Manzanillo

Sierra Maestra

⑬ *Pico de Turquino*

Guantánamo

⑭ Santiago de Cuba

Caribbean Sea

© 2010 Meighan Cavanaugh

CONTENTS

The

SUGAR KING

of

HAVANA

INTRODUCTION

C uba has known many rich men since Christopher Columbus first
introduced sugarcane to the island. At the start of the twentieth
century, one Cuban sugar baron tiled the floors of his Havana
palace with Italian marble bedded down in sand imported from the Nile.
Tomás Terry, the most successful sugar planter of Cuba's colonial years,
left $25 million on his death in 1886—not bad considering that the then
richest man in the world, William Backhouse Astor, left just $50 million.
Yet Cuba does not have to look back more than a century to find extreme
riches. In Havana today to have Croesus-like wealth is referred to as *ser
rico como un Julio Lobo*—to be as rich as a Julio Lobo. After almost five
decades of communism, Lobo's fabled wealth has become folkloric, and
he has become emblematic of a way of life that existed in Havana before
the dictator Fulgencio Batista fled the island on New Year's Eve 1958.
Julio Lobo was the richest man in Cuba before Castro's revolution did
away with such men.

Every Cuban schoolchild knows Columbus's description of the island
as being "more beautiful than any I have ever seen"; it is Cuba's first exaggeration. Yet, like so many beautiful tropical places, the island has also

suffered a commensurately cruel history. Lobo's life frames and measures a poorly understood period of that history—the sixty-odd years of the prerevolutionary Cuban Republic. He was born in 1898, the year that Cuba won independence after thirty years of fighting against Spain, and he left the country in 1960, two years after Castro's guerrillas came down from the hills. In his heyday, Lobo was known as the King of Sugar, not just of Havana but of the world, with an estimated personal fortune of $200 million, about $5 billion in today's dollars. Yet he was also a financier of such talent that Castro's government, which was Communist, asked Lobo, a full-blooded capitalist, to work for them after the revolution had begun. So Lobo captures the period's contradictions too.

I had been fascinated by those elegant, decadent, and whirligig years all my life. The curiosity was an inevitable outgrowth of my mother's exile. She was born in Havana and raised into a conventional upper-class Cuban world: her father owned a department store in the center of town; her grande dame mother presided over the home. Her haute bourgeoisie parents mingled in the same world as Lobo's, and my mother was a close friend of his younger daughter. Years later, in England, when I was a child and couldn't sleep, my mother would stroke my hair and murmur descriptions of her life in Cuba until I closed my eyes. The props for her stories of an almost dreamlike prerevolutionary life were the photograph albums that she kept on a bottom bookshelf in our living room in London. They had ragged brown leather spines, which creaked when you opened them. The stiff black pages inside were separated by tissue paper, which crackled as you turned them. Some of the photographs had slipped their bindings and stuck together. Then you could only glimpse croppings of a disappeared world: an empty table at a cocktail party, the back of someone's head, a man's ankle disappearing into a polished black shoe on a marble step. But most of the photographs had survived intact.

There she is in one faded polychrome, seventeen years old, beaming, dressed casually, sitting cross-legged on a wall, her loafers tucked under her shins. A later photograph, this time in black and white, shows her standing next to her first boyfriend. The handwritten caption underneath anticipates later boyfriends and later pages; *Victor y Yo*, Victor and I, soon

My mother. Havana, 1955.

becomes *Antonio y Yo*, and then *Walter y Yo*—the characteristic concerns of a Cuban debutante. One sequence of photographs shows her uncharacteristically demure in a white ball dress, walking down a spiral staircase at the Havana Country Club during a fashion gala. Turn the page, carefully, and there she is again, this time performing an elegant arabesque while ice-skating at Havana's Blanquita Theater on First Avenue and Ninth Street, since renamed the Karl Marx Theater. Another shows her with a group of friends standing in the shallow end of a swimming pool, cocktails in their hands, all laughing. It looks like a scene of bourgeois American life in the 1950s, perhaps in Connecticut. Only it is a photograph of a swimming pool at one of Julio Lobo's many estates outside Havana, where my mother sometimes stayed. It is also the same pool that Lobo supposedly filled with perfume so that Esther Williams, the Hollywood starlet of *Bathing Beauty*, could practice her swimming routines when she visited the island. Such are the legends from which revolutions are made, and then justified.

Even as a schoolboy growing up in London, I knew that prerevolutionary Cuba with its perfumed waters had indisputable failings. Everyone in 1970s England told me so; the message seemed to be in the very air I breathed. The red double-decker bus that I took to school each day passed a fashionable clothes shop on Kensington High Street called Red or Dead, which later became Che Guevara, and when that shop finally closed down a restaurant opened opposite, called Bar Cuba. Not only was that distant island ruled by one of the world's longest-serving heads of state—whose accomplishments in health and education I was perforce quick to recognize—everybody seemed to revere him too. It was, in that most characteristic of English emotions, embarrassing. Yet even as a British schoolboy wearing shorts, a cap, and scuffed black shoes, I wondered if Cuba's failings had been so exceptional as to have nurtured a revolution that had once brought the world to the brink of nuclear war and had dispersed my mother's family and so many others around the world. It was so at odds with the stories that my mother and her family told me, even though I recognized them as tales of privileged, upper-class Cuban life.

Then I became interested in Julio Lobo. His life and business empire helped shape the troubled years of the Cuban Republic, the very era I was interested in. If any story could reveal how Cuba worked in the prerevolutionary years and disentangle the contradictions that I held inside me, I thought, it would be his. Remarkably, there was no biography. Even the best history books mentioned Lobo only briefly. Such fragments were tantalizing; they suggested a richer and more complicated life, lived on a bigger canvas.

Some writers believed Lobo was Dutch and his name a Hispanicization of "Wolf," which lent him the ruthless air of a restless egoist, the evil speculator of Communist lore. Others praised his philanthropy. I look at his jowled hound's face in an old photograph, glowing like white stone, and see the look of a solitary man who loved reading and books. In another I examine his stilled gaze, focused on an event taking place outside the frame. Unfreeze and rewind these single images, though, and Lobo's life has the explosiveness of a Hollywood movie, one that might have screened in an elegant art deco Havana theater in the days when the city

Julio Lobo. Cuba, c. 1956.

had 135 cinemas—more even than New York. Lobo swam the Mississippi as a young man, fenced in duels, survived assassins' bullets, was put against the wall to be shot but pardoned at the last moment, courted movie stars, raised a family, made and lost two fortunes, and once told Philippe Pétain, Marshal of France (perhaps apocryphally but also in character), *Je veux dire un mot: merde*, shit.

More than all this, though, is how Lobo's life mirrored, in extreme Technicolor, the repeating rises and falls of the Republic. This is more than a literary conceit because Cuba, as is often said, constantly relives its past. Certain events and themes—bewitchment, prosperity, decline, revolution, exile, and return—repeat themselves in recurring cycles that are as old as the island itself. Telling are the first words of the memoir that the Condesa de Merlin, "Cuba's Scheherazade" and a Havana-born ancestor of Lobo's first wife, wrote 170 years ago as she watched the island appear on the horizon from the poop deck of her sailing ship: "I am enchanted!" Yet telling too, for me, was the apprehension she felt disembarking again in Havana after a long absence. The condesa, whose father's house survives in the Plaza del Mercado, worried she might not know the city after living in Paris for forty years. Worse, she feared that it might not know her.

I had held that same fear inside me for many years, teasing away at its anxieties in only a tangential way. After college, I left England and worked as a journalist and economist in Colombia, Mexico, and Venezuela. I was searching, of course, for echoes of my mother's family's prerevolutionary Cuban past: the music, some of the food, the fast almost slurred Spanish, the mixture of social casualness and Latin formality, the beauty of the mornings before the heat burned away their color, and the unforgettable smell of guavas rotting in the sun that always draws one back to the Caribbean, as Gabriel García Márquez once put it. Yet while I spent a decade living around the Spanish Caribbean, I never visited Cuba. One reason I stayed away from the island, I told myself, was to inoculate myself against tropical lyricism. When I eventually traveled to Cuba, I wanted to be able to see through its vehement sunsets, palm trees, and romantic colonial past in the same way that I wanted to see beyond the glamorous life captured in my mother's photographs. More important, I avoided Cuba because I feared that I wouldn't recognize the island from her stories. Worse, I feared that it wouldn't recognize me.

Finally, I began to make short trips. For a while, in the 1990s, I even ran a newsletter out of a London basement that described the travails of the Cuban economy and what it meant for the island's future. It was a confusing time. The collapse of the Soviet Union had ended Moscow's thirty-year patronage of Fidel Castro, and many exiles hoped that his revolution would finally end too. In Miami, expectations swelled of an eventual return and, among the older generations, maybe even something of those glorious prerevolutionary days as well. In Havana, Castro deftly turned those expectations in on themselves. Even as the Cuban ship of state seemed to be sinking beneath him, he conjured up a mythic image of prerevolutionary Cuba, only it was an abject vision rather than golden. There can be no going back, he exhorted. *¡Socialismo o muerte!*

I objected to Fidel; I objected also to the feverish hatred of many exiles' anti-Castroism. From England, the vehemence of their passions, their bitterness and rage, sometimes had the feeling of a flat-earth society. Publishing the newsletter, I became briefly what others called an expert. I gave talks in Europe and the United States, at universities and in government departments. Yet the more expert I became, the less truth I recognized in much of what I read or heard. Even the best commentary from the island was driven by a government-sponsored sleuthing that aimed to uncover a malignant force—usually capitalism. Yet neither did I recognize a rounded picture in the sugar-coated memories told to me in Miami. In time I came to see that exile imposed a kind of selective censorship, a critical numbing that might otherwise tarnish glorious memories, which can be all that is left when everything else is taken away.

When I began to write this book, Castro was still strong enough to stand in the midday sun and give two-hour-long speeches. As I finished it, he had vanished from view, suffering from a severe intestinal disorder, having handed power over to his then seventy-six-year-old younger brother, Raúl. "The Revolution is stronger than ever," Raúl had proclaimed in 2009 on the occasion of the revolution's fiftieth anniversary. "Glory to our heroes and martyrs." News photographs of the event showed Raúl dressed in military uniform, addressing an invited audience of elderly army officers under the hot Caribbean sun. It was a significant symmetry: half a century before, a young and charismatic lawyer, Fidel Castro, had taken power in Havana, displacing a corrupt dictator, while an old general, President Eisenhower, sat in the White House. Now, fifty years later, a young, charismatic, and black lawyer was in the White House, while an aging white general, Raúl, sought to maintain the dream of a flawed revolution in Cuba.

Far too much, whole libraries, has already been written about the revolution. As the island limps toward the end of the Castro brothers' rule, what interests me more are the events, some of them very distant, that preceded and caused it. A famous historian once suggested to me that recovering a better knowledge of this history could play as crucial a role in the country's future as it did in Russia before the fall of the Soviet Union. If so, thinking about Cuba's "before," therefore, also meant thinking about its "after." In

Havana, a wise friend counseled me that this was a vain and preposterous task. Better, he said, to ponder something else, as so many people had been proven so wrong over so many years. I took only half his advice, though, as it is impossible not to wonder about Cuba's future, even if I have done so through the lens of its past.

I think of a speech that Winston Churchill gave in the House of Commons when Neville Chamberlain died in 1940. The great British wartime prime minister—who first saw action in Cuba as a young man, where he began to smoke large cigars—described to Parliament how history, "with its flickering lamp, stumbles along the trail of the past, trying to reconstruct its scenes, to revive its echoes, and kindle with pale gleams the passion of former days." So it is that my concern here is with the flickering myths, untold stories, and simple facts that surround the life and businesses of Cuba's once-richest man, Julio Lobo, and the Cuba in which he lived. Sometimes I have turned to my mother's family to help reveal these half-hidden times. This is not out of any sense of vanity. Rather it is because they also played a small but not always insignificant part in helping shape a prerevolutionary way of life that supposedly heaped so many inequities on the island that civil war, the exile of a tenth of the population, and the enduring struggle of those who remained were somehow inevitable. Shrunken, their stories form part of a calumnious revolutionary narrative that diminishes prerevolutionary Cuba's past—sometimes inglorious, sometimes the opposite. Expanded and brought back to life, they also suggest happier futures.

PART ONE

One

A TRISTE TROPICAL TRYST

❦

There's a violent smell of sugar in the air.

—Agustín Acosta, *La Zafra*

On October 11, 1960, Ernesto "Che" Guevara summoned the sugar magnate Julio Lobo to his office at the Cuban central bank in Havana. It would be a midnight meeting—odd, but not entirely unusual during those chaotic times. The Cuban revolution was barely eighteen months old, an inexperienced government was remaking the island, and, anyway, Guevara often worked through the night, if only to keep up with events and as an example of his iron will and revolutionary discipline. Stories abounded in Havana of foreign dignitaries turning up at the central bank for a meeting at three o'clock in the afternoon, only to be told that their appointment was at three in the morning.

Lobo hastily called his lawyer and consigliere, Enrique León. "Che wants to see me," he said, and hung up the phone. León arrived shortly after at Lobo's neoclassical mansion in Vedado, a residential area west of the old city. The two men conferred briefly in the hallway and then left in Lobo's car, driving east through the Havana night.

Lobo sat behind the wheel of the humming black Chrysler, his lawyer by his side, the car headlamps picking out a few sudden faces on dark

Lobo in his trading room.

street corners. Curiously, in letters written a few months earlier, Lobo had often depicted himself driving a machine. Sometimes it was a vast ship, Lobo the captain on the bridge, confidently guiding his empire through the rough waters of revolution toward a safe harbor. "We are going through very difficult times, though I am a confirmed optimist," he wrote in one letter. Yet just as often the machine was a more modest contraption. "I often feel like a man on a bicycle: if I stop, I will fall. . . . I am quite incorrigible and in a way irrepressible," he wrote in another. There is a sly humor to these words, a quiet, self-confident gloss, which suggests that when Lobo drove to meet Comandante Guevara that evening he was resolute, hopeful, perhaps deluded about what would happen, but certainly not scared. Fearful was not Lobo's style.

Short and stern-faced, balding but with a strong jaw, Lobo was then the most important force in the world sugar market. Sixty-two years old, he was known as an authoritarian empire builder who handled about half the six million tons of sugar that Cuba produced annually. As part of his personal fortune, he controlled fourteen sugar mills in Cuba, owned hundreds of thousands of acres of land, and had trading offices in New York, London, Madrid, and Manila. He also owned a bank, Banco Financiero, an insurance company, shipping interests, and the telecommunications firm Inalámbrica. Some of Lobo's wealth derived from his father, who had fled to Havana from Venezuela in 1900 and entered into a profitable partnership with a Spanish private banker and importer. But Lobo had built most of his empire subsequently, by himself. A speculator and financier of genius, one business competitor observed with grudging awe that Lobo "doesn't sense a trend, he smells it."

There was more to Lobo than money and sugar, though. He was a cultured man, famed for his private collection of art and the largest holding of Napoleonica outside France, including one of the emperor's back teeth and his death mask—the revealing interest of a man who sought to project his ambition and sense of self by association with Napoleon. Politically, he was an enigma. Lobo's wealth made him an emblem of prerevolutionary Cuban capitalism, of everything that Fidel Castro would eventually purge from the island. By marriage, he was linked to the remarkable Condesa de Merlin, who had married one of Napoleon's generals and whose uncle, Lorenzo Montalvo, the Julio Lobo of his day, introduced the first steam-powered sugar mill to the island. With a due sense of dynasty, Lobo had even christened his eldest grandchild with cane juice in the same baptismal font that Napoleon had used to baptize his own son, the king of Rome. Yet despite these trappings of imperial grandeur, Lobo had also fiercely opposed the corrupt Batista government. "We didn't care who overthrew Batista so long as somebody did," he once said. A receipt nestled among Lobo's papers and stamped with the swirling red and black Cuban revolutionary logo shows that he had even helped finance Fidel Castro's rebels a few years earlier. That, however, was before Castro's plans and eventually his Communist leanings had been fully revealed.

On that October night, as Lobo drove across Havana, less than two years had passed since President Fulgencio Batista had packed his bags on New Year's Eve and fled to the Dominican Republic, his departure cheered by nearly all. Since then much of Lobo's land, although not yet his sugar mills, had been confiscated by the rebel leader whom Lobo had once helped. Yet Lobo still refused to leave the island, unlike many other middle- and upper-class Cubans. Nor had Lobo lent his voice to the growing flood of anti-Castro protest. Now Che Guevara was going to put Cuba's King of Sugar to the test.

LOBO'S CAR TURNED DOWN LINEA and toward the old city. October lies in the middle of the hurricane season, when high sea spray can spume over the broad wall that lines Havana's waterfront drive, the Malecón. Lobo took this route every day to his office in the old town. The view from his car was little different from that evoked in Graham Greene's *Our Man in Havana*, published two years before:

> The long city lay spread along the open Atlantic; waves broke over the Avenida de Maceo and minted the windscreens of cars. The pink, grey, yellow pillars of what had once been the aristocratic quarter were eroded like rocks; an ancient coat of arms, smudged and featureless, was set over the doorway of a shabby hotel, and the shutters of a night-club were varnished in bright crude colors to protect them from the wet and salt of the sea. In the west the steel skyscrapers of the new town rose higher than lighthouses.

Yet while Havana looked the same, the atmosphere was quite different from that absorbed by Greene and depicted by his fictional British vacuum cleaner salesman, Wormold. A year ago, Havana was still an exciting city. It boasted casinos, nightclubs, bordellos, and a fabled live sex show popular with tourists in Chinatown's Shanghai Theater, which featured a performing stud called "Superman." Drugs such as marijuana and cocaine were freely available. It was Havana's very seaminess—existing in a parallel universe to Lobo's world and that of my mother's parents—that had attracted Greene. "In Batista's day, I liked the idea that one could obtain anything at will, whether drugs, women or goats," he wrote.

Indirectly, Lobo himself had been involved in the manufacture of

Havana's steamy nightlife, sensual glamour, and racy reputation. Alongside his other business interests, Lobo had helped finance the Riviera and the Capri, two of the glitziest casino-hotels to open in the 1950s, when Cuba was known as the American Riviera. The latter had a flashy casino and a rooftop swimming pool; the former, a futuristic Y-shaped tower overlooking the sea, was the first major Havana building with central air-conditioning, and had an egg-shaped windowless casino at its heart. Both hotels' links to the Mafia were an open secret. George Raft, the movie tough guy of the 1930s and '40s, worked as a greeter at the Capri, glad-handing and joking with customers. Havana's hotels would later gain further notoriety in the movie *The Godfather: Part II* when one breezy terrace, overlooking the Caribbean, provided the setting for a Mafia birthday party and a famous scene in which sixty-seven-year-old mob leader Hyman Roth carved up his birthday cake—a map of Cuba—for the assembled guests.

A grayer and more militaristic mood had fallen over the city since Castro assumed power. The atmosphere was tense with invasion rumors. The purifying uniformity of the revolution that visitors such as Jean-Paul Sartre and Simone de Beauvoir would comment on had started to set in. The days of privilege for Cuba's upper and middle classes were coming to an end, and increasing numbers were leaving on the ferries and shuttle flights to Miami. As many as sixty thousand had already left by the late spring when the northerly *vientos de cuaresma,* or Lenten winds, would have whipped the bay of Havana into whitecaps, leaving the city feeling airy and fresh and at its most beautiful. Indeed, around that time Lobo had written to a former girlfriend, the daughter of a Danish aristocrat, that her invitation to stay with him remained a standing one. He warned, though, that Havana would not be as pleasant as she remembered. "Gracious living has practically disappeared," Lobo wrote. "We are entering a period of austerity." Then he had added the surprising afterthought, ". . . which may have some good points and perhaps even benefits in the long run." Lobo, the billionaire businessman, could be a revolutionary patriot too.

By October, the roulette wheels were still spinning in Havana's big hotels, but most of the prostitutes were off the streets and the world of exclusive yachts, private beaches, and casinos had disappeared. Instead, groups of uniformed and armed *guajiros*, poor farmers from the Cuban interior, chanted revolutionary slogans and roamed the streets. In the hotels, trade and cultural delegations from the Soviet bloc took the place of American tourists. Simone de Beauvoir wrote that compared to her visit the year before, there was "less gaiety, less freedom, but much progress on certain fronts." In the half-empty Hotel Nacional "some very young members of the militia, boys and girls, were holding a conference. On every side, in the streets, the militia was drilling."

MY MOTHER'S FAMILY, Sanchez y Sanchez, would soon join those sixty thousand Cubans who had already left the island—although my mother had moved abroad several years earlier for reasons that had nothing to do with politics. After the Havana cardinal visited her house to explain why her wedding to an American divorcé the next day had to be broken off, she went to live in New York. There she reveled in the anonymity of a big city, free from what she viewed as the claustrophobia and pettiness of upper-class Havana's social mores. She got a job as a buyer for the department store Bergdorf Goodman, and met my father, an Englishman, who worked in advertising. They returned to Cuba to get engaged a year and a half before the revolution and were married in Havana on September 3, 1960, just five weeks before Guevara summoned Lobo to his midnight meeting.

In many ways, my mother was typical of her generation, which included Julio Lobo's younger daughter, María Luisa, one of her circle of closest friends. Like most Cubans, my mother and her family hated the Batista regime. Although she lived a privileged life, she viewed the revolution with excitement. During a trip to the island from New York in early 1959, she turned out, dressed in revolutionary red and black like much of Havana, to watch Castro's victorious army enter the city.

"Havana was buzzing, there was excitement and hope in the air," she wrote in her diaries. "The whole country seemed to be behind Fidel. Cuba

Wedding of John Rathbone and Margarita Sanchez.
Havana, 1960.

was free of Batista and all that he represented, we were on our way to true democracy. . . . It was a spectacle that I shall never forget. He and his young bearded men all dressed in battle gear, walking beside their army vehicles, being kissed and hugged by the multitude, red carnations strewn in their path. . . . We were jubilant."

In the following days, my mother watched the televised show trials of Batista's henchmen, led by Che Guevara, and succumbed to the hypnotic chant of "*¡Paredón! ¡Paredón!*," "Against the wall! Against the wall!" She felt there was no real difference between a mock and a real trial, as the outcome would have been the same. But my grandfather viewed the proceedings and subsequent firing-squad executions with distaste, and maintained that they marked the beginning of the end.

He was right. Much had changed when my mother married my father in Havana eighteen months later. Their wedding was a strange and beautiful occasion, a melancholy mingling of Cuba's old ways with the uncertainty of the new. The ceremony was held in the family home; the drawing room was converted into a chapel, the arrangements completed with the help of Milagros, Miracles, the firm that traditionally handled Havana high-society weddings. My mother's nieces acted as flower girls and her nephews walked in front of them dressed in white drill suits, hair slicked into neat partings, carrying lit candles. Only a few people attended, partly because the revolutionary government had banned large private gatherings, partly because most of the people my mother knew had already left the island.

A few weeks later, Castro nationalized my grandfather's department store on the corner of San Rafael and Amistad streets in central Havana. All of his employees followed him as he was marched out of the shop. They insisted that they would not go back to work without him. But there, in the middle of the street, at the foot of the two-story red art deco building topped with the elegantly silver-lettered name of his business, Sanchez-Mola, he convinced them to return. It would be dangerous not to. Shortly afterward, everyone in my mother's family—her mother, her father, her sister and brother with their spouses and seven children— packed a suitcase each, took their scrapbooks filled with memories of a life that had already passed, and boarded a scheduled flight for the United States.

LOBO WOULD HAVE KNOWN hundreds of stories like this. Indeed, he had made plans for his own family to emigrate. Leonor, his elder daughter, who was married to a Spaniard, had stayed behind for now, but his younger daughter, María Luisa, with an American husband, had already left.

Lobo's car pulled up outside the central bank, a columned building on Lamparillo Street in the old city. It lay just three blocks west of Lobo's sugar trading house, Galbán Lobo, on San Ignacio. This was the nerve center of Lobo's sugar operation and, lest anyone needed reminding, a huge mural surrounded one of the colonial building's leafy inner patios.

A machetero *from a Galbán Lobo mural, Old Havana.*

Like the fourteen Stations of the Cross that lined the interior of the baroque cathedral nearby, its 170 square meters of mosaic illustrated key
stages of the sugar harvest. From planting to milling, it showed scenes of
workers and oxen in the fields under high Cuban skies, all in the elon-
gated and clean art deco style then in favor. In another paean to sugar,
Lobo had earlier also commissioned a sugar symphony, and envisaged it
beginning with the song of plowmen breaking the earth and ending with
the fading sound of sirens as ships carried their cargos of sugar away from
Cuba and over the sea.

Lobo and his adviser León got out of the car and headed into the
building. Lobo walked with a limp due to a murder attempt fourteen years
before that had blown a four-inch chunk out of his skull after he had
supposedly refused to pay $50,000 in protection money to a gang of

Cuban mobsters. The machine-gun bullets had also shattered his right leg and left knee. One bullet had lodged near his spine.

Inside, the central bank was a mess. Guevara had only been central bank president for a few weeks. But the once-pristine financial building was dirty and disorganized, with papers all over the floor.

Guevara certainly made for an unlikely central banker. He loved telling the story of how he got the job. Supposedly, at a cabinet meeting to decide who should be the new bank governor, Fidel Castro had said that what he needed was a good "*economista.*" Guevara stuck up his hand, much to Castro's surprise. "But Che, I didn't know you were an economist!" "Oh, I thought you said you needed a good *comunista,*" Guevara replied. The response gives a good measure of his priorities. He casually signed the new Cuban banknotes "Che," and only a few days before Lobo's meeting had cut short an architect in the middle of a presentation of his plans for a new state-of-the-art central bank building. The foundations had already been laid at a site on the seaside Malecón, and because of the autumn storms, as the architect explained, the thirty-two-story American-style skyscraper needed hurricane-proof windows too. "Look," Guevara said. "For the shit we're going to be guarding here within a few years, it's preferable that the wind takes the lot."

None of this boded well for Lobo. But when he climbed the stairs, Guevara greeted him politely in the doorway of his office on the second floor. "Señor Lobo, it is good of you to come," Guevara said. "Apologies that we bothered you at this late hour." They shook hands, and Guevara invited Lobo into the room and to take a seat.

I read in Lobo's diaries how he felt surprised by Guevara's cordial, if formal, mood. He mentions this twice in his written recollection of the evening, having probably expected more brusque treatment. Lobo also stressed, again twice, that he and Guevara had never met before, although their paths had already crossed several times indirectly, and in ways that illustrate the intimacies and deeply personal social networks that still characterize Cuba.

Celia Sánchez, Fidel Castro's confidante and secretary since the earliest days of the revolution, was the daughter of the dentist on one of Lobo's eastern plantations, El Pilón. Several years before, Lobo had built what he called "a dovecot" on the estate where Sánchez, an eccentric woman in her thirties, could "sleep, write or dream," as he put it. She was also a close friend of Lobo's daughter María Luisa. Together, they had set up clinics and other help for indigent sugar workers at and around Lobo's mill.

Guevara had also stumbled through one of Lobo's eastern cane fields on December 5, 1956, shortly after landing in Cuba for the first time. It had been an inauspicious introduction to the island. The sea voyage that Guevara had made with Fidel Castro and eighty other rebels across the Gulf of Mexico had been an unmitigated disaster. It had taken seven days, instead of five. Then, weakened by seasickness, the rebel force had landed at the wrong spot on Cuba's coast. Their navigator had fallen overboard just before landing, and the boat had run aground on a sandbar, turning their arrival in Cuba into more of a shipwreck than a landing. The expedition had then slogged through mangrove swamps, jettisoning most of its equipment, leaving the rebels with only rifles, cartridge belts, and a few wet rounds of ammunition. They had tried to satisfy their thirst and hunger by chewing on sugarcane in the fields of Lobo's Niquero mill. Foolishly, they also left a careless telltale trail of bagasse, or cane peelings, all over the place. The next day they were ambushed by Batista's forces. In the melee that followed, Guevara was hit by a ricochet bullet in the neck. Blood poured from his wound, and Guevara, who had trained as a doctor, believed himself mortally wounded and went into shock. "I lost hope for a couple of minutes," he wrote in his field diary.

Of the eighty-two men who came ashore, only twenty-two ultimately regrouped in Cuba's eastern mountain range, the Sierra Maestra, where they were helped by Celia Sánchez and a truck driver from one of Lobo's plantations, Cresencio Pérez.

Now at the central bank, Lobo and Guevara faced each other for the first time. They could not have looked more different. Che, the guerrilla, the bearded thirty-two-year-old revolutionary, was dressed in green battle fatigues, a revolver slung across the glass desk. This was the man who would later explain to Cubans that the reason visiting Russians were so poorly dressed and often smelled of sweat was that deodorant and soap were superfluous in a genuine revolution.

By contrast, Julio Lobo, the arch-capitalist, was a dapper dresser who used Eau de Cologne Imperiale de Guerlain and hosted literary parties at his favorite sugar mill, Tinguaro, which he believed to be the "Cliveden of Cuba." While Guevara was the face of Cuba's "New Man," Stakhanovite in his labor and fervent in his belief that individualism should disappear, Lobo was a friend of Hollywood stars such as Joan Fontaine, Esther Williams, and Maurice Chevalier, who often stayed on his estates.

Lobo and Guevara were opposites in so many ways, yet they had more in common than what might have at first been apparent. Both were lucid and deeply rational men. Guevara looked to the various intellectual constructs of international communism. Lobo hewed to the modernizing enlightenment ideals that had shaped the beliefs of some of his Cuban sugarcrat predecessors. Both were loners. Guevara's terrible asthma attacks often kept him apart from others, while his mordant Argentine humor didn't always gel with the more flippant Cubans. As for Lobo, he used to say that Napoleon was a lonely character, and so was he.

Both men were austere in their habits. Lobo might have lavished gifts on others, and decked out his house with original paintings by European masters like Sisley, Utrillo, Vlaminck, and Turner, but his personal life was almost spartan. His bedroom had once been a reconstruction of his bachelor quarters from student days, with a simple wooden bed, a side table, and a solitary chair—similar to the simple living arrangements of Guevara.

Both men were candid to the point of brutality. Both engendered fierce loyalty. Contrary to the usual stereotype of the heartless and absent sugarcrat, Lobo visited his plantations often and was well regarded by employees. After the revolution his workers even sent delegates to Havana to request that Lobo's mills not be nationalized. Like Guevara, Lobo was scrupulously honest too. He claimed to have refused the secretaryship of the Cuban treasury under a former president on the grounds that the administration was too corrupt.

Indeed, that night in October 1960, Lobo believed that Guevara had ostensibly sent for him to talk about certain monies owed in connection with the construction of the Riviera and Capri hotels. But Guevara, with his usual frankness, explained to Lobo that he and his aides had examined Lobo's accounts and found no irregularities. "Not a stain, or a blemish," as he put it.

"What did you expect to find?" Lobo interjected.

". . . and because of that," Guevara continued, ignoring Lobo's question, "we have left you to last."

Lobo said nothing; he was used to playing the cipher and, facing Guevara, he put on his bravest face to hide the uneasier emotions that ran underneath. Some of these are revealed in a letter written the year before, when Lobo had quoted the eighteenth-century Irish writer Oliver Goldsmith: "Man wants but little here below, nor wants that little long." Might Lobo, the billionaire who lacked for nothing, have had an early presentiment of his own fate? Perhaps. Lobo, who had suffered morbid thoughts lately, then mused that everyone would be so much better off if they could only remember the wisdom of Goldsmith's words. Typically, Lobo then changed tack quickly, shrugging off any sense of fatalism, and asked rhetorically: "But what is the point of life if there is no desire to create, to build, to construct? Probably only fishing and hunting with a g-string, as our millennial ancestors used to do." The letter closes suddenly on a firm note, Lobo apparently having made up his mind. "One of the most human of all desires is to perpetuate what you have created, and I think for the time being that is the business at hand."

That was indeed the business at hand for Lobo that night at the Cuban central bank. When Guevara said that he had been saved until last, Lobo knew that his time had come, the moment when his bicycle might wobble, when the great machine of the empire that he commanded from the bridge of his ship might flounder, when it might sink.

GUEVARA FINISHED HIS PREAMBLE. He had led the talking for the past half hour, and had even complimented Lobo on his honesty, albeit in a backhanded way. Lobo sat in silence in an overstuffed chair, his adviser Enrique León beside him. A clock ticked on the mantelpiece; it was twelve thirty at night and, outside, most of the city was asleep. Lobo waited for Guevara to continue.

Sitting in that government room in downtown Havana, papers scattered around the floor, Lobo knew that to the revolutionary government his sugar mills were an emblem of two hundred years of subjugation, not only of slaves but of a whole country. That March, Guevara had called sugar "economic slavery." Yet Lobo also knew that to unpick and roll back Cuba's sugar history would take more than the bureaucratic stroke of a pen, or even a revolution. "*Sin azúcar no hay país*," without sugar there is no country, is the famous, damning phrase that had continued to define the island—even more, perhaps, than Fidel Castro's revolution would come to do.

Cuba and sugar had been tied at the hip since the British had captured Havana in 1762 and thrown the island open to the slave trade. Sugar, the wealth it generated, and the slaves that its plantations required had set the course of the country's economy, culture, and political life ever since. The slaves who worked in its sugar plantation economy had transformed Cuba from a mainly white and Spanish colony into the more variegated island it is today. It was the riches of sugar that alternately acted as an engine for, and then a brake on, Cuba's independence movements of the nineteenth century. It had also shaped Cuba's ambivalent relationship with the United States. Agustín Acosta had struck a deep chord with his anti-epic poem *La Zafra*, the harvest, published in 1926, in which wagons carrying sugar to U.S.-owned mills

... ford the streams ... they cross the mountains
Carrying Cuba's fate in sugarcane.
They go towards the nearby colossus of iron:
They trundle towards the North American mill,
And as though complaining on their approach,
Loaded, heavy and replete,
The old carts creak ... creak.

Acosta's poem is an emotive portrait of resignation and woe, yet it is also a more complicated and richer picture than it first seems. Those "colossuses of iron" of which Acosta writes, magnificent monuments to capitalism, were not all foreign-owned. Sugar mills also defined Cuba's own restless, entrepreneurial, and worldly planter class. In the eighteenth century, there were resourceful planters like the creole economist and anglophile Francisco Arango y Parreño, who traveled, cloaked and with a false mustache, to Liverpool in 1788 to spy on England's latest technical developments such as the steam engine. Just as Arango and his patrician friends, often viewed as the fathers of the nation, looked to the world for technical and political inspiration, so too had Cuba looked to them as banners of modernity and sources of homegrown power in opposition to its then colonial master, Spain. In one typical incident in 1834, General Miguel Tacón, the survivor of various wars of Latin American independence and one of Cuba's most reactionary governors, was outraged that railways should come to Cuba before Spain, and freely expressed his contempt for such "Anglo-Saxon ironmongery."

Cuba's liberal creole tradition continued through the nineteenth century when some planters, including some of my ancestors, fought in the wars of independence against Spain. Many years later, Fidel Castro cast his revolution against the Yankee imperialists as a continuation of their heroic struggle. Finally, in the twentieth century, there was Julio Lobo, the embodiment of Cuba's erudite and cosmopolitan sugarcrat elite, indeed its apogee, a man who had used his sugar wealth to wrest the industry out of foreign hands, who knew better than any the byways of the international sugar trade, who had even supported Cuba's homegrown creole rebels just as some of his predecessors had done. To separate sugar from Cuba, Lobo knew, one might as well chop away the arterial system of a body and imagine that it could somehow survive. So despite Guevara's plans for Soviet-style industrialization and self-sufficiency, Cuba's revolutionary government needed sugar. Because of that, it also needed men like Lobo.

This was the aim of Guevara's meeting that night. Castro was going to seize Lobo's sugar mills in a few days and Guevara wanted to convince

Lobo to stay—and keep his expertise—in Cuba. Alfredo Menéndez, who administered the revolutionary state's sugar mills, knew in advance the offer that Guevara was going to make Lobo: a relatively modest salary and the right to keep one of his palatial homes. "We really didn't want him to leave," said Menéndez. "All that talent . . . was what Che wanted."

Lobo's skill was without doubt. A few months before, the sugar market had tumbled after U.S. refiners had refused to buy Cuban sugar in the hope that it might weaken the revolutionary government. Lobo had found himself stuck with a large cargo of sugar on board the Japanese freighter *Kimikawa Maru* that no one wanted to buy. Lobo had then executed an almost insanely audacious move: he cornered the global sugar market and rammed his prices down the U.S. refiners' throats. To Guevara, the memory of Lobo's business daring must have chimed with the military heroism of the revolution's own rebels.

Lobo first ordered his agents in London and New York to start buying sugar futures to put the price up sharply. In the Galbán Lobo office, telex machines chattered out cables addressed to SUG, Lobo's code name, which then trolleyed past his desk on a special conveyor belt. As the market began to climb, other producers around the world decided to withhold their raw sugar in the hope that prices would climb higher still. Then Lobo launched his masterstroke. He lifted the phone and reserved virtually all the cargo space available on the charter ships that carried sugar to the United States. He was now in the position of being the only major seller of sugar to the United States. Lobo proceeded to tighten the noose around the necks of the North American refiners by forcing up his price.

At first the U.S. buyers held fast. Then Pepsi-Cola bowed and meekly paid 5.40 cents a pound for sugar that only a few days ago had sold for 5.30. Twenty-four hours later, Pepsi bought again, this time at 5.70. Others followed suit. In two weeks, Lobo pushed up the price by almost a half to 7.58 cents. For the Cuban revolutionary government, this was capitalism fighting capitalism at its best. It was also why Guevara had left Lobo until last.

. . .

LOBO'S LEG BOTHERED HIM; he shifted in his seat. He knew that Guevara was laying the ground for a proposition, and readied himself calmly for it. "I will not whine," he once said, "business is not a kissing game."

Guevara leaned forward in his chair, still formally polite, firm, and clear. In so many words, he told Lobo that the time had come for him to make a decision: the revolution was Communist, and he, as a capitalist, could not remain as he was. Lobo could either stay and be a part of it, or go.

"It is impossible for us to permit you, who represent the very idea of capitalism in Cuba, to remain as you are," Guevara said.

Lobo was used to playing all the angles as a speculator. He may have remembered Napoleon saying, "I am sometimes a fox and sometimes a lion, the whole secret . . . lies in knowing when to be the one or the other." Lobo played fox. He pointed out that Nikita Khrushchev believed in the peaceful coexistence of the two systems of production, capitalism and communism. Guevara replied that that was all very well *between* nations, but not *within* one. Stymied, Lobo asked Guevara how he could integrate himself with the revolution. Guevara laid out his terms.

Lobo would become general manager of the Cuban sugar industry under the revolutionary government. His job would be to nationalize all aspects of the business: commerce, agriculture, and industry. He would lose all his properties but keep an income from Tinguaro—some $2,000 a month, about what Lobo paid the mill's manager.

In the past, Lobo would have relished the opportunity for modernization that such an offer represented. He had often been frustrated by labor laws that were enlightened, by any American standard, and that had protected Cuban jobs from mechanization, even if there were few such jobs to go around. "Harder to get rid of a worker than of a wife" was the cruel joke told by American businessmen over daiquiris at the Havana Biltmore. ("Harder to find a job than a wife" might have run the workers' riposte.)

But the offer was also absurd. As León told me many years later, remembering that night: "Julio wasn't really interested in money. Perhaps he was interested in power, although this was really a by-product of his businesses. What he was interested in was creation—almost in an artistic sense."

León had just celebrated his ninety-first birthday when I talked to him in his modest three-room apartment on the twenty-third floor of an anonymous-looking condominium that overlooked Miami's South Beach. His body was thinned by age, and his powerful glasses looked strangely large on his face. Yet León also moved easily around the room when he got up from his sofa to consult a Cuban almanac from the 1950s, and his eyes, magnified by the giant lenses, sparkled with intelligence and vivid memories. The notion that Lobo might surrender his empire, his "creations," to anyone else, let alone a Communist government, was "impossible," as León put it, "bizarre."

Lobo stalled for time. He told Guevara that it would be hard for him to change his ways, having worked for so long, as he had, in a capitalist system. He would like a few days to consider the offer, and would give a definitive answer next week.

"Unfortunately, I leave for Russia in a few days," Guevara said. "I will send two of my colleagues to discuss the matter with you and see if we can reach an agreement."

They both stood up. They had been talking for at least two hours. Guevara accompanied Lobo to the door of his office and they shook hands again, still formally polite.

"I look forward to meeting your colleagues" were Lobo's last words to Guevara as he turned to leave, although Lobo had already made up his mind. Outside on the street, as he got back into the car, Lobo wondered if his refusal to reveal that decision had consigned him to prison, or worse.

THE CARIBBEAN IS SOMETIMES described as an American Mediterranean. Both seas face a barbarous and modernizing north, and are cupped by patriarchal and older cultures to the south. In that light, Cuba becomes a kind of Caribbean Sicily—an important sugar producer in its own right—and Havana a version of Palermo, another city, as Goethe once said, with an impossible-to-describe beauty. That may be why when I think about Lobo at that moment, leaving the central bank, considering his future but still straddling two epochs divided by a revolution, my mind cannot escape the similar image of Don Fabrizio. He is the Prince of Salinas in Giuseppe di Lampedusa's magnificent novel of Italian revolution and Sicilian decline, *The Leopard*. Specifically, my mind keeps returning to a scene toward the end of the book that with its faded colors and sense of decay exudes a smell of autumn and the sound of rustling leaves.

Don Fabrizio attends a ball that marks the end of the Palermo social season and where the few hundred people who make up the inbred world of aristocratic Sicily are gathered. At his peak, Don Fabrizio had been a model of health and vitality, who governed his province with uncontested authority. Now he is in decline, as is his class.

A mob of young women huddled in an explosion of rustling taffeta on a pouf in one gallery—"incredibly short, improbably dark, unbearably giggly"—remind him of monkeys. He imagines them swinging from the chandelier and throwing nuts and showing their behinds to visitors below. The older women, dressed in waves of silk that smell faintly of violets, do not please him either; several had been mistresses. And the conversation of the counts, princes, and dukes of his generation, all wearing stiff white shirts and black tailcoats, is about money only. Don Fabrizio, who is more interested in mathematics and astronomy, takes this as another sign of the rise of coarser values that have come to permeate Sicily following Garibaldi's overthrow of the Bourbon kings, the unification of Italy, and the birth of the new Republic. The prince slips away from the gay music to a silent library, where a print of Jean-Baptiste Greuze's gloomy painting *The Death of a Just Man* catches his eye. He reflects on his own mortality, the passing of one regime for another, the tombs of his ancestors, and makes a mental note to repair their graves. Suddenly the library door opens and Don Fabrizio's favorite nephew interrupts his reverie. "Uncle, you're looking wonderful this evening. Black suits you perfectly. But what are you looking at? Are you paying court to death?"

Cuba at the dawn of the revolution is contained in this moment: in Sicily's dust and oppressive heat, the formal decadence of its parties, the fading seignorial grandeur of the prince's estates, and his nostalgia for a way of life submerged after years of gentle decline by a heroic leader. That Garibaldi, the first revolutionary to wear a red shirt, also mastered the techniques of guerrilla warfare in a series of military actions in South America, and his romantic rallying cry "*Roma o mòrte*" was echoed by Castro's own exhortation "Fatherland or Death" many years later, only amplifies the resonance of the image.

Lobo's life is there too, condensed that night in the distress of the more refined and pessimistic prince. Both men are incompatible with the new age, and shrunken by it. The prince's ball finds its counterpart in the parties Lobo liked to give at Tinguaro, in the smallness of Havana's social register that my mother sought to escape, and in the feelings and events that pressed down on Lobo after his interview with Guevara.

When Lobo returned from the central bank, he climbed the stairs of his Havana home and shut himself away in his bedroom above the Napoleon library to think. Only a few months before he had been saturated with power that smelled as pungent as a fox; now the scent had left him. Lobo's daughter Leonor banged on his door several times that night but her father never let her or anyone else in. Instead, he sat immobilized and silent in a house filled with Napoleonic symbols of demise. There was the letter that Marie Antoinette wrote to her children before she was guillotined: "4-½ in the morning—farewell children, farewell, no more tears to cry!" There were the thousands of books that described the life of Lobo's hero, including his final years in exile, slowly dying, on the desolate and windswept English prison island of St. Helena. And there was the bronze copy of Napoleon's death mask that Lobo kept on a special desk by a bookshelf in his library.

Lobo spent hours locked in his room, in a house filled with these morbid reminders of the emperor's fate, recriminating with himself over plans wrongly laid, miscalculations made, trying to recalibrate his life. That night, and for much of the following day, a man who had once ruled vast swaths of Cuba and had taught himself to sign checks with both hands so as to save time was paralyzed by inaction. Lobo simply couldn't conceive that his empire had gone.

The great difference between the death-gazing of Lobo and Don Fabrizio is that the Sicilian nobleman understood that his life was coming to an end and was reconciled to his mortality and the new age. He knew, in the book's famous phrase, that everything was going to have to change in order to remain the same. Lobo had also thought a lot about death, having confronted a would-be assassin's bullets. But while the prince was prepared to compromise with the new order to save his family's fortunes, Lobo had just learned that he could not and that he would have to reinvent everything as he was about to lose it all.

Other planters and businessmen had already taken their money out of Cuba. The powerful Falla Guttiérez family had moved $40 million abroad, fearing revolution, yet Lobo had continued to invest in Cuba to the last. In part, this was sheer hubris. Lobo ignored early warning signs of trouble, such as a bomb that damaged Tinguaro in 1957. In part, it was because Lobo believed, like so many others, that he could somehow control Castro, or that the Americans—only ninety miles away—would. Conversations Lobo said he had had with Allen Dulles, the head of the CIA, may have convinced him of that. In part it was because Lobo believed deeply in Cuba and was critical of anyone who did not. And in part Lobo continued to invest in the island because events moved so quickly that it soon became too late to stop. Even in early 1960, the year that followed Castro's triumph, Lobo had insisted that letters of credit worth millions of dollars for sugar cargos dispatched to the United States should be remitted to Havana rather than to his office in New York. "If I don't do that, the Revolutionary government will take everything," he explained to León at the time. Now it was clear that the government would take it all anyway.

Lobo finally regained his composure the following evening. The next day, he went to his office in Old Havana. The building sat atop a network of old tunnels that had been used during the colonial years to store gunpowder and food. Lobo had a vague plan to gather up what he could and use the tunnels as secret storerooms. When he arrived, the building was roped off, guards were posted around the doors, and a former office boy wearing a militia man's uniform was sitting behind his desk, his feet up, smoking a large cigar.

"Now we've got you where and how we want you," he said to Lobo, without getting up.

"How is that?" replied Lobo, standing in front of his old desk.

"Stripped of everything, almost naked."

"*Chico*, I was born naked, I will probably die naked and some of the happiest moments of my life were when I was naked," Lobo shot back, and then left.

That afternoon, Lobo caught a crowded airplane flight to Mexico and from there to New York. He took with him a small suitcase and a toothbrush. He left behind his El Greco paintings, his palaces, his vast enterprises, and his locks of Napoleon's hair. Lobo was then sixty-two, eight years younger than Don Fabrizio, and if not an old man, then at an age when most people think of retiring rather than starting again. The day after his departure, the Cuban government nationalized his sugar assets and made itself "custodian" of almost all the art and artifacts, leaving Lobo with virtually nothing.

Lobo foresaw all of this after his midnight meeting with Guevara. As he had readied to leave the island, he told his secretary, "This is the end." Of course it was not the end, it was just another beginning, and everything that came before or that follows after flows from this thought.

Two

THE BETRAYAL OF JOSÉ MARTÍ

*Liberty is a condition, a way of being, not a real and
positive thing, and that is why we see how a civilization
which takes liberty as its creative principle without
troubling about anything else, leads to no result
or to negative results.*

—Bishop Josep Torras i Bages,
La Tradició Catalana, 1892

always wanted to de-exoticize Cuba—land of palm trees, championship
women's volleyball, and machete-wielding rebel heroes. Yet whenever I
traveled to the island, it seemed to require me to step into another state.
Once, in 2004, my nerves about the forthcoming trip even prompted a
fever. It came on while I waited in an airport lounge in Madrid. It rose as
the Iberia flight crossed the Atlantic, and by the time the plane landed at
José Martí airport in Havana, I was jittering with cold sweat. The night
drive into the city passed in a hot blur—I was normally so attentive to the
details: the sugar train railway tracks that crisscrossed the road into town,
the billboards carrying political messages on the outskirts of Havana, the

finishing loop around the one-way system circling the university, the persistent elegance of the art deco mansions that surrounded the campus, and
the old graffito Abajo Batista Asesino, "Down with Batista the Assassin," still proclaiming its message in faded red paint on a white wall at a
crowded intersection at the head of Neptuno Street.

I checked into a state-run hotel and went to my room. The brown
carpet was blotted with stains and there was a threadbare patch one step
in from the door. The shabby brown curtains smelled of damp, as did the
brown bedspread and the brown chair with a dark patch on the headrest
that marked where others had sat before. I lay down and turned the knobs
of the broken radio set built into the headboard that dated from the
1950s. I switched on the modern television made in Japan and then
clicked it off when I found only static and dancing black specks on the
screen. I flicked through a copy of the state newspaper *Granma* that I had
picked up in the lobby, and a small story caught my eye. It paid tribute to
Ignacio Agramonte, a hero from Cuba's war of independence against

Spain, and described in four crisp paragraphs how a group of sixty international students from thirty-five foreign countries had accompanied a
small band of aging rebels from the Sierra Maestra on a march to the
Cuban battlefield where Agramonte had died 170 years before. I put
down the newspaper and opened the window. I listened to the sea breeze
swish past the building; it sounded like a long dress trailing on the floor.
Hot and thirsty, I went downstairs to ask at the bar for ice. A waiter
emerged from the kitchen, shrugged, and said there was none. "I know:
for a bar man to have no ice is like a *puta* not having a *coño*," he admitted
without mirth. I went back to my room, pulled the sheets over my head,
and sweated into a dreamless sleep.

It wasn't always so dismal, although I had felt similarly despondent
the first time I visited Cuba thirteen years before. I remember a cool
September weekend, Havana gray with gentle rain, and a muffled city—as
though covered with a thick layer of dust. It was the beginning of *el
periodo especial*, the special period, the time of severe rationing that followed the end of Soviet subsidies in 1991 and has never formally ended.
I wandered through Havana's back streets and felt safe in a way I never
would have in Caracas, Bogotá, or Mexico City. Yet as I walked around
Havana for the first time, I also heard no music filter through the open
doorways of people's homes and saw none of the Spanish Caribbean's
usual bustle. The city lacked buoyancy. Compounding the disillusionment was my companion, a well-meaning English girl. Like her, I saw
the pathos and crumbling beauty of the once-grand buildings that lined
the Malecón. I saw the irony of the dilapidation of my grandfather's
old store, the roof caved in, just two naked mannequins standing in a
cracked display window on San Rafael Street. But I also felt anger and,
outside Havana's Museum of the Revolution, had launched into a neo-
conservative tirade about the merits of capitalism that had surprised
me. My companion rose to the revolution's defense—its education and
health care, the greater Latin American poverty elsewhere. Yet she too
then felt confused, and struggled through the rest of our short visit with
a splitting headache, as she tried to reconcile the ambiguities we saw
around us.

. . .

DESPITE MY GRANDFATHER'S DEPARTMENT STORE in Havana's former shopping district, the wealth of my mother's family was rooted, like so much else on the island, in sugar—not as encompassing as Lobo's but still substantial. Just like Lobo's family, it was also contained in one man: Bernabé Sanchez, owner of the Senado sugar mill in Camagüey. The first of my mother's forebears to arrive in Cuba, Don Mateo Sanchez-Pereira, a Spanish soldier, had landed in Havana at the dawn of the seventeenth century from Mexico's Yucatán. Predating that even, my maternal grandmother's family is distantly related to the bastard conquistador Vasco Porcallo de Figueroa, who arrived in Cuba in 1511. Figueroa joined Hernando de Soto in the invasion of Florida in his doomed quest to find the fountain of youth, wisely turned back to Cuba to found Camagüey's capital, among other cities, and made an immense fortune from Indian slaves, marrying the Taíno princess Tínima, daughter of the local *cacique* Camagüebax. The stories of such men are fables, though. Three hundred years later, Bernabé, my great-great-grandfather, is the first figure to really come alive in family lore. He is the benign but epic patriarch of our imagination.

A tall and wide-shouldered man with a broad chest, thick mustache, and close-cropped silver hair, Bernabé was born in 1841, when Cuba was still under Spanish rule. His father was a merchant in the provincial port of Nuevitas, and when he retired, Bernabé took over the business, expanded it, and in 1883 built his first sugar mill, Congreso, the Congress. Bernabé later rechristened it Senado, the Senate, another name that hints at his political beliefs. A progressive modernizer, like Lobo many years later, Bernabé achieved a modest renown after he used sturdy burlap sacks to bag sugar at Senado. These replaced the wooden boxes made from imported North American pine that had been the norm before; although expensive, U.S. pine was preferred to Cuban woods, such as sandalwood or mastic, which scented stored sugar with their resin. While an apparently small innovation, Bernabé's sacks changed the way sugar was handled, stored, shipped, and measured.

Bernabé's mill was also among the first of the newly mechanized sugar

Bernabé Sanchez at Senado with his eldest son, Bernabecito, and eldest grandson, Bernabé.

operations to spring up in eastern Cuba after the abolition of slavery in 1880. Such mills were called *centrales*, literally centrals, which gives a sense of the system of lands, machines, transport, workers, and credit that revolved around the biggest of them. Their hub, the nucleus of every *central*, was the *batey*, a town square around which were arranged the huge buildings that housed the grinding machines, the railway shunting yards where cut cane was unloaded into wooden carts pulled by oxen or locomotives, the homes of the mill owner and senior managers, as well as the provisions warehouse, perhaps a church, a school, and a hospital. Behind these buildings, in smaller one-story houses, lived the skilled and semi-skilled technicians who measured the pressure of the rolling mills, the heat of the boilers, the viscosity of the sugar solution, the rate of crystallization, and the polarization of the sugar—a measure of its whiteness. Farther out lay the barracks of the field hands.

Centrales were more like factories than farms. The largest were industrial giants, such as the American-owned Las Delicias or the United Fruit Company's Boston, which looked like cities set down on the edges of vast rolling fields of cane. There, foreign managers lived with their families in mosquito-screened bungalows set in gated communities, a world apart from the rest of the island. By contrast, *cachimbos*, the smallest mills, re-

The batey *at Senado.*

tained a sense of almost artisanal production. At the start of every harvest, in a creole vision of the sugar idyll, the yeoman planter fired his boiler, and tufts of white smoke would float over Cuba's green and peaceable countryside. Senado lay between these two extremes.

Among my family, Bernabé is known fondly as Papa Né. His local nickname, though, was *El León de Camagüey*, the Lion of Camagüey. And, like one of the stud bulls he also raised around the mill—including a rather special breed called the Santa Gertrudis, a kind of walking steak—Bernabé allegedly sired tens of illegitimate children, as well as two legitimate families of his own. His first wife, María de la Caridad, my great-great-grandmother, had six children and died when Bernabé was in his mid-forties. His second wife, Elizabeth Laurent, the twenty-two-year-old daughter of the French governess at Senado, bore him six more. Bernabé looms in my mind like one of Robert Graves's great-bellied ogres of yore:

So many feats they did to admiration,
   with their enormous lips they sang louder than ten cathedral choirs,

and with their grand yards
they stormed the most rare and obstinate maidenheads.

Whatever his virility, Bernabé was also a clear-thinking man. "One has to be lucid" is the parting instruction in a letter that he wrote over a century ago. Written in a cramped hand on thin onionskin paper that is stained with age and damp, the letter is bound with 499 others in a copy-book, through which a bookworm has since drilled a neat hole from the first page to the last. Although they were written at the end of the nine-teenth century, what strikes me each time I read them is their enduring relevance. Because of the way time seems to repeat itself in Cuba, when Bernabé wrote all those years ago of the U.S. president's "silly games" and the Cuban revolutionary government's "foolish rules," his words seem strangely pertinent today.

The first letter is dated September 28, 1898. Bernabé, then fifty-seven years old, has just returned to the island after spending two years in New York. It is also a significant date: one month before Lobo was born, one month after peace has been declared after three decades of fighting for independence against the Spanish, and a marker for the new Cuban Re-public which is about to begin.

CUBA, "THE EVER FAITHFUL ISLE," had been the last great bastion of Spain's vast empire in the Americas. The patriots had fought a first bloody ten-year war against Spain that began in 1868, when the planter Carlos Manuel de Céspedes freed the 30 slaves on his small sugar estate in east-ern Cuba and added them to his army of 117 men. Céspedes then torched the surrounding cane fields: "Better . . . that Cuba should be free even if one has to burn every vestige of civilization" was his rallying cry. An in-conclusive truce was signed in 1878, and the patriots rebelled again the following year, but their offensive soon fizzled out. The next revolt began in 1895, organized from New York by José Martí, Cuba's "Apostle of Independence." Martí's great feat was to unite a host of factions both within Cuba and its émigré communities in the revolutionary cause, and his success persuaded two celebrated leaders from the first war, Máximo Gómez and Antonio Maceo, to come out of retirement and take up arms against Spain again.

Martí, an extravagantly gifted poet and diplomat, was the most brilliant and contradictory of Cubans. He came of age in Havana during the Ten Years' War, and was as passionate about independence as he was in his hatred of slavery. Aged sixteen, he founded his first newspaper, *Patria Libre*, and was later sentenced by the Spanish to six years' hard labor after writing a letter that accused a friend of being a traitor to the independence cause. Although a central figure in Cuban history, Martí spent most of his forty-two-year life outside the island in exile. Most photographs show a short and unsmiling figure with a high forehead and big mustache, dressed in a funereal black suit and white shirt. But Martí also had a wonderful sense of humor, as the Cuban-American writer Alfredo José Estrada wisely points out. So he might see the joke in the frightfully solemn reverence that has since attached to his name—although not always, nor by all.

Bernabé, for one, disagreed with this ardent figure, who wore an iron band on his ring finger with the word *Cuba* carved on its rim. Nor was Bernabé the only planter to do so, although Bernabé was the only planter (or so I believe) that Martí called an "Enemy of the Revolution." These are harsh words from a man whom Cuban history has since elevated to the stature of saint, or a writer whose most famous poem, "La Rosa Blanca," "The White Rose," enjoins the reader to turn the other cheek. Bernabé and Martí certainly had political reasons to disagree—the clash between Bernabé's material interests and Martí's revolution is an enduring one. Yet their differences were also marbled with personal reasons, the most important of them being the simple fact that Bernabé came from Camagüey, the hot and flat ranching province three hundred miles east of Havana.

Camagüey held a special place in Martí's revolutionary plans, especially those of his senior military commander, Máximo Gómez. "Without Camagüey, the Revolution will be nothing," he told Martí. This was largely due to the general's long admiration of the province and Camagüey's unusual place in Cuban history. Accessible during the colonial years only by boat or a hard slog along rutted roads, Camagüey's jagged coastline meant its inhabitants placed more importance on watching out for threats of pirate attack than on obeying the letter of distant Spanish laws. Its grasslands and wild forests were also better suited to banditry and ranching than to sugar. To the west, closer to Havana, planters were wont to sit on thrones, built by slaves, surrounded by the Spanish flag and coat of arms, their feet and hands kissed by old Negroes when they asked their owners for a blessing. Camagüey, by contrast, lived free of the slave-owning tradition that haunted much of the rest of the island. Its landed families formed huge clans that intermarried with each other, and were sometimes described as the "Wasps" of Cuba: White, Aristocratic, Spanish, in their tastes rather than allegiances, and Proud. All this gave the province a "special, freedom loving mentality," as the great Cuban historian Manuel Moreno Fraginals described it. It also explains why Camagüey's creole cattle barons fought so bravely and willingly in the first rebellion against the Spanish. Agramonte, still a venerated revolutionary figure as the *Granma* news story I had read in my hotel bedroom showed, came from Camagüey. So did his right-hand man, Colonel Enrique Loret de Mola, Bernabé's brother-in-law and my other Cuban great-great-grandfather. One of their most daring feats of arms occupies a place in Cuban revolutionary mythology similar to Lord Cardigan's charge of the Light Brigade at the Crimea in English history—although Agramonte's attack with the colonel at the head of Camagüey's famed cavalry corps against a larger Spanish column in 1871 met with success and only one death. "Trumpeter sound the charge!" Agramonte had ordered. Outnumbered almost four to one, the Cuban troops routed the Spanish, rescued a captured general with a slight wound to his right hand, and reports said the rebel cavalry's movements were so synchronized that they appeared to act "as if just one body." Gómez, who was Dominican, had fought alongside such men during his first battles against the Spanish, and remembered them proudly. "Without Camagüey's support I will feel like a warrior, but not a true revolutionary," he told Martí.

Martí had a more anguished relationship with Camagüey. Although he never visited the province, not once in his life, it often occupied his thoughts. In the twenty-eight volumes of his collected works, Martí mentions it 110 times; Puerto Príncipe, as its capital was then known, another 31; and people from the region on innumerable occasions. His wife, Carmen Zayas-Bazán, the daughter of a rich landowner, came from Puerto Príncipe. But Martí was a generous womanizer, theirs was an unsuccessful marriage, and when it finally fell apart in 1881, Carmen left her husband in New York and returned to her family home in Camagüey. She took with her their only child, José Francisco, whom Martí never saw again.

From that moment on, Camagüey became for exiled Martí a place forever linked not only with his lost country but also with his lost son. In Manhattan, Martí's brilliant and restless mind continued to feed Cuba's independence movement. He raised funds. He organized. He wrote, prolifically. It was through Martí, also the New York consul for Argentina and Paraguay, that South America learned about North America—not just the bustle of Yankee life, which Martí admired, but its cult of wealth too, which he detested. "I have lived inside the monster, and know its entrails" is his famous quote, taken from a letter written the day before he died. Yet, as Martí admitted to a friend in New York, "My mind is not here with me, but in Puerto Príncipe, where Carmen is and my son—the distance almost forces me to go to Cuba."

Martí shaped this loss into his first published book of poetry, *Ismaelillo*. Its tender poems are filled with feverish longing, and have titles like "My Kinglet," "Son of My Soul," and "Fragrant Arms":

> . . . two small arms
> that know how to tug me,
> and hang tightly
> from my pale neck
> and of mystic lilies
> weave me a chain!
> Forever far from me,
> Fragrant arms!

But Martí also wrote in his diaries, "I love my duty more than my son." He remained in New York, plotting revolution from the junta's dingy office near Wall Street.

Martí is central to Cuban history, especially Castro's vision of it, which goes something like this: For four centuries the country was a colony of Spain, with the last thirty years spent fighting for independence. For sixty years after, Cuba was a neo-colony of the United States. It was only in 1959, with the triumph-of-the-Revolution, that Cuba achieved true independence, or "dignity," as Castro has called it. The rhetorical vanishing point of this "one-hundred-year struggle" is that it elevates Castro's revolution by making it the logical culmination of a fight for freedom that is embodied in the haloed but eventually thwarted figure of Martí. "The Revolution begins now," Castro had proclaimed to a jubilant crowd in Santiago in January 1959. "This time, luckily for Cuba, the revolution will truly come into being." That is why "patriot" leaders have ever since been elevated to the heroic status of Agramontes, while anyone with an opposing point of view has been condemned and vilified. "Within the Revolution, everything; against the Revolution, nothing," Castro was fond of saying. Yet little was predestined about Cuba in the 1890s, or in 1958 on the eve of Fidel Castro's revolution, or even now. Nothing is immutable, except perhaps geography. Time can reduce even history's most ardent revolutionary ideas to ashes.

Indeed by 1893, fifteen years after the Ten Years' War ended and a decade after Bernabé set up his first mill, the heroic Camagüey that Gómez remembered had changed. Age had softened the revolutionary resolve of the province's old war heroes. Gómez himself was in his sixties, Agramonte had died, and his adjutant colonel, Loret de Mola, had sworn never to raise arms again, as he could not bear for his wife and children to suffer another war. The devastation of the fighting that followed Céspedes's exhortation to ruin in the first war of independence had left many of Camagüey's once-proud families homeless, penniless, and with only their names—often on the headstones of graves. Now in his fifties, the colonel was more interested in prosperity and reconciliation than revolution, sentiments captured by what was then called the Autonomist movement. Although now often forgotten, the Autonomists remain of current interest as they represented a stream of political thought, honorable rather than heroic, that held out the possibility of a different Cuba, a country-that-might-have-been, rather than the blood-drenched cradle of revolution it became.

"Headed by Cubans of great bravery," as Martí described them, the Autonomists did not seek independence from Spain or annexation by the United States. They looked around South America and saw that independence had not brought the continent what it promised: Colombia was locked in civil war, so too Venezuela, while Mexico was a dictatorship. Instead, they imagined Cuba as part of a Spanish commonwealth, took Canada or Australia as their models, and were, in general, middle-class reformists who wanted the same rights in Cuba as the Spaniards already had, but no more. They hewed to a middle path of self-rule. They were Cuba's "Third Way," and were particularly strong in Camagüey—Rafael Montoro, their most eloquent proponent, was Camagüey's representative to the Spanish court.

Bernabé and the Colonel supported the Autonomist project. In May 1893 they formed part of a group of Camagüeyano notables that wrote to Martí in New York, condemning the idea of a new war of independence. Their unsigned letter began by expressing the usual courtesies and then politely explained that a successful rebellion required that all Cubans have a revolutionary spirit "beating in their hearts" and "only a few felt that." Bernabé's opposition subsequently went even further when he actively foiled a revolutionary plot the following spring. It was led by Enrique Loynaz del Castillo, a twenty-two-year-old patriot rebel from Camagüey who idolized Martí. In New York, Loynaz had recently given Martí a photograph of his son, José Francisco, taken on on a rocky Camagüey hilltop beside a rough tree branch hung with a Cuban flag. The picture showed Martí's son flanked by Loynaz's friends, standing "in a rough line, like a squadron of rebels." Martí kept the photograph on his cluttered writing desk.

In March 1894, Loynaz sailed from New York with a smuggled cargo of two hundred Remington rifles and 48,000 bullets hidden under the seats of six trams in the ship's hold. After landing at Nuevitas, he disembarked the gun-laden trams at the wharf. Proudly sporting a silver-plated revolver he had bought a month before at Tiffany's, Loynaz then liaised with Emilio Luaces, a Ten Years' War veteran who worked with Bernabé. In New York, Martí had urged caution on his brave if impetuous protégé. But in Cuba, Loynaz was flush with the early success of his mission. Feeling his blood rising, he told Luaces about the smuggled cache of arms, adding that he wanted to start a revolution "right there and then." Luaces panicked at the thought that the revolutionary junta in New York was planning to start war in Camagüey and told Bernabé of Loynaz's plans. Uncertain as to what to do, they handed over the munitions to the Spanish, having passed word to Loynaz, who fled at dawn in a small boat. "No well-established person in Camagüey wants to back any revolutionary plans," Bernabé later said.

Landing at Key West, Loynaz wrote to the revolutionary junta's military leaders about what had happened. Gómez hesitated when he read the report, and the uprising, originally planned for later that year, was delayed. "The main reason for the setback is that I haven't received assurances from Camagüey, which I consider the central nerve of the Revolution," Gómez told Martí. Martí also knew that Cuba wouldn't respond to calls for an uprising so long as the Autonomists' hopes of reform might become a reality. "Martí was very clear about that.... War will be impossible," Gómez later wrote. "It was only afterwards, when the [Autonomists'] reforms collapsed and Cuban disenchantment grew, that revolution became a real possibility. And that's what we did."

The war of liberation, launched on April 11 the following year, had an uncertain start. Martí put in with a small group of men at a rocky beach on the far southeastern coast of Cuba to begin the offensive. They landed on the same stretch of coast as Castro would on the yacht *Granma* sixty-one years later, and their landfall was as equally haphazard. "The boat is lowered," Martí wrote in his war diary:

> Hard rain as we push off. Wrong direction. Opinions on boat varied and turbulent. More squalls. Lose rudder. We set course. I take the forward oar ... We strap on revolvers. Making for the cove. A red moon peers out from under a cloud. ...

Martí and his men trekked inland though bramble-covered hills, living off sour oranges, forest honey, and wild pig. It was sixteen years since Martí had last been in Cuba, and he reveled in the countryside and the delights of being on the march. "Climbing hills together makes men brothers," he wrote. He met with his generals, Gómez and Maceo, at the sugar mill La Mejorana at the beginning of May, but the three leaders squabbled. Six pages torn from Martí's diary that have never been recovered supposedly record a violent argument. Whatever happened, they parted afterward: Maceo for the mountains, Martí and Gómez inland to prod Camagüey into war.

Seeing what was coming, but believing that fighting was not the answer, Bernabé sailed for New York the following year. He left behind Antonio Aguilera, his son-in-law, charged with safeguarding the mill, a canny decision given the impeccable rebel credentials of Aguilera's father. Francisco Vicente Aguilera, a fabulously wealthy eastern planter, had sold his vast estates to fund the Ten Years' War and died penniless in New York in 1877 (but was fittingly rewarded during the Republic with his portrait on Cuba's 100-peso bill). Bernabé's eldest son, Bernabécito, also remained in Cuba to join the rebel *mambí* ranks.

The rebels made steady progress west across the island, singing the rebel anthem, "Hymn to the Invader," which Loynaz had composed: "Every march will be a victory, the triumph of good over ill." They gathered support as they marched, especially after General Valeriano Weyler, the Spanish commander in Havana, adopted radical tactics to blunt their advance. Weyler ordered his troops to force huge numbers of Cuban civilians into fortified settlements, where thousands of the *reconcentrados* died in what were in effect the first concentration camps. Having drained the countryside, Weyler then declared all of Cuba outside the Spanish-held towns a free-fire zone. The rebels responded by burning farms, destroying mills, and slaughtering cattle. Thousands of acres of sugarcane and tobacco went up in flames. Soon much of the population was starving, bitterly angry, and passionate in its support of independence.

Martí never saw these glimmerings of victory. He died five weeks after landing, shot by the Spanish in a surprise skirmish, conspicuous on a white horse, a life of Cicero in his saddlebags. Eager to prove his fighting ability, and against Gómez's instructions, Martí had rushed forward into the line of fire. Ironically, a raw recruit called Angel de la Guardia, literally guardian angel, rode by his side. Like so many other nineteenth-century Romantic poets, Martí had anticipated his own death. Seven weeks before he was shot, Martí wrote a brief letter to his son: "I leave for Cuba tonight: I leave without you, even though you should be by my side. If I should disappear on the way, find with this letter the watch chain that I used when I lived. Farewell." José Francisco was then sixteen. Learning of his father's death, he immediately abandoned school, joined the revolutionary forces, and rose through the ranks to become a captain. It is said that he rode the same white horse from which Martí fell.

Three years later the U.S. Army intervened. It was the culmination of an impulse that had been building almost since the days of the founding fathers. In 1821, after the United States won control of the Florida peninsula, Thomas Jefferson wrote to President James Monroe that he had "ever looked on Cuba as the most interesting addition which could ever be made to our system of States." The image of Cuba as a ripening fruit that would one day fall into the hands of Uncle Sam had endured ever since. A cartoon published in *Puck* magazine in 1897 had shown him standing beneath a fruit tree with a basket, staring intently at "Cuba," a ripe plum hanging from an upper branch. On February 15, 1898, the United States finally gained its pretext when the USS *Maine*, a battleship on a "friendly" visit to Havana, exploded mysteriously in the harbor. Two months later, encouraged by William Randolph Hearst's newspapers ("Remember the Maine. To hell with Spain"), the United States declared war on Spain. Ostensibly it was to help the Cuban rebel cause. But at the Spanish surrender only a few months later, the authorities raised the American flag over Havana—not the Cuban. And when Spain and the United States signed the treaty ending the war, the Cubans were not even invited.

Just before he died, Martí wrote a note that his comrades had pinned to a pine board at their campground. "It is my duty to prevent through the independence of Cuba, the USA from spreading over the West Indies and falling with added weight upon other lands in Our America." If Martí had survived, he would have become Cuba's first president and history might well have been different. Instead, in dying, he left a figure so disturbingly necessary in Cuban history: the martyr. Judged by his own high standards, Martí's plans had also failed.

THIS THEN WAS THE CUBA that Bernabé found when he returned to Camagüey from New York in 1898, the autumn of peace. Martí was dead, and Weyler and the rebels had left the country a smoking ruin. One journalist, traveling from Havana to Matanzas, described it as a "country wrapped in the stillness of death and the silence of desolation." It was a beautiful land, he said, but he did not see in it a single house, man, woman, child, horse, mule, cow, or dog—not one sign of life, except for an occasional vulture circling in the air. After three decades of fighting for independence, the island was as quiet as a grave.

At Senado, Bernabé found that many of the houses, sheds, and warehouses around his *batey* were roofless. Nearby, where once had stood a village, there were only scattered piles of rubble and charred wood. Bridges had fallen and the railway lines that snaked though Bernabé's land and had once carried cut cane to the mill from the fields were unusable: the wooden sleepers had rotted. A yellow fever epidemic broke out.

It began to rain. Bernabé grew anxious. Deep in debt, he was desperate to prepare for the *zafra*, which begins with the dry season in December. But the weather was like a curse. "We are living in the mill but it is raining so much that it is impossible to do anything, even leave the house," he wrote to his brother. "You know what the rain is like here." As rainstorms pounded the fields and the world around him turned brown—red-brown earth, damp-brown wood, black-brown clouds—Bernabé's frustration became palpable. His handwriting grew smaller, more urgent, and he broke off his words at the margin of the page, continuing on the line below:

. . . it is still rai
ning . . .

Papa Né.

When the rain paused, Bernabé set to work immediately, rebuilding the mill's chimney. The oxen he hoped to find to plow his fields were dead. So he bought mules that had pulled Spanish cannon only a few months before. He tried to hire disbanded Cuban troops to work in the coming *zafra*. But the fever epidemic complicated his plans; most men remained camped in distant hills, where they were safe from disease and could also forage for food. Then one of Bernabé's grandchildren died of malaria, and his son Pedro caught dysentery. "It is true that Rome was not built in a day," a despondent Bernabé wrote to his banker George Mosle in New York. "But Rome did not have debts to pay, nor was it subject to the caprices of nature and the consequences of war."

Martí was right to call Bernabé Sanchez an "enemy of the revolution" when he learned of Loynaz's betrayal to the Spanish. But Bernabé was not a selfish old fool. He was a pragmatist and a survivor. At the very least, autonomy would have preserved the island from the ravages of a dreadful war and the ambiguity of U.S. military rule that followed it. Alejandro Rodríguez, a young soldier who had carried the Camagüey Autonomists' first message of protest to Martí in New York and then went on to fight as a general against the Spanish, confided as much to a friend after the war. "You know that abandoning my interests and family, I was among the first to reach for arms and support the revolution. . . . But I who have served my country, for which I have sacrificed everything, cannot even have my family by my side for lack of means to support it. I cannot embark on any business or reconstruct my farm due to lack of funds. I see myself perhaps forced to emigrate in search of bread in a strange land." In letters written from his mill at around the same time, Bernabé had similarly contemplated his age, his looming poverty, and the destruction of his mill and his country. "Is this the price of a Free Cuba?" he asked sarcastically. Many Cubans have wondered the same ever since.

Three

A SENSE OF HOME

❦

*The house is no longer known to me,
it does not speak to my memories.*

—THE CONDESA DE MERLIN, *Viaje a la Habana*

Havana's Prado is a magnificent shaded boulevard nearly a mile long that stretches from the city's central park down to the sea. In the colonial era it was a fashion catwalk, the place to be seen, the women wearing white muslin, the men dressed in frock coats, linen trousers, and ties, all riding in *volantes* with a liveried black footman in high boots and silver spurs driving the horse-drawn carriages up front. Later, my grandmother remembered the evenings in the 1920s when men still promenaded up one side and women down the other, while orchestras played among the Prado's open-air cafés and laurel trees.

At the end of 1898, though, when the occupying U.S. Army set up camp in Havana, the Prado became a tent city. Habaneros looked on with bemusement and some horror as U.S. soldiers pitched canvas, drove tent pegs into tree beds, and strung their laundry between the lampposts. General John Rutter Brooke described the city as a place of "desolation, starvation and anarchy." The mast of the wrecked USS *Maine* could still be seen sticking out of the harbor water, and the remnants of the old *recon-*

centrado dwellings, grim tenements, lined the city walls. Yet Havana had also escaped the worst of the fighting and even then was what it remains today, one of the Americas' great capitals, a city of cobbled streets, graceful balconies, and grilled windows, the names of past sugar barons carved into massive stone lintels above studded wooden doors.

Cubans were humiliated on New Year's Day 1899 when they saw the Spanish flag come down over the old fortress in the harbor and the U.S. flag take its place. "Neither a colony nor a free state, Cuba suffers all the disadvantages of the former and none of the advantages of the latter," the old Autonomist newspaper *El Nuevo País* lamented. When the U.S. military governor moved into the former captain-general's residence, they also wondered who their real enemy was and what progress really meant. At the same time, they marveled at the speed with which the occupying troops transformed the island.

In Havana, the first car arrived, then the first tramway, and the Mutual Incandescent Company turned on the city's first electric streetlamps. Drains were dug and modern bathrooms installed in old Spanish homes. Public buildings were repaired, streets paved, dock facilities improved, and new telephone lines installed. The scruffy bathing huts and fishermen's houses that lined the city seafront were razed, the ground leveled, and the beginnings of a seafront corniche, the famous Malecón, built in a broad sweep across the bay. Three-story houses rose in new suburbs to the west, and a capitol building was commissioned for a site outside the old city walls that had been used as a garbage dump in colonial times. Looking much like the White House in Washington, D.C., but thirteen feet taller, it cost $20 million to build—enriching at least one generation of politician-contractors—and squatted athwart the Prado, top-heavy with bronze and Italian marble.

It is hard now to imagine the wealth that sugar once created—especially as it has become such a mundane commodity. After the war, there may not have been the same fortunes to be made in Cuba as during the colonial years when the Condesa de Merlin said Havana life recalled *les charmes de l'âge d'or*. Still, there was great excitement in the United States about the island's prospects. Cuba was variously depicted as "virgin land," a "new California," "a veritable Klondike of wealth." The destruction of the war also created stupendous business opportunities, and American carpetbaggers, speculators, and investors descended on the island.

Old Cuban businesses struggled during what became known as the "second occupation." Racked by malaria, Bernabé contemplated selling Senado to one of the foreign syndicates buying land around Camagüey for "$2 or $4 an acre, depending on the want of the owner." The weather still seemed bent on ruining his enterprise: after the rain came drought and fires that crackled through the cane. Mortgaged, sick, and without enough money to attend his eldest son's wedding in Havana, Bernabé wrote in a moment of despair: "The life of an *hacendado* is hell."

Yet Bernabé did dig his mill out of the mud and eventually prosper. For this, the "enemy of the revolution" was lauded as a patriot. It was a sign of how fast Cuba had changed. The new Republic had many deficiencies. The first president, General Tomás Estrada Palma, was honest but ineffective, drawn from the rebel ranks like the Cuban presidents that followed him, and all better warriors than governors in times of peace. Worst of all was the new constitution's hated Platt Amendment, by which Washington arrogated the right to intervene after U.S. troops left in May 1902—they would twice return. Even so, Cubans, bored with their colonial past, turned to the future with excitement, and the first decades of the century were optimistic years, the time of the *self-made man* as he was referred to in English; adroit, hardworking, and socially mobile. The island glittered with promise. After independence, some 100,000 exiles returned to the island with small amounts of capital or credit and valuable work experience gained in the United States. Despite the ferocity of the war, half a million Spaniards also came to try to make their fortune. Then there were men like Heriberto Lobo, Julio Lobo's father, the epitome of the *self-made man,* who had recently lost one fortune in Venezuela and arrived in the new Cuban Republic at the start of the century, like so many others, to start again.

IN FACT IT was a quirk of fate that brought Don Heriberto, his wife, Virginia, and their two young children to Cuba in the autumn of 1900.

Heriberto and Virginia in Caracas, 1899.
Leonor stands at the front, Julio on the table.

A tall and moderately good-looking man with a broad forehead, aquiline nose, and deep dark eyes, Heriberto was born in 1870 in Puerto Cabello on Venezuela's Caribbean coast to a long Sephardic line that almost embodied the medieval image of the wandering Jew. Since the Jewish expulsion from Spain in 1492, Heriberto's ancestors had lived in Portugal, Amsterdam, London, Amsterdam again, then Saint Thomas, Venezuela, and now Cuba. Arriving penniless in Havana, Heriberto had already pulled his life up by the bootstraps once before. Just fourteen when his father died, Heriberto joined the Banco de Venezuela, the national bank, working as a clerk to support his mother and family. Six years later, after learning accounting, French, and English in his spare time, he was appointed chief accountant. By the time he was twenty-two, Heriberto had joined the board of directors. Three years later he ran the bank; it was a remarkable achievement.

Virginia Olavarría, his wife, was six years older. The eldest daughter of an aristocratic Basque family that had settled in Venezuela in the sixteenth century, she had wavy dark hair and was handsome rather than beautiful. They married in Caracas in 1896, after Heriberto converted to Catholicism; their first child, Leonor, was born the following year and Julio the year after. Life seemed to be full of promise for the young couple in Caracas on the eve of the new century, until President Cipriano Castro threw them out of the country.

Castro was an *andino*, a native of the mountainous Venezuelan state of Táchira near the Colombian border. A brave military leader, like his unrelated Cuban namesake, and a vain man, Castro had a shock of dark hair and burning black eyes that many commented on; he was "a cockerel," as his father described him, "made for fighting and women." In 1899, he marched on Caracas from the Andes with a thin column of sixty men— "whistling, happy, clean dressed, as if for a party." Armed, ironically, with rifles called *cubanos*, they took the capital five months later. But the country was bankrupt, the treasury empty, and Castro soon summoned Heriberto to the Presidential Palace and asked him to open the Banco de Venezuela's vaults. When Heriberto refused, saying that would "ruin the bank," Castro threw him in jail and thirty days later expelled him and Heriberto's immediate family from the country. The Lobos sailed to the United States, planning to settle, but an American banker read an interview that Heriberto gave to a newspaper on arrival in New York. Impressed by how Heriberto had stood up to Castro, the "Monkey of the Andes," he offered Heriberto a job in Havana as deputy manager of the North American Trust Company, which acted as fiscal agent for the U.S. troops on the island. ("The American people," Heriberto commented wryly, "are easily impressed by anyone they believe is a victim of injustice.") With no better immediate prospects, Heriberto accepted and arrived with his family in Havana on October 21, 1900, the eve of his thirtieth birthday. Leonor, his eldest daughter, was two years old at the time; Julio, one. "I came to Cuba with the new century," as Lobo later liked to say.

The Lobos had arranged lodgings in Vedado, now a residential area of stately mansions to the west of the old city, then an almost rural area with cows tethered on vacant lots. Heriberto reported for work at the North American Trust. Shortly thereafter, when the bank's American manager died of yellow fever, Heriberto was promoted to the top in a macabre leap over his boss's corpse. This stroke of fortune, along with his Venezuelan experiences, left Heriberto with an enduring sense of equanimity and generosity of spirit; it also made him alert to the possibilities of luck. Vaulted into the commercial world of postcolonial Havana, Heriberto met Luis Suárez Galbán, a gruff and hardworking Canary Islander. Galbán had arrived in Cuba in 1867, aged fifteen, first sleeping on the floor of his uncle's struggling import business. Several bankruptcies and restructurings later, the diligent Galbán had transformed it into a prosperous merchant house. Heriberto joined in 1904 after the U.S. troops left. He arranged the financing that planters needed to harvest their cane and, after the *zafra*, with his fluent English, French, and Spanish, sold their sugar abroad.

Galbán's business survived the onslaught of the American carpetbaggers, his firm "emerging more powerful than ever from the struggle," as Galbán put it. And it continued to prosper thereafter, with Heriberto deploying his talents as a prudent and humane administrator alongside Galbán. Virgilio Pérez, later a senior manager and close friend, remembered meeting Heriberto on his first day as a nervous young employee. He reported to Heriberto's office and grew even more alarmed when he heard shouting inside. The door suddenly swung open and a distressed clerk scurried down the hall. Before him stood Heriberto, smiling broadly and entirely at ease.

"Come in, don't worry, *mi hijo*, my son," he told Pérez. "Sorry that I made you wait. . . . All those harsh words you heard for that *mozo*—pure fiction. He thought I was furious. But it's the only way of getting these youngsters to work. You know the saying, *quien bien te quiere, te hará llorar*, who loves you well will make you cry."

Cipriano Castro in 1913, the year of Virginia's revenge in Havana.

From Heriberto, Lobo inherited ambition and humor; from his fiery mother, a sharp temper. "May the mountains fall on your head," Virginia had shouted at Castro's Presidential Palace as she left Caracas, shaking a fist at the despot who had run her family out of the country. A small Venezuelan earthquake almost did just that ten months afterward, although Virginia exacted a more satisfying revenge thirteen years later. Castro, by then deposed from power, had arrived in Havana to drum up support for a counterrevolution. He sped through customs, clad in white flannels, swinging a silver-topped cane, and his drive through the city turned into a procession as a fifty-strong orchestra playing national Venezuelan and Cuban songs led the way. Virginia, meanwhile, headed to Castro's hotel, the Inglaterra, and waited in the lobby. When Castro appeared, she rushed him with her parasol, and hotel staff had to pry the umbrella from her hands as she beat her old enemy around the head.

Cuba's self-made men pursued their interests. The island prospered. Senado now milled some fifteen thousand tons of sugar a year, a crop worth almost $1 million, and Bernabé had become a *personage*, a man who could ride in his own Pullman carriage direct from his mill in Camagüey to Havana's central railway station. Galbán's business also expanded; he bought three mills, operated the Westinghouse concession in Cuba, and opened a trading office on Wall Street with equity capital of $1 million. Heriberto remained in Havana as co-head of the Cuban operation.

By now the Lobos had put down roots. Heriberto and Virginia bought the Vedado house they had first settled in, paying six thousand pesos to Doña Lucia, a Sicilian who owned the building with her Cuban husband, a failed sugar planter who sported a white mustache with sharp ends that pointed upward like the kaiser's. Three stories high, the house stood on a breezy rise in Vedado, shaded by ficus trees. Although roomy, its simple white stucco front seemed plain compared with some of the other palaces built around them in Renaissance, Moorish, or belle époque styles. Among the string of markers that locate the Lobo family in Havana's prerevolutionary social geography, there was the house of Mario García Menocal, a general in the War of Independence and one of Cuba's first presidents; Jacobo later married Menocal's cousin, Estela. There were also the homes of the Gelats, leading Cuban bankers; the Condesa de Revilla de Camargo, who lived in an ornate mansion built with Carrara marble by her brother, the sugar baron and amateur racing car driver José Gómez Mena; and the imposing Sarrá family residence next door to the Lobos', with its gardens and chapel. The Sarrás were well connected, big in pharmaceuticals and real estate, and renowned for their wealth, a source of gentle rivalry with their neighbors. Pérez tells the story of how Heriberto tripped and fell while on a business trip abroad. Surprised by the attention he received from some of the female guests in his hotel when it became known that a "Cuban millionaire" had hurt his leg, Heriberto asked his traveling companion: "Do you see any change in me?" "Not really, you seem the same," Pérez replied. "Ahh, just as I thought," Heriberto mused. "I've no extra magnetism, or animal charisma, or sex appeal. What these noble women are responding to is my Sarrá-appeal."

By the 1910s, the Lobos were a well-established presence in Havana. After Galbán retired in 1914 to return to the Canary Islands, Heriberto became president of the company, which was renamed Galbán Lobo

Helena, Leonor, Julio, and Jacobo. Havana, c. 1910.

shortly after. He and Virginia invited their Caracas relatives to stay, adding other Venezuelan touches to their life in Havana, such as the traditional Christmas meal of *hallaca*, a mixture of pork, beef, capers, raisins, and olives packed into a cornmeal mush, wrapped in plantain leaves. They had two more children, Jacobo and Helena, fussed over by nannies and governesses, as was the norm. Leonor grew into a striking teenager; an accomplished pianist, she was Virginia and Heriberto's favorite. Julio apparently vied for his parents' attention; although he had a happy childhood, this may have been an early spur to his ambition. Jacobo was the mischievous younger son. Although he is scowling in the photograph, his humor and charm could make his elder brother look sullen by comparison. The youngest, Helena, everyone agreed, was the sweetest-tempered.

Heriberto later built further homes next door as his children established their own families, so turning the house into a homestead. As
adults, Helena lived across the street; Julio in the middle building on
Eleventh and Fourth streets next to his parents' house on the corner; Jacobo on the far corner on the other side, with a garden interconnecting
them all around the back. After so many centuries of wandering the world,
this family compound in Vedado perhaps seemed to Heriberto like a place
which the Lobo family would never need to leave again. To the south,
inland up the hill, lay the university. To the north glittered the sea, beyond
the domed mosaic tower of St. George's School. And around them sprang
up embassies and other large residences, the highest fronds of the trees
planted in their central courtyards reaching above the rooftops, rustling
in the sea breeze and giving Vedado a sense of permanence and peaceful
lushness. But then Fidel Castro came down from the Cuban Sierra, just
like Cipriano Castro had come down from the Venezuelan Andes many
years before, and the appropriated Lobo house became an annex to the
Culture Ministry, watched over by a stern guard with dark glasses behind
a barred gate. "The Castros have always had it in for the Lobos," Lobo
liked to quip as an old man.

A SHORT WORD about Cuba's old homes, if only to preempt arguments
that will surely arise later. They are a touchstone of exile experience. No
other place gives such a sense of belonging. The fact that former owners
may not have lived there for almost fifty years does not change that. The
old home may have been altered and subdivided by postrevolution resi-
dents so that it is unrecognizable. It may now exist only in a yellowing
photo album. Yet every detail captured by a camera half a century ago is
burnished with memory and association, providing a still point from which
life's unsteadiness in exile can be measured and met. "I will never forget
the view from my window," Lobo's younger daughter María Luisa wrote
in a poignant evocation of the house on Eleventh and Fourth streets,
where she grew up. "I yearn for my childhood and that distant world, lost
forever." These old houses also provide a fantasy of escape, nostalgia.

Lobo's old home, glimpsed through the trees. Havana, 2002.

Few issues are more contentious on either side of the Florida straits. The Havana government often invokes the specter of exiles returning one day and turning people out of their houses. For some older émigrés, the nostalgic dream may still include a hope of reclaiming the house and the wealth it once represented. Yet for most, this nostalgia is less a wish for return than a dream of flight, the old house in Cuba becoming a lottery ticket out of the despair of old age. Younger exile generations have meanwhile raised children and perhaps grandchildren abroad, and so created new memories and new nostalgias. One Miami lawyer in his mid-fifties told me a typical story. He had traveled to Havana and, after much searching, found his father's old house in the city center. It was half fallen down, the walls and window frames eaten away by the damp and sea air. The door, he said, was open but as uninviting as a wolf's mouth, and inside there was the sense of a muffled multitude moving about. Although he well

knew that some governments in former Soviet bloc countries had resti-
tuted confiscated properties, the last thing he wanted, he said, was to try
to reclaim the house one day and become the landlord of a slum property,
where several families lived in permanent danger of the roof collapsing on
their heads. Sometimes there is no going back because there is nothing to
go back to. Then the idea of return has to take on broader meanings. Often,
it is less a thirst for revenge than a desire to recreate a new home in the
old country.

My mother discovered this when she first revisited the island in 1994.
Like the Lobos, her family lived in a group of white stucco houses gathered around a Vedado town block. Her parents occupied one corner of the
compound in a house built by their father, Don Pedro, Bernabé's third
son, who gave it to them as a wedding present. Her parents had grown up
together in Senado, presided over by Bernabé the great patriarch, *recto
como una palma*, as upright as a palm, as the saying went. They were also
first cousins, so their marriage prompted endless family mirth about how
it could only produce children with pig's tails. Pedro built more houses
around them for his other children, much as Heriberto had done, and they
all opened at the back to a central patio, where my great-grandfather, a
thin white-haired man whose uniform was a white guayabera and white
linen trousers, reigned from a park bench.

Standing outside on the pavement again for the first time in thirty-
four years, my mother saw the old neoclassical mansion on Nineteenth
and Second streets, still shutterless, shaded by flower trees and adorned
with columns and metal grillwork. She noticed the rubber trees that she
had climbed as a young girl, collecting white resin and rubbing the sticky
globules together in her hands to make bouncy balls. She saw the elegant
terrace that circled the back of the house, and remembered the green
lizard that one day fell from its eaves and tangled itself in her hair. Suddenly she recalled her old telephone number—F2032. The house is now
part of the North Korean diplomatic compound, but the door was open.
Propelled by old habits, my mother walked in.

Of course not all the grand old families left Vedado after the revolution. Some stayed, out of belief in the revolution's ideals, others because

they could not bear to leave. That was the case with one of my great-uncles, who died soon after the rest of the family had left. Government officials promptly sealed off the house, having been alerted that bourgeois treasure was hidden inside. They eventually found the hoard—silver plates, utensils, parasols, a wedding dress—in closets sealed with concrete, and the story played in local newspapers for a while.

Other Cuban grandees who stayed on in their Vedado homes passed the years living like ghosts among their old possessions. One of the most dramatic of these figures was the Cuban poet Dulce María Loynaz. She lived five blocks north of Don Pedro's house, six blocks east of Heriberto's, and was the youngest daughter of the impulsive and brave General Loynaz whom Bernabé had betrayed to the Spanish.

Dulce María was born in 1902, four years after Julio Lobo. A friend of Federico García Lorca and the Chilean Nobel Prize winner Gabriela Mistral, she wrote and published poetry through her youth and middle years, and then stopped suddenly in 1960. She lived for the next thirty-eight years in virtual seclusion in her Vedado home, like a tropical Miss Havisham, with her two sisters and one brother, some servants, and an exquisite collection of paintings, sculpture, and delicate china. The authorities thought Dulce María's spare and classically inspired poems too effete or otherworldly to be published in a country where issues were painted in black and white, for or against, and were described with sledge-hammer words like Sacrifice, Solidarity, and Revolution. But mostly they treated her neither badly nor well; they simply left her alone. "Yo Soñaba en Clasificar," "I Dreamed of Classifying," is one of her most popular poems:

I had a dream of classifying
Good and Evil, the same way scientists
classify butterflies:

I dreamed that I pinned Good and Evil
on to the dark velvet background
of a glass display case . . .

Below the white butterfly
a label that read "Good".
Under the black butterfly,
a label that said "Evil".

But the white butterfly
was not so Good, nor the black butterfly
so Evil . . . And between my two butterflies,
all the world's green, golden and infinite butterflies flew.

Dulce María had to wait until 1991 for her first book of poems to be published in Cuba. The following year, she unexpectedly won Spain's prestigious Cervantes literary prize. Dulce María was eighty-nine years old when she traveled to Madrid, and so frail that she had to take the Spanish queen's congratulatory call from a sickbed, surrounded by flowers that she was too sick to smell, and chocolates that the doctor said she was too old to eat. Shortly before her death five years later, an interviewer asked this most aristocratic of writers why she had never left the island after the revolution. Dulce María simply replied: "I was here first."

For some reason, my mother carried a Dictaphone when she walked into the North Korean diplomatic compound. On the recording you can hear the click of doors, her gasps of surprise and disappointment as she looked into the rooms of her old home, her voice echoing in the empty corridors. She saw the same black-and-white tiles in the hallway that she remembered, the same glass sliding door to the drawing room, and the same curved marble staircase that she walked down in her wedding dress on her father's arm after the revolution had begun. She also remembered the side table, on which sat a bronze Medusa's head with serpents en-twined in its hair; the two black wicker chairs that flanked it, where her aunts would place her *en penitencia*, for punishment, whenever she lied or stole; and the piano, where her mother played pieces by the Cuban com-poser Ernesto Lecuona or the latest popular American hits, like "Saturday Night Is the Loneliest Night of the Week" and "Ac-Cent-Tchu-Ate the

Positive." The table, the Medusa, the telephone, the piano, and the black chairs were all gone, of course.

Suddenly there is a gabble of foreign voices in the background and the sound of footsteps on stairs. "The North Koreans are coming," my mother whispers into the tape recorder, and then giggles like a naughty schoolgirl caught in a prank. The North Korean voices grow louder, my mother makes a polite protest, everyone switches to Spanish, and there is a rustle as she jams the Dictaphone to the bottom of her shoulder bag. Then there is a click, and the recording goes dead.

Four

SUGAR RUSH

✈

*While the ancient countries of Europe are consumed
by war, in little Cuba there reigns a
carnival of madness and laughter.*

—Rafael Antonio Cisneros,
La Danza de los Millones

L obo's childhood is also suffused with nostalgia, although of a different sort. If a lonely adult recalls early loneliness, an adventurer remembers moments of excitement, and Lobo was both a loner and
an adventurer. The incidents that he remembered from his childhood
show the same determination and picaresque impulsiveness of his later
life. It was an explosive mix, as Heriberto foresaw. *Domina tus pasiones*,
control your passions, he used to counsel his son. Because from an early
age it was apparent that Lobo sought not only wealth but glory too.

As a young school boy, he went to Colegio de La Salle, which had just
opened its doors five and a half blocks from his house. Founded by lay
brothers in 1906, La Salle became one of Havana's two great schools, the
other being El Colegio de Belén, where Fidel Castro and his younger
brother Raúl later received their Jesuit education. It was at La Salle that
Lobo first realized his talent for speculation. Lobo's classmates used to

trade pencils during school breaks. When the games ended, Lobo usually found that he had collected the lot. He also showed an unusual interest in Napoleon at an early age, buying his first artifact from his father, an autograph. Heriberto asked for thirty pesos. Lobo, not yet a teenager, said he had only fifteen, so Heriberto, wanting to impart a useful lesson to his son, loaned him the remainder.

There was a tradition among wealthy Cubans that dated from colonial times of sending their children to be educated in the United States. And in 1910, just before his twelfth birthday, his parents dispatched Lobo to New York to board at Columbia Grammar in preparation for the more famous university fifteen blocks north. Bernabé's sons also went to school in the United States; so did their sons—my grandfather went to Storm King in New York State. Lobo eventually sent his daughters north for a "proper education" at a young age too. From there, the usual route was on to an Ivy League college.

Lobo was being groomed for this path. In 1914, sixteen years old, precocious but "still wearing short pants," he enrolled at Columbia University, one of the six youngest boys among the almost four hundred freshmen to join that year. He roomed at 738 West End Avenue, between Ninety-sixth and Ninety-seventh streets; mingled with the sons of other Cubans studying at Columbia, including his two future brothers-in-law; and attended lectures on mathematics, English literature, and philosophy. He continued the fencing lessons begun at preparatory school—at home, many Cubans still settled their differences with swords. In the evenings he went to Broadway shows, drawn by an early attraction to the stars of the stage, even if he could hardly see them from his cheap seats up in the highest balcony.

By his seventeenth birthday, Lobo looked set for the predictable education of a child of the Cuban well-to-do, studying law perhaps. But he was too restless and ambitious for that. "I decided to become a sugar expert," Lobo remembered. "It was so intimately linked with what was going on." Sugar prices had risen with the outbreak of World War I, and foreign investment had flooded the island chasing the profits to be made. While millions of men mobilized in Europe, Cubans planted sugarcane

Manuel Rionda. Tuinucú, 1905.

and reaped the riches. Sugar production doubled during the first decade of the century. It doubled again in the eight years to 1918 in a boom led by figures such as the merchant and planter Manuel Rionda.

A patrician Spaniard with dark hair, piercing eyes, and a Vandyke beard, Rionda bridged the worlds of Cuba and Wall Street with his old Spanish manners, and the scale of his operations at their peak was immense. He was copartner of Czarnikow Rionda, the powerful London-based trading house, and handled some 60 percent of Cuba's sugar sales to refiners in the United States. His family had interests on the island that predated the wars of independence, and already owned three mills. In 1912, after raising the then huge amount of $50 million on Wall Street as president of the newly formed Cuba Cane Corporation, Rionda oversaw the purchase of seventeen more. He lived on a vast New Jersey estate at Río Vista overlooking the Hudson River, reputedly had oranges tied to the trees in his garden to remind him of his Spanish roots, and spent at least four months of every year in Cuba overseeing the *zafra*. He began the 1,300-mile migration every December in a private railroad car with his family and secretaries. The train left vaulted Pennsylvania Station for Key West, then they continued by boat to Havana, traveled east across Cuba by train again, the last leg completed when his carriage was un-hitched from the Havana Special and hauled by one of Rionda's own engines to the two-story, yellow *casa de vivienda* at his favorite mill, Tui-nucú. From his bedroom suite on the first floor, Rionda could hear the steady beat of the mill grinding day and night next door, the shrieks from the whistle as shifts were changed, and the clanging of engine bells and the crash of cane as it was dumped from railroad cars and ox carts into the chutes. In its heyday, Cuba Cane was the largest sugar company in the world. Rionda called it his "baby."

Lobo was spurred on by the fortunes that men like his father and Rionda made. He left Columbia after just one year, and in 1915 enrolled at the sugar engineering institute at Louisiana State University. Now a huge university of 28,000 students, LSU was then a small college campus on a deep and fast-moving stretch of the Mississippi River, about 140 miles upstream from New Orleans. Although far from the genteel Ivy League world, where most of his Cuban peers moved, Lobo felt imme-diately at home. New Orleans and Havana were entwined in the same Atlantic world, shared a common Caribbean culture, and had a common history; during the late eighteenth century, New Orleans had even an-swered to the Spanish garrison in Cuba. New Orleans and Havana also shared the same economy. On both sides of the Gulf of Mexico, tens of thousands of tons of sugarcane were planted, hoed, cut, lifted, and hauled every year. It was in Louisiana that Lobo first inhaled the acrid stench of burned cane, akin to roasted corn, and the sweet smell of molasses. "Once that perfume invades your nostrils, it permeates your whole body," he liked to say. "You will never be able to get rid of it. Such was my case."

Lobo lodged in rooms near the campus in Baton Rouge, dallied in

"El Veneno." Louisiana, 1917.

New Orleans on weekends, staying in plush hotels like the Grunewald or the Monteleone when he could afford it, and spent his winters gaining work experience at nearby sugar refineries. Clad in rough overalls, he rolled exhausted into his dormitory bed every night after long days spent in the laboratory, monitoring the sugar produced in the giant milling and centrifuge sheds next door. Lobo sent home samples of sugar he had made for his father to inspect. Less innocently, he made hand copies of the refineries' balance sheets and also mailed them to Heriberto, until he was caught and stopped.

Friends remember Lobo working hard, often late into the night, proudly encouraged by his father. "Your average mark in October was 85 per cent. In November it was 88 per cent," Heriberto wrote halfway through Lobo's second year. "If you keep on going at this rate, you will reach 100 per cent in May," he teased. Yet there were also moments of

Huckleberry Finn foolhardiness—Mark Twain's book had been published only thirty years before.

One Easter, Lobo canoed with two friends to New Orleans. They paddled during the day, camping on the banks of the Mississippi at night, the canoe upturned and raised on blocks to make a rough shelter. They drifted lazily downstream, and made it to New Orleans two days later, having capsized several times in eddies. It was wartime and the Military Police, on the lookout for spies, arrested the bedraggled trio after they sneaked ashore through the wharves.

On another occasion Lobo swam the Mississippi, endangering his life and a friend's, Charlie Coates, the son of the dean, and therefore his university education as well. It began as a student lark. They set off from the foot of Main Street in Baton Rouge, where the river was a mile wide and swept by at eight miles an hour. They swam safely to Port Allen on the other side, sliding downstream with the current, but struggled on their return. Coates lagged behind Lobo, the stronger swimmer. When they finally pulled themselves out of the water back at Baton Rouge, Coates's mother was waiting on the shore, her eyes, Lobo never forgot, "full of fire over what she considered a virtual suicide jaunt."

This was typical Lobo. Even as a young man, he focused on everything with a passionate and single-minded determination, be that studies, high jinks on the river, or women. Friends nicknamed him El Veneno, the poisonous one, for his charm and sibylline tongue. José Tiglao, a Philippine classmate at LSU and one of Lobo's closest friends, remembered him as an "individualist, who does not spare himself any sacrifice to attain his objectives." He also recalled Lobo's golden touch. One Friday in their fourth year, Tiglao asked Lobo for a $5 loan to tide him over the weekend. Lobo, usually generous to a fault with friends, demurred. Instead he took Tiglao to the Hibernia Bank, where the Lobos banked, saying that he had a scheme which he hoped would bear fruit over the weekend. If he loaned his friend the money, Lobo explained, the interest he could charge would not match the profits he hoped to make.

There is a sharpness to this anecdote that can seem like unattractive tight-fistedness. Tiglao simply took it as an example of how Lobo viewed money. This depended on what end it was being used for; carousing with friends was one matter, business another. Clearly the scheme Lobo had in mind over that weekend worked, as did others like it, because when he graduated, Lobo repaid Heriberto his college fees. The show of independence angered his father, despite the lesson of the Napoleon autograph he had taught several years before. It was also central to Lobo's belief that if he made it to the top, it would be from his own efforts. That is why he later avoided the corruption that enmeshed so much of Cuban business life. As Lobo saw it, turning to others for favors, let alone stealing, was a lesser man's game. Making it on his own, whatever the cost, was not only a point of honor, it was a matter of pride.

Such pride brings costs. Acting the lone wolf also means suffering failure alone, as happened with one harebrained scheme that literally blew up in Lobo's face. In 1916, the Allied troops were bogged down in the trenches in Europe, and the grenade was still a rudimentary weapon that often exploded in soldiers' hands. Lobo imagined an improved model that would explode on contact with water when lobbed into the damp mud behind enemy lines. He dreamed that it would bring him the riches of Alfred Nobel, the inventor of dynamite, and help the Allies win the war.

Lobo worked on the device in the school's chemistry labs during the evenings. Tiglao was dismissive, seeing it as "nothing more than a pipe dream, common to all students." But Lobo worked on, ultimately to his own detriment, when the glass retort he used one night to mix chemicals had not properly dried. Tiglao was outside when he heard the explosion. He rushed into the building and found Lobo lying unconscious on the floor, broken laboratory apparatus strewn around him, his body peppered with shards of glass. An ambulance rushed Lobo to the Touro infirmary in New Orleans, where doctors painstakingly picked over his body and face. Lobo spent the next week with his eyelids clamped open, crying glass, the slivers floating out on his tears. Yet the only mark left by the accident was a shallow gouge on the end of his nose that looked like the faint shadow of a lunar sea on the face of the moon. In certain lights, as Lobo later liked to say, it resembled a question mark, a fitting scar for such a curious speculator.

Lobo, the young executive.

LOBO GRADUATED IN June 1919 and returned to Havana that autumn. A photograph taken the year before showed him standing in a muddy Louisiana yard, smiling, wearing dungarees and scuffed boots, holding a pipe. In a portrait taken some ten years later, he had become a powerful businessman dressed in a suit and tie, dripping savoir-faire, albeit with less hair, staring out at the viewer with an unflinching gaze and an inquisitorial raised eyebrow. Unfortunately, most of Lobo's transformation from grinning student to titan of finance takes place in the shadows. Correspondence during this period survives only from his parents and siblings, and the letters that Lobo wrote to them have been lost. Thus one learns from Jacobo in March 1919 how dawn masses were being held daily at St. Gregory's Church in Havana after their sister Leonor died during the great flu pandemic. Leonor had given birth to a son, Carlos

Todd, just five months before, and her death was an emotional low water mark for the family. To ease Virginia's grief, Heriberto built a country residence in Wajay on the outskirts of Havana and planted the garden with fruit trees, peonies, and ylang-ylang. He also encouraged Virginia to travel, taking their youngest daughter, Helena, as a companion. Six years after Leonor died, Lobo's mother scribbled a chatty and tender letter to Lobo from her bathroom at the Waldorf-Astoria in New York while Helena slept next door. "She went out last night," Virginia explained, "and did not get back until 1.30 in the morning having danced at the Lido with Menocal," the former Cuban president. In Havana, Lobo worked hard, Virginia often urging him to take life more easily. "Why unhappy *mi corazón*, my heart? . . . You are too young to be so pessimistic. Grab life by its better side," she wrote in one letter after what must have been a miserable message from Lobo himself. But he romanced too. "Helena says you are in love!" Virginia wrote. "Can I ask—with whom?!"

Most of the surviving letters, though, are from his father. They begin offering sage advice to a young man about to begin his career, evolve into sharp business letters during Lobo's early years at work, and end in tones of respect toward a man he regarded as his equal. "Take care, work with faith, cultivate the spirit and dominate your passions," Heriberto had counseled Lobo at his graduation. "Do not concern yourself about finding a job," he added, as "there will be no lack, and it will be well paid."

He was right. Lobo returned to Havana in the autumn of 1919 and found the city infected by a dreamlike fever. Fittingly, because so much on the island is characterized by music, it was called the "Dance of the Millions." Sugar prices had risen in the run-up to World War I and then been fixed. After peace was declared in November 1918, the controls were lifted. Sugar prices soared, and Cuba was gripped by a speculative sugar rush that is one of the landmarks in the history of capitalism, the dot-com boom of its day. Money seemed to waltz down from the heavens. Enrico Caruso, the world's greatest tenor, was contracted for a Cuban opera tour and paid the outrageous sum of $10,000 per performance, even though he was well past his prime. Small-time sugarcane farmers from the deep Cuban country shopped the jewelry stores in Havana in collarless shirts,

wearing studs of diamond or gold embossed with their initials. The shops
bulged with North American manufactured goods—radios, refrigerators,
and sewing machines, all the appurtenances of the modern age. The
National City Bank of New York asked: *¿Qué sucederá si no deja Ud. un
testamento?* What will happen if you don't leave a will? Cuban women,
bored with their Spanish past, meanwhile modeled themselves on the Jazz
Age's independent-minded "flapper girl."

How times had changed! In 1840 the Condesa de Merlin wrote how
she spent all her days closeted inside her house in Havana avoiding the
heat, and in the early evening might venture into the city in a horse and
carriage for a *paseo* on the Prado. Now, when the Condesa's descendants
wanted to travel about town, they rode in a luxury North American or
European motorcar with a chauffeur outfitted by Montalvo y Corrales,
the firm that advertised its smart uniforms in the pages of *Social.* "Havana," the magazine had trilled in 1917, "is progressing with giant steps
in every field." Amid the prosperity, Cuba seemed more like a rapidly
emerging country than a developing one. Habaneros outdid one another
in the lavishness of their parties as if to prove it. "A ball that never ends,"
Social described one costumed dance given by Lily Hidalgo during the
1916 season. "An elegance that is enrapturing, a luxury that casts its spell,
a beauty that bewitches; the men in their red tails, the ladies in period
gowns, all so admirably classical, of exquisite taste, of extreme chic."

Cuba was gripped by a sugar frenzy. New mills were built at great speed
and older mills expanded. At Senado, my great-grandfather Don Pedro,
who now managed the mill with Bernabé, tripled the amount of sugar it
produced each year. They also built a church and a baseball field, which
unusually for those times hosted mixed-race games; Senado remained a
progressive mill, a place where no child, as the saying went, lacked for
shoes. Elsewhere Cubans planted sugar wherever they could. "If things go
on at this rate, we'll be sowing cane in the patios of our houses," *El Mundo*
remarked. Around the country, the huge trees under whose shade the early
Spanish chroniclers insisted one could walk from one end of the island to
the other, and which the Condesa de Merlin had described so vividly to
her friends in Paris, were burned in a terrible conflagration to clear fresh

land. At night the fragrant aroma of smoldering hardwoods—cedar, ma-hogany, mastic, and pomegranate—covered the island with a smell like church incense.

For a young man seeking his fortune, Lobo's return to Cuba could hardly have been better timed. He was fluent in English and Spanish, technically up to date—unlike the sons of most local sugar men, he also liked to get his hands dirty—and well connected. He could work wherever he wanted. His first job offer came from Manuel Aspuru, a contemporary and later close business associate, who had inherited the sugar mill Toledo two years before. A second prospect followed soon after. Rionda offered Lobo $500 a month to work as assistant superintendent at the Lugareño, a midsize mill adjacent to Bernabé's property that had changed hands several times since independence. The Galbán Lobo office balked at the prospect of their president's son working for the competition and invited him to join them instead. Lobo, just twenty-two years old, named his terms, aiming high: the princely wage of $1,000 a month, 5 percent of profits, and managerial authority to sign off on large deals. The office agreed, Heriberto apparently absenting himself from the negotiations.

On January 2, 1920, Lobo reported for his first day of work. The Dance of the Millions was in full cavort. Any sugar price over five and a half cents per pound was reckoned to be enough to "stimulate the coun-try to extreme prosperity." By February 1920, sugar traded at nine and one-eighth cents, almost twice as much. As prices rose, planters sought huge advances on future crops. The banks—many of them American—were happy to lend. National City had opened twenty-two branches in Cuba in 1919 alone. When local funds ran low, New York was tapped for more. Every bank had portfolios thick with mortgages on plantations, credit notes on standing and future crops, and liens on bagged sugar. Notoriously, one grower famously planted cane quickly around the edges of his fields. His bank loaned him an advance on the crop on the assump-tion that all his land was cultivated, and the grower absconded to Paris before the lender realized its mistake.

By the end of March, the sugar price had risen to twelve cents, at the end of April to eighteen cents, and by mid-May it stood at twenty and a

half. Up, up, up rose the price of sugar—as did the harvest, to 3.75 million
tons, the second highest in history. Then, just as fast, down, down, down
the price fell. By August it had dropped to eleven cents, by September to
eight cents. November saw it halve again, and by Christmas it had dropped
to three and three-quarter cents a pound. During his first year in the
business, Lobo, the future King of Sugar, the man who would later say "I
am the market," watched fortunes balloon and collapse. He had missed
the biblical seven years of feast. He would witness and sometimes suffer
the years of famine that followed.

YOUTH IS A time of promise and ambition. Questions about the costs of
that ambition only come later, when its fruits are lost to old age or catastrophe. In his middle age, Lobo occasionally asked himself whether the
prize of Sugar King had been worth it. So too in the 1920s did Cuba
during the calamity of the ensuing bust.

The banks were the first to go, as in every credit-fueled boom. There
was understood to be $80 million in loans outstanding, made on sugar
prices between fifteen and twenty-two cents a pound. With the price
fallen to a third of that, several U.S. banks teetered on the brink of insol-
vency. As much as 80 percent of National City's entire capital had been
loaned against Cuban sugar during the height of the boom. For the Royal
Bank of Canada, Chase National, and the Guaranty Trust, the situation
was almost as serious. For many Cuban banks, the case was hopeless. In
the spring of 1921, the locally owned Banco Nacional closed its doors.
On March 28, José ("Poté") López Rodríguez, the wealthiest man in Cuba,
committed suicide and was found hanging from his balustrade. Eleven
days later, Cuba's leading sugar speculator, José Lezama, met his creditors,
declared himself bankrupt, and fled the country, leaving debts of $24 mil-
lion behind. Mills folded, with more than forty taken over by U.S. banks
in settlement of their debts, almost a quarter of the total on the island. It
was a sea change for the industry. Before the crash, Cuban-owned mills
produced almost 40 percent of the island's crop, a tenth of world production. Afterward, they accounted for half that amount. Nationalist resent-

ments, papered over by Cuba's early prosperity, began to grow. The cartoon figure Liborio captured the national mood, becoming the popular face of Cuba. But while Uncle Sam is shrewd and wiry, and England's John Bull jocular and fat, Cuba's Liborio was skinny, big-nosed, and mute, a perpetual victim of North American power.

Senado escaped the worst of the crash, Bernabé having sold most of his sugar before the peak. So did Galbán Lobo, thanks to Heriberto's prudence. The firm had sold the three mills it owned for a handsome price to Rionda's Cuba Cane just as the Dance of the Millions made its last magnificent sweep around the floor. For Rionda, the bust and the decade of low sugar prices that followed were his undoing. He still controlled much of the sugar produced on the island and sold in the United States. Yet his star was dimming, and he passed the next ten years mediating an ignominious series of squabbles between sugar producers everywhere, trying to sort out the mess.

The problem, as seen objectively, was simple. Sugar production was too high. This depressed world prices. So output had to be cut. The question was, by whom? The prevailing opinion was Cuba. It alone accounted for a quarter of the world crop. In Rionda's view, it was "consequently the greatest one to blame." The Cuban government took it upon itself to prop up the market, passing a series of laws to restrict local production in an attempt to boost the world price.

The policy was unpopular with many of the larger Cuban planters. From London, John Maynard Keynes did not think it sensible either, at least not for Cuba over the long run. As well as being a distinguished economist, Keynes was a successful commodities speculator: between 1923 and 1928, he made around £47,000 trading on his own account. For men like Keynes, the economics were clear. Cuba was the "cheapest sugar-producing country in the world," as Rionda put it. It therefore made sense for Cuba to produce the most sugar too. Instead, Cuba cut back. Keynes referred to this as the "paradox of artificial limitation in Cuba." The reasons were largely political. Havana feared that lower prices would bankrupt the smaller Cuban-owned mills. Control of the industry would then pass entirely to the larger and more efficient North American concerns.

This was seen as politically untenable, as it would reduce Cubans to the role of dogs at a rich man's table.

The gambit failed. When Cuba cut back sugar production, other parts of the world—cane growers in Java, beet growers in Europe and the United States—simply increased their output. World prices stayed low and all of Cuba suffered. The Lobos, both father and son, had disagreed with the doomed strategy from the start, Heriberto doing so from a front seat. In July 1927, he sailed to Paris to witness another attempt by Cuba to convince European beet producers to join its efforts to stanch world sugar production and prop up prices. Despite the urgency, it was still the golden age of the ocean liner when a transatlantic crossing took five days, and evening dress was required at dinner. En route to Europe from Havana, Heriberto stopped in New York. His colleagues on Wall Street were pessimistic. They saw the Paris talks failing. Many had already sold all the sugar that they held, fearing that the price would only fall further. One told Heriberto that Rionda believed "the bankruptcy of Cuba was inevitable" unless sugar prices rose. Yet past attempts to restrict production and boost prices had not worked. Why, wondered Heriberto, would this time be any different?

Heriberto wrote to his son when he arrived in Paris. Most communication was then by mail, with only the most urgent situations requiring a cable, and very rarely a telephone call. On Waldorf-Astoria Hotel–headed paper, Heriberto wrote that he hoped "this crazy plan does not prosper." In the end, economic efficiency would prevail and, as Heriberto added, underlining each word, it would all boil down to "The Survival of the Fittest." He was concerned as a patrician, but his letters showed that he believed it would happen anyway.

Lobo, meanwhile, was in Havana. When he had started at the office seven years before, he had been put through his paces first, hawking *frijoles, harina y garbanzos*, beans, flour, and chickpeas. Now he directed Galbán Lobo's day-to-day sugar trading operation. It was a fast promotion to a senior position, but as Heriberto told him: "I would much rather you make your mistakes now than later when I may not be around to pick up the pieces." In 1921, showing early promise, Lobo had made the supposedly highest-ever priced sale of sugar to a U.S. bottling company, three thousand tons at twenty-five cents per pound. But now Heriberto was away, the market had crashed, and the firm's senior vice president, Enrique Sosa, was suddenly absent because of an urgent medical operation. Lobo was in sole charge of the Havana office. He was twenty-eight years old.

Heriberto's concern shows in his correspondence, even though he had become managing director of the Banco de Venezuela three years younger. He asked Lobo to make Pepe Rodríguez, the office treasurer, joint manager in his absence. He wrote on August 2, disagreeing with his son's view that the sugar price would reach three and a quarter cents (events subsequently proved Heriberto right). Heriberto also upbraided Lobo for failing to promptly forward the firm's weekly trading positions. On September 14, Heriberto played golf with Bernabé Sanchez's son-in-law, Julio Cadenas. I was surprised to find Bernabé's name cropping up in Heriberto's correspondence. But Bernabé, the Lion of Camagüey, had died the year before, aged eighty-six. His obituaries described a man of simple habits and "an Anglo-Saxon frame of mind," who woke at five o'clock every morning and worked at his standing writing desk until the last. He left twelve children, thirty-two grandchildren, sixteen great-grandchildren, and a mill, worth some $8 million, that was inherited by the children of his second marriage. Soon after, most of my mother's family, including Pedro, Senado's manager, moved to Havana. Bernabé's death also left the Senado account open; Heriberto suggested that Lobo pitch for it.

Perhaps Lobo did, although he was then at work on far bigger and more important matters. On October 12, he brokered the sale of 150,000 tons of surplus Cuban sugar to Britain's Tate & Lyle for $6 million. At the time, it was the largest sugar deal in the world, and Lobo had stolen it from under Rionda's nose by shaving a fraction of a cent off the expected selling price. The news came as a thunderclap to *El Viejo*, the old man, as the Lobos called Rionda. His office had lost a handsome commission, his prestige had been dented in the trade, and he felt personally betrayed. The deal meanwhile catapulted the firm of Galbán Lobo onto the international stage. It also gave Lobo the confidence that he might truly one day become the world's Sugar King.

"The sale was solely due to your skill and hard work," Heriberto congratulated Lobo from Paris. "The profits you have made take second place to the importance and prestige you bring both to the house and to yourself, inside and outside the country." Galbán Lobo had long been a thorn in Rionda's side; now El Viejo considered it an equal. "He sees advantage in getting down from his high horse and discussing matters with us," Heriberto wrote Lobo the following year from New York.

Yet the sugar market remained in the doldrums, and not even the Lobos, mixing the sage caution of Heriberto with flashes of brilliance from his son, could escape that. "This is a very delicate time. . . . I'm losing sleep over it," Heriberto wrote in late 1928. Heriberto was then in the United States, meeting with congressmen in Washington and sugar traders and financiers in New York. Notably, Heriberto had a confidential meeting in October with Colonel José Miguel Tarafa, who was in charge of determining Cuba's sugar policy. Their conversation provides a window onto the corruption of Cuban political life at the time.

Tarafa was the most conspicuously successful businessman to rise out of the revolutionary *mambí* ranks. He had cherubic if puffy features, was a planter in his own right, was also the owner of Cuban Consolidated Railways, and had risen to prominence in large part thanks to his control of Cuba's Congress, which he managed through a mix of nationalistic propaganda and large bribes. In one incident, while Tarafa was working to push through a bill that favored his railway interests, he had invited Havana's most senior politicians on a private railway trip through eastern Cuba. A fellow U.S. investor asked to come along too. Tarafa refused, a colleague politely explaining to the North American that:

> Mr Tarafa . . . did not think it advisable that you should accompany him on that trip, because he had to make representations of a certain nature to the Senators, and he would have to refer to the obnoxious foreign elements that are getting the control of the sugar industry all over Cuba, and your presence might restrain the Senators from patri-

otic exuberance, which he desired to arouse in attaining the purpose
in view.

The meeting with Heriberto was held discreetly in Tarafa's New York
hotel suite, as all of Wall Street was on the lookout for the Cuban sugar
minister—speculators could make or lose millions from his decisions.
Tarafa spelled out to Heriberto why he thought it was a good idea to curb
Cuban sugar production. He droned on and on. Heriberto finally butted
in. Given the seriousness of the situation, Heriberto asked, wouldn't it be
better to leave sugar output unrestricted? Prices were already so low that
it should be easy to sell off any surplus crop, and prices could hardly fall
much further. Tarafa, unmoved, replied with a pointed question of his
own. He had been trading sugar on the New York exchange, he explained,
had already made a handsome profit, and still held a short position—a
speculative bet that prices would fall further. But after he made public his
proposed policies to cut Cuban output again, the sugar price would likely
rise. When would be the best time to close his short position? Heriberto
drily suggested that if Señor Tarafa already had a profit, he should get out
while the going was good.

Such insider trading explains why Heriberto and Lobo were so against
the government restrictions—a controversial position, as the measure was
supposed to help Cuban planters. It fostered corruption and also went
against market principles, "whose rules can be no more easily ignored than
the laws of gravity," as Lobo later wrote. Nor did Tarafa's policies obviously help. When Cuba signed a restriction agreement in 1930, called the
Chadbourne Plan, Lobo wrote a stinging counterblast, calling it a social
cancer that unnecessarily robbed Cubans, both rich and poor, of work.
"In civilized countries, they create occupation for the unemployed," he
wrote. "Here [by cutting production] we are doing the opposite, which is
so absurd as to be incomprehensible, even criminal." It was a battle that
Lobo would fight many times again.

Lobo showed early skill in trading and dealing during the 1920s, yet
he was far from infallible. Lobo's most spectacular mistake came in 1926,
when he bought Agabama, a small mill in central Cuba, from a British

bank that owned the mortgage. With sugar prices so low, it was the worst possible time to buy. His first *zafra* was also a disaster. Lobo brought in two new Boulager rollers to grind the cane, but they were mounted on a concrete base mixed with sea water. When the machines started to roll, their mounts collapsed, the heavy grinders fell over, and much of the harvest was lost. Lobo suffered what he called a "dark night of the soul," sitting under a mango tree in the *batey*, pondering losses that subsequently ballooned to 600,000 pesos. Later harvests at Agabama were little better, although by then every planter in Cuba was losing money.

The sugar price continued to drop. It was reckoned that two and a half cents was enough to cover production costs. In 1932, during the world depression that followed the New York stock market crash, the price dropped to 0.7 cent a pound. Cuban cutbacks only made matters worse. That year, Cuba produced the same amount of sugar as it had in 1901, when the country had been emerging from the devastating war of independence. Mills closed. Unemployment grew. In April 1932, Lobo wrote to his father of "the disastrous results suffered by the house over the past four years, due solely and exclusively to me," and asked formally to be relieved of his management duties. I would rather work "as a foot soldier," he wrote. It was a gallant move, especially as Lobo had married a young Cuban aristocrat, María Esperanza Montalvo, only three months before and was starting a family. The comparison between this honorable gesture and Lobo's early confidence is stark. Lobo had been humbled, for a moment. But by then all of Cuba had been turned upside down.

Five

DEATH IN THE MORNING

*Morris of Lykes Brothers . . . saw a Negro in the street
with a red flag so he stopped his car and called the Negro
over and asked him if he was a Communist. The Negro
proudly said, "Sí Señor." Morris enquired as to just what
a communist might be. The Negro stopped and thought a
second and then said, un hombre muy guapo con una
bandera roja [a gallant man with a red flag].*

—RUBY HART PHILLIPS, *Cuba: Island of Paradox*

Certain dates cut deep gashes into Cuba's history, like blows from
a machete. There is the moment when Fidel Castro first rose to
Cuban prominence after he stormed the Moncada military barracks in Santiago in 1953; the day gives the name to Castro's rebel front,
the 26 July movement, and is now commemorated as "national rebellious-
ness day." There is January 1, 1959, the moment from which Cuban time
has been subsequently reset. (I was born, for example, in the sixth year of
the Revolution and I write this in 2009, the "fifty-first year of the Revolution.") Then there is Independence Day, although Cubans dispute when
this is. Some celebrate when the U.S. governor general handed power over
to Cuba's first president on May 20, 1902. Havana, by contrast, insists the

correct date is thirty-four years earlier, when Carlos Manuel de Céspedes freed his slaves and began the first war of independence against Spain.

All Cubans agree, however, on the portentousness of the revolt of September 4, 1933. It is a moment roughly halfway through the sixty-odd years of the Cuban Republic, a mathematically neat division because there was one kind of Cuba before it and another that followed after. It is also a negative date, a valley rather than a peak of Cuban history, because nobody celebrates what happened then. As Lobo put it in his old age from exile: "All our misfortunes in Cuba date from that fateful day in September 1933 when Batista being a sergeant took over in a coup d'état."

GERARDO MACHADO WAS then the island's president. He was also the country's first dictator. A former butcher who had lost two fingers on his left hand to a meat cleaver as a young man, he had risen to the rank of brigadier general during the War of Independence. An astute-looking man, dapper in a dark suit, white shirt, and tie, with horn-rimmed spectacles and short silver hair, he had since become a successful sugar planter and businessman.

Although he is now painted in the darkest of tones, everyone applauded Machado when he took office in 1925. He promised strong rule, national regeneration, and an end to corruption. He built a central highway through the country, expanded the Malecón, and said he would "discipline these Cubans," the "Italians of the Americas." U.S. tourists flocked to Havana, escaping Prohibition, charmed by the island's architecture, climate, music, and rum. Machado joined in the Havana high life and could be seen at nightclubs such as the Château Madrid.

Yet four years later Machado had become a tropical Mussolini. His fawning supporters called him El Supremo, and when the president asked what the time was, the reply came back, "any time you like." In 1929 he changed the constitution to allow himself a second term. Student unrest grew. Then came the New York stock market crash and the onset of the Great Depression. In the United States and Europe, banks shut their doors, farm prices collapsed, and there was talk of an Apocalypse. Keynes told an audience in Chicago in mid-1930: "We are today in the middle of the greatest catastrophe—the greatest catastrophe due entirely to economic causes—of the modern world. I am told that the view is held in Moscow that this is the last, the culminating crisis of capitalism, and that our existing order will not survive it." Cuba, so often apart from the currents that affected the rest of the world, was sucked into the maelstrom. Foreign tourists no longer came to Havana. The sugar price fell and unemployment grew. For those mill hands who still had jobs, wages collapsed to a third of their level in 1929—the lowest since the time of slaves. For the first time, phrases such as "class struggle" and "anti-Imperialism" rose from Cuban lips. Machado clamped down on the growing unrest with uncommon ferocity. By 1933, he was literally feeding his opponents to the sharks.

Ernest Hemingway captured the mood in his first Cuban novel, *To Have and Have Not*, begun that October. In a dramatic opening scene, Harry Morgan, a bootlegger and the book's central character, meets secretly at the Pearl of San Francisco café with three anti-Machado revolutionaries,

> . . . good looking young fellows, wore good clothes; none of them wore hats, and they looked like they had plenty of money. Talked plenty of money, anyway, and they spoke the kind of English Cubans with money speak.

They were members of the ABC, a secretive rebel movement, who wanted to buy safe passage out of Cuba to escape the clutches of Machado's secret police, a goon squad known as La Porra, literally, The Bludgeon. Morgan refused their request.

> As they turned out of the door to the right, I saw a closed car come across the square toward them. The first thing a pane of glass went and the bullet smashed into the row of bottles on the show-case wall to the right. I heard the gun going and, bop, bop, bop, there were bottles smashing all along the wall.

The ABC—so named because of its cellular structure, whereby if a member of, say, cell B1 was captured, he could not betray his superiors in any of the A cells, nor his peers in any of the B or C cells—continued to plant bombs and assassinate Machado supporters. There were nightly shootings in Havana, on the streets and in theaters and cafés. Unperturbed, Machado proclaimed he would serve out his second term, which ran until the middle of 1935, and "not one minute more, not one minute less." But that spring Sumner Welles, the new U.S. ambassador, arrived. Tall, condescending, and patrician, a classmate of Franklin Roosevelt at Groton and Harvard, Welles landed in Havana on May 8, 1933, immaculately dressed in a three-piece suit. His brief was to mediate an end to the crisis. Further violence and unrest soon made it clear to Welles that Machado had to go. On August 4, the country was paralyzed by a bus stoppage that turned into a spontaneous general strike. In Havana not a wheel turned and not a factory was open; no cigar workers sat at their tobacco rolling tables, and all offices and businesses were closed. "Outwardly Havana was a tomb," wrote one observer. "In reality it was a seething cauldron." Seven days later, Machado learned he had lost both the United States' and his own army's support. He fled Cuba by plane the following morning, bound for the Bahamas with his family, five revolvers, and seven bags of gold on board. As he flew over the island, he saw the Cuban sky stained red by the fires of the burning homes of his former supporters.

The violence unleashed by Machado's departure was unlike any other that Cuba had experienced since independence. Fed as much by desperate hunger as by a thirst for revenge, the printing presses of pro-Machado newspapers were smashed to pieces and the mansions of former Machadistas and the president's mistresses were looted. Throughout the island, gunshots and shouts summoned witnesses to impromptu executions. Ruby Hart Phillips, the *New York Times* correspondent in Havana, watched one Machado supporter reach his end outside the Capitolio building.

> As he crossed the street someone recognized him and cried out his name. The horde was upon him. He drew his revolver, backed up

against a huge light post and prepared to die fighting. A huge stone smashed against the side of his head; a bullet struck him in the breast. He sagged clinging to the post for support, his revolver empty. The crowd howling like devils closed in. Across the street on the balcony of the hotel, his wife and two children saw him beaten to death before the bullet could take effect. Several soldiers standing on the sidewalk looked on calmly and finally one pushed his way through the mob and sent a bullet crashing through the brain of the victim. The body was completely unrecognizable when the mob finished their work.

Welles tried to reinstate order by installing a new government. It collapsed after just twenty-one days. Then, in early September, Fulgencio Batista, an unknown army sergeant, took control of the Camp Columbia army base outside Havana to press for better housing and pay. What started as an act of military insubordination soon escalated into a full-fledged coup. Strike leaders and the ABC student rebels saw the opportunity and joined forces with Batista and other dissident sergeants. The two groups formed an uneasy alliance.

Batista and his sergeants were men of action, generally from poor backgrounds. Batista was then thirty-three years old. The charming and quick-witted son of a mulatto cane cutter, he had grown up in poverty in rural Cuba and raised himself through the army ranks as a stenographer. It was a deceptively useful role: transcribing orders had exposed him to the flow of military orders and intelligence. The student and labor leaders, by contrast, were mostly middle-class radicals. They spent hours debating the finer points of public policy and were led by Ramón Grau San Martín, a forty-six-year-old man of inherited wealth who spoke cultured Spanish and was a professor at the university. Under the slogan "Cuba for Cubans," Grau unilaterally abrogated the hated Platt Amendment, and instituted a minimum wage and a 40 percent cut in utility prices.

Taking power had been easy. Keeping it would prove difficult. "Who is ruling Cuba?" *El Mundo* newspaper asked on September 23, three weeks after the coup. Nobody knew for sure. The students and the sergeants were surrounded by powerful enemies. These included the U.S. ambassador; Welles was uncomfortable about Grau's apparently socialist agenda and refused to recognize his government. There were also the Communists, a growing and insistent force on the island, backed by Moscow. Finally, there were the military officers that Batista had ousted and who disdainfully regarded the upstart mulatto sergeant as a *guajiro*, or country boy. Each made their challenge in turn.

The first confrontation came on September 29, when soldiers fired on a Communist rally at Havana's Parque de la Fraternidad, Brotherly Park, killing at least six, although some estimates ran as high as thirty dead and more than one hundred wounded. A second battle followed three days later at the Hotel Nacional, where a group of two hundred military officers were making a stand against Batista's army. The officers stationed sharpshooters in the Nacional's red-tiled *miradores*, killing as many as one hundred. Batista summoned naval artillery, armored cars, and cannon to shell their positions. Crushed by this onslaught, and running low on ammunition, the officers surrendered. When they filed outside the building, a crowd opened fire from the tennis courts, killing eleven and wounding twenty-two.

The skein of violence and confusion that threaded through Cuba that year twisted itself around everybody, including Lobo. Shortly after the Nacional siege, a group of armed guards came to the Galbán Lobo office in Old Havana, arrested Lobo, and took him to La Cabaña fortress, a short boat ride across the bay. The soldiers told Lobo he was to be shot the next day for plotting against the government. Suspicions may have arisen because Lobo and his father knew Sumner Welles. When the American ambassador had first arrived in Havana six months before, aides had advised him to seek out the Lobos' counsel, as Heriberto was "one of the soundest, if not the soundest" businessmen in Havana, someone "who avoided politics and so could be trusted to keep confidential matters inviolate." It is also possible that Lobo was arrested because of his openly critical views about Cuba's restrictive sugar policies. Lobo saw them as responsible for the immiseration of the country, and had long campaigned for their removal. The year before, he had even traveled to Albany to explain this to Roosevelt. The president-elect had wanted the Lobos' opinion on how to relieve Cuba's growing state of unrest under Machado. Lobo told him that "unless Cuba was able to sell more sugar and at higher prices . . . a general upheaval would come about on the island." And so it had proved.

Lobo was held overnight in a subterranean dungeon. From the darkness of his cell he heard "the sea pounding against the rocks outside." His cell mates were common criminals: a mulatto from Santiago accused of raping and killing a young girl; a black shopkeeper from Camagüey accused of murder; and a Spaniard who had stabbed his Cuban wife to death after finding her in bed with another man. Lobo protested his innocence and was released the next day when the authorities realized they had made a mistake. Later, Lobo breezily dismissed the incident, but it was still a close call. Other Cubans—such as the marching Communists killed at Brotherly Park, or the officers at the Nacional—were less fortunate.

The whole island was in a state of unrest. Outside Havana workers marched on the sugar mills, potent symbols of foreign capitalism. In Camagüey, five hundred armed workers took control of the Lugareño mill. At the Central Soledad, in the neighboring province of Las Villas, the manager—Llewellyn Hughes, the son of a Welsh village priest from Caerphilly and a longtime Cuba resident—was imprisoned in his house by a mob. "It is so comforting to hear an English voice that I must speak. But I must be careful," he told a British reporter who called from the *Daily Express*. "This wire is tapped by the Communists. . . . The situation is so tense here that the slightest incident would undoubtedly lead to the loss of a good many lives." The strikes spread. By the end of September, thirty-six mills were occupied, a third of the total, and at Welles's request North American warships surrounded the island to glare over American property. Fearing intervention, Batista dispatched several columns of soldiers by train to the east of the island to bring order. It was a fateful decision. Many bloody and tragic events took place that year in Cuba, but one of the saddest happened at a sugar mill that my family once proudly considered their own.

. . .

NOBODY KNOWS, FOR sure, how many people were killed at Senado on November 18, two and a half months after Batista's coup d'état. At the time, some said three died; others, ten. An investigation in the 1980s suggested that as many as twenty-two were killed. All versions are plausible, but nothing is sure, because the more I looked into the incident, the more confused everything became, and instead of a hard kernel of bitter truth, I found other stories, intermingled and contradicting each other.

The only part that everybody agrees on is that the incident began with a strike in the first week of September. Led by a Russian (or a Pole) called Pedro Stodolsky (or Stolovski), a thousand workers took control of Senado. Stodolsky's red beard gave him the very image of an agent provocateur but was in fact a mask for his youth; Stodolsky was then only in his mid-twenties (police reports of the time were uncertain about his precise age). He organized Senado's strikers. Some guarded the *batey*; they carried sharpened machetes and spiny branches cut from thorn trees. Others gathered supplies and food. Grau sent them a message from Havana: *firme con ustedes*, I stand firm with you. But then Grau fell out with the Communist Party and turned his back on the strikers. Stodolsky sent an *estaca*, a large wooden stake, to Havana in protest, a defiant response.

Senado was then a medium-sized mill. It provided employment for around four thousand workers and their families, and its St. Louis Fulton triple crushers produced around 200,000 bags of sugar, some 25,000 tons, every year. It was run by Don Emilio, the eldest son of Bernabé's second wife. Don Pedro, the former manager and my great-grandfather, had moved to Havana a few years earlier after the mill had passed to his half-brother's family following Bernabé's death.

Emilio had a playboy reputation—as did his brother Julio, who knew Churchill, apparently well enough to invite him to Senado where they had played tennis on a mahogany court laid down by Bernabé many years before. Perhaps unfairly, I think of Emilio as a cold-hearted man. One family story, although it may be apocryphal, told of a mill worker who asked Don Emilio for help after he suffered an accident that threatened his sight in one eye. "There is so much unhappiness in the world that it is much better to have just one," Emilio supposedly replied. "Two eyes would be too much misery to bear." He had only one son, also called Emilio, who later became a successful painter in New York. Emilito, little Emilio, was apparently estranged from his father and, while this may only be a coincidence, in Emilito's copious sketchbooks I have seen drawings of everything from teapots to roosters to skyscrapers and palm trees, yet never a drawing of a stalk of sugarcane.

Emilio was in Havana at the time of the strike, staying at the Nacional. A workers' committee came to talk to him directly to try to end the standoff. It was two weeks after the Nacional's siege, and the group met in the battle-scarred gardens of the hotel, its balconies shorn off by artillery fire, the insides looted to the walls. In the distance, the group could hear gunshots and the occasional bomb going off. Emilio was apparently befuddled and confused. Many years later, one of the five workers from Senado recalled their brief conversation. Emilio told the delegation that everything was too chaotic.

"When the situation in the country is sorted out, then we'll sort ourselves out too," he said.

Disappointed, the workers made to leave. As they turned to go, Emilio asked them: "You must be feeling the pinch, no?"

"Yes," they replied. "But we are still on our feet."

"Surely you need some money. Do you need any?" Emilio asked.

"No, we still have some left," the men said proudly, rejecting the offer. But on the way back to Camagüey, they had an accident in their car and had to borrow ten pesos to continue the journey home.

Parsing this snippet of conversation, I figure it is possible that Emilio had tried to offer the men some kind of bribe, although his concern for their well-being could just as well have been genuine. Emilio had already arranged for weekly provisions to be distributed to mill workers and their families during the strike. He had also instituted an eight-hour day, one of the workers' demands, even before the strike began. Furthermore, around 80 percent of Senado's employees had paid work for the whole year—

generous terms, on which the mill lost money, especially as sugar workers elsewhere were then lucky to be employed for seventy days, let alone a whole year. The mill had also allowed the formation of a union, albeit in opposition to the Communist group that Stodolsky had organized.

Similar confusions blurred the traditional lines of class warfare elsewhere on the island. Indeed, many of the strikes in Cuba that year were less because of worker dissatisfaction than a reflection of the country's militant mood. At the Bacardi rum company in Santiago, a newly established union had also gone on strike, even as it paradoxically complimented the company in its founding statutes, while simultaneously affirming its own Marxist ideology:

> Although we know the capitalist class is always antagonistic in its relations with the proletariat . . . we recognize the Bacardi Rum company of Santiago, making an exception to the rule, has always maintained the most cordial and friendly relations with its employees, to whom it has been most considerate.

All this suggests that reconciliation at Senado should have been possible. Indeed, on November 5, nineteen days after the Nacional meeting, a second group of Senado workers met in Havana at the newly formed Labor Ministry, with a follow-up meeting with Emilio arranged for three days later. Officials said that "a harmonious end to the conflict is expected on that day." Instead, events disrupted the plan. As dawn rose over Havana on the day the Senado strike was due to be resolved, an air attack led by army officers and members of the ABC bombed Batista's troops and President Grau in the Presidential Palace. The fighting continued in a series of skirmishes and ended with an artillery barrage on the rebels, who took shelter in the Atares fortress at the head of Havana's harbor. The final death toll ranged between two and five hundred, with many more wounded. Amid this mayhem, the meeting between Emilio and the striking workers never happened. Ten days later, some six hundred kilometers east of Havana, the killings at Senado took place.

. . .

THIS IS WHAT I now understand happened at Senado on the morning of November 18, 1933, another inglorious date from an inglorious year that no Cuban commemorates but which shaped the island's bitter history thereafter.

The events took place at a nondescript railway crossing called La Loma de Cortaderas, or cutters' hill, a dusty rise two kilometers outside the mill. On one side there was a hoisting yard and the small house of a local farmer. On the other, next to the railway tracks, lay a field of sugarcane and beside it another of sweet potatoes. Three large trees relieved the desolation of the landscape. They stood over the crossroads and had thin green leaves, spiny branches, and distinctive yellow cat's-tail flowers. Cubans know the trees as *algarrobo americano*; North Americans call them mesquite. I imagine a quietness in the air, something like the stillness that Emilito captured in an early-morning sketch of a Cuban back road, the calm only emphasizing the explosive presence of the men who would soon fill the scene.

A large group—some said two hundred men, others a thousand—topped the rise at about 9:30 that morning. A few were on horseback at the head of the column. The rest walked. They were mostly Haitians and some Jamaicans, imported to do the hard field labor that many Cubans and Spaniards felt beneath them; cane cutting is literally back-breaking work. The group reached the crossroads and one of the riders raised his hand as a signal. Everyone stopped. "Wait here," he shouted. Another horseman drew alongside. "We will go ahead first to ask permission to enter the mill," he explained. Together they rode off at a canter, their horses' hooves throwing up small bursts of dust.

What the men now waited for at the crossroads, nobody knew for sure. Some believed they were waiting to join a rally at the mill to press home their demands. Others thought the rally was to celebrate the mill owners' agreement to these demands, such as the eight-hour day. Some believed they were marching on the mill to take it over. They carried pointed sticks and sharp machetes—some even had rusty old guns, relics

Caribbean landscape, by Emilio Sanchez.

of the War of Independence—and wanted to advance right away. The mix of languages—Spanish, English, and Haitian patois—only increased the confusion.

After perhaps an hour, the railway tracks pinged, announcing a wagon's approach. The waiting men looked up. There was no sign of the two horsemen who had left earlier. Instead, they saw a small group of uniformed rural guards walking toward them, led by a sergeant. Some of the guards carried rifles; the rest had .45-caliber pistols slung around their hips. One of the workers, mounted on a horse, pulled up next to a friend. "Hey buddy," he said. "This looks strange."

In the most folkloric version of the story, the sergeant then told the workers that the mill owners had agreed to the union's requests and suggested a group photograph to mark the occasion. The workers lined up in front of the box camera, with its characteristic tripod and dark hood. The sergeant told them to huddle closer to fit into the frame. Then he drew back the black cowl and sprayed the men with bullets from the machine gun hidden underneath.

Eyewitness accounts gathered by a Cuban researcher fifty years later do not mention this camera–machine gun. Instead, they suggest that the sergeant approached the group, stopping close enough to see that the whites of the eyes of the men waiting there were yellow. To better hear what he had to say, the crowd formed a half-circle around the increasingly nervous sergeant. "There aren't going to be any problems," he said. "But if you want to come into the mill you have to throw down your weapons. Order please!"

The workers put their weapons on the ground as the sergeant told them and started to walk toward the mill, still in a half-circle. The sergeant and the other rural guards, feeling surrounded, panicked. Four of them suddenly dropped to their knees, lifted the muzzles of their weapons into the air, drew the rifle butts tight into their shoulders, and let loose a volley. The cane workers saw and heard the flashes of the gunshots, yet for a moment nothing happened. Then a shower of twigs, leaves, and yellow flowers fell on them from the branches of the trees above. The crowd began to swirl in panic. Some men threw themselves onto the ground; those on horseback ducked. When they looked up again they saw the soldiers' rifles pointing directly into their midst. Then the scene really exploded. The horsemen dug their heels into their horses' flanks and charged forward, trampling the others lying by them on the road. Everything spun out of control. There were more gunshots. The cane cutters started to run. Some scrambled into the cane field. Others climbed the high earth banks that flanked the railway lines. From the top, they tumbled into the gulley below, where some later said a squadron of soldiers was waiting. According to some reports, they did have a large machine gun, mounted on a tripod on an open railway truck, and opened fire.

One of the many inconsistencies that thread through this terrible incident is that when I asked my immediate uncles and aunts, none of them had even heard about it. I showed them a macabre photograph that I found in my grandmother's photo album. It lay incongruously between charming scenes of her childhood at Senado: simple interiors of her uncle Pedro's house with clapboard walls and bare wooden floors; my grandmother on a swing in the yard; the amateur league baseball games, where the famous

The macabre photograph in my grandmother's Senado picture album.

Cuban slugger Roberto Ortiz, "the Giant from Senado," first swung a bat. This gruesome picture, by contrast, showed three men in military uniform sitting around a machine gun on a tripod loaded with a bandolier of ammunition. *¿Qué?* my relatives had all exclaimed in horror and doubt.

I thought perhaps my great-aunt might remember something. So on a sultry July afternoon, I drove to her roomy ranch house in Belle Glade, a featureless agricultural town seventy miles north of Miami set amid grass and sugarcane fields that run straight to the horizon.

Tía Angelita is ninety-five, old enough to have known about the strike and sharp enough to remember it. She was sitting in a cane rocking chair when I walked into her front room, dressed in a floral print dress with a small gold chain and cross around her neck. A portable radio played tangos on a small table by her side. "The music keeps me company," she explained, as I bent down to kiss her on the cheek. Angelita is a warm and courageous presence: although half-blind, she has lived alone since Don Alvaro, her husband, died a few years ago. One of Bernabé's grandsons by his first wife, Alvaro had remained in Senado to manage its ranch, a kind of Camagüeyano *High Chaparral*. Indeed, in his swaggering youth Alvaro looked like the Marlboro Man, and cowhands would remove their hats, bow their heads as a token of respect, and murmur "Don Alvaro" when he did his morning rounds. Alvaro and Angelita lived at the mill after marrying in 1935.

Yes, Angelita said, she recalled the strike. She remembered that Emilio was staying in Havana at the time. She remembered the baseball player Ortiz, and certainly the Russian, Stodolsky. "He wanted to close down the warehouse, or only have it open for an hour a day," she said. "Alvaro often spoke to me about that."

We sat around a glass-topped table, and Angelita started to caress the surface as we talked. A large wooden bookshelf ran along one side of the room behind her, filled with the histories of great men. On a middle shelf, a bronze statuette of a solemn heifer stood guard next to a biography of Franklin Delano Roosevelt. In one corner, on the books' spines, I saw the names of the English Romantic poets, Shelley, Keats, and Byron, that Alvaro liked to read. I asked Angelita about the massacre.

"What massacre?" she replied. I described what I knew. She looked puzzled and thought about it for a while.

"Well, I am not sure there was a killing," she said. "I never heard of such a thing, and I talked to everyone in the mill, you know. Not just the *Sanchezes*," she added with gentle emphasis.

Angelita's brow furrowed above her one good eye, magnified in the spectacles. She riffled through her memories. Then she made up her mind.

"No, there was no killing," she said firmly, and patted the table softly with her left hand.

Two days later, Angelita telephoned me in Miami to say that she had spoken to a friend whose uncle had also once worked at Senado and he thought that, yes, something might have happened, maybe there had been a killing after all, someone in Cuba had even written a book about it apparently. At the time, though, it all felt very much like Macondo, the mythic town of *One Hundred Years of Solitude* in which Gabriel García

Márquez describes a historic and similarly disputed massacre of banana workers that took place in northern Colombia in December 1928.

> "There must have been three thousand of them," he murmured.
>
> "What?"
>
> "The dead," he clarified . . .
>
> The woman measured him with a withering look. "There haven't been any dead here," she said. "Since the time of your Uncle . . . nothing has happened in Macondo."

MAYBE TWENTY-TWO PEOPLE did die that morning in Senado in 1933, maybe less. Maybe there was a machine gun disguised as a camera, or mounted on a tripod in an open railway carriage, or maybe not. Probably not; it wasn't in keeping with traditions at the mill. The British ambassador who subsequently investigated the death of Elijah Sigree, a forty-one-year-old Jamaican worker killed that day, noted in his dispatches to London that Senado "always had a good reputation as regards its treatment of . . . laborers." Still, the times were such that a massacre *could* have happened that morning.

The events of 1933, such as the killings at Senado, set Cuba's political course for the next three decades. For one, they secured Batista's position. When Welles made it clear that he would never recognize Grau's government, Batista shifted his support to a more acceptable leader. Grau resigned, and within five days the new government received recognition and a twenty-one-gun salvo from the battleship *Wyoming* anchored off the Malecón. Henceforth, Batista would dominate Cuban politics, either as president or as head of the army from behind the throne. Welles's refusal to recognize Grau's progressive government also left Cuba with a feeling of unfinished business, the sense of an incomplete revolution. Castro's revolution therefore grew out of this revolution, as Hugh Thomas writes in his magisterial Cuban history, in the same way that the Second World War followed the First. Furthermore, the bloodletting—led by the anti-Machado movements of the ABC, the students, the unions, and the Communists—glorified violence in the pursuit of that unfinished revolution.

In a presentiment of events to come, the poet and Communist leader Rubén Martínez Villena wrote in 1933 of the red flags that would one day fly over the island's sugar mills. "Eyes still young today," he foretold, "will not yet be old when they look upon this marvel." Chilling prophecy and unheeded warning: Fidel Castro—living in the foothills of Oriente province, near the United Fruit Company's Miranda mill, and born to a wealthy landowner and his common-law wife—was seven years old at the time.

PART TWO

Six

A TALENT FOR
SPECULATION

The sun slices through gaps in the wooden shutters of a small walk-up apartment in Havana, and I wake slowly in a wooden rocking chair where I had fallen asleep. I had just lunched with a Cuban historian at her home, we had discussed Lobo, and afterward she had retired to her study, asking if I would like to stay in the front room and sit out the midday heat. I watched television; there was a program state-broadcast from Venezuela. President Hugo Chávez, Cuba's closest ally in the Americas, was inaugurating a new hospital, and Evo Morales, the Bolivian president, was at the opening ceremony, as was Mahmoud Ahmadinejad, the president of Iran. I had listened to Chávez tell the audience that Che Guevara was a doctor, and Fidel Castro the greatest doctor of them all, "a doctor of the soul," which made him "a father, our father of all the Latin American revolutions, and my father." And then I had dozed off.

Stirring from my sleep, I switch off the television and look at the dust in the air, normally invisible, glitter and dance in the light. I turn the handle on the shuttered windows and force them open, pushing against the sunlight as if it were a wind. I look across the street and see an old woman, as brown and wrinkled as a raisin, sitting in a dark room on the first floor of a rundown building opposite. I watch her, watching me, both of us motionless, separated by fifteen feet of still afternoon air. In the silence and the heat it feels as though time has stopped again in Cuba, and with that as though the past might come alive.

Even today, a mysterious aura surrounds Lobo's success, as is so often the case with the very rich. Before the revolution, envious competitors believed he had an almost occult ability to create wealth. As early as 1937, one Havana newspaper described him as:

> The new sugar magus
> Who turns his knowledge into gold,
> And like a bull holds sway
> Over all that is bought and sold.

Many years later, Lobo's Midas touch won him a walk-on part in Alejo Carpentier's last novel, *The Consecration of Spring*. The great Cuban writer described him as "the Sephardic millionaire, renowned for his miraculous ability to weather the market's ups and downs"—a halfway accurate description. Others believed his wealth was evidence, surely, of some great crime. Such distrust was more than just tropical malice or the usual suspicion of corruption. It grew out of the misgivings that speculators face everywhere.

Lobo's office was in Old Havana and I had an appointment there. I closed the shutters, washed my face, and said goodbye to the historian, who was now half-dozing, an open book across her lap. I let myself out the door, walked down a narrow staircase with blue walls, and stepped out into the street. In the distance I saw the pale, porous stone of the old city, filigreed with late afternoon sun.

LOBO HAD AN almost mystical attachment to the firm. He called it *la casa*, the house, the same as stockbrokers did in London when English finance was still a cottage industry and city gents wore bowler hats and carried furled umbrellas to work. It stood on a corner in Old Havana, two blocks west of the Plaza de Armas, the old seat of the Spanish governors. Down one side ran Obispo, Havana's traditional street of bookshops. Down the other was O'Reilly, known as Havana's street of banks. It was an apt address for a bibliophile and speculator such as Lobo.

I walked through the colonial splendor of Old Havana. In Lobo's day, it was not the pretty town that it has since become, the buildings freshly restored and painted, the streets newly laid with cobblestones. Then it was an almost dingy place, filled with architectural inconsistencies, much of it simply falling down. There was little space, no vacant lots, no rustling trees, and few tourists—except for the American sailors who spilled out of bars like the Floridita and Sloppy Joe's and wandered into the colonial quarter. There were somber government ministries and dark churches, pathologically baroque, filled with candles and the smell of incense. Many of the old colonial palaces had been turned into dismal flats. *Es anticuado vivir en la ciudad,* it is old-fashioned to live in the city, real estate developers had advertised in glossy magazines like *Social.* And by the 1930s, most of the grand families that once lived in the old city had sold out and bought new homes in the leafy suburbs of Vedado and Miramar. They were followed in turn by the jewelers, tailors, milliners, artificial flower makers, and hairdressers that had once lined Obispo. Most of these set up shop a few blocks west in the new town center, by the department stores around San Rafael Street that had improbable names such as El Fenix (the Phoenix), El Encanto (the Enchantment), Fin del Siglo (End of the Century), and my grandfather's own shop, Sanchez-Mola. The colorful goods they displayed in abundance were as much a reflection of American-inspired consumerism as traditional Cuban hedonism, the desire to live, dress, and eat well.

The banks, though, remained in Old Havana while the rest of the city moved on. Among the most important Cuban lenders there were Banco Gelats, Banco Pedroso, and the Falla-Gutiérrez family's Trust Company of Cuba. By the late 1950s, *Fortune* magazine ranked them among the world's five hundred biggest banks. Meanwhile, among the sugar brokers, there were Galbán Lobo, the houses of Luis Mendoza and García Beltrán, and Rionda's Cuban Trading Corporation, run by his nephew George

Braga. ("The only other trader," Lobo once said, "to whom I would tip my hat.") In the 1920s, Cuban merchants had all looked up to Rionda and his organization as an emblem of success. But as the Cuban economy recovered from the Great Depression in the years leading up to the Second World War, Lobo had grappled his way to the front and led the field. "G[albán-Lobo] with his organization in Cuba can today wipe the floor with anybody else," one of Rionda's partners in London cabled Havana in early 1940.

I wandered down O'Reilly, Havana's former "Wall Street," where brokers and lenders had once financed the island's sugar crop. The buildings still look austere, massive, and pompous, as was the long-held custom. In 1859 the American writer Richard Henry Dana described the stone floors, panels of porcelain, high rooms, and colossal windows of one Havana sugar merchant's stately offices. Inside, amid rich and heavy furniture, sat the merchant, dressed "in white pantaloons and thin shoes and loose white coat and narrow neck tie, smoking a succession of cigars, surrounded by tropical luxuries." These opulent buildings have long since found new use. Through one open door, a massive entrance flanked by Doric columns and white stone plinths, I saw how the cavernous vestibule of the old Royal Bank of Canada had become a garage, filled with parked cars, yellow Coco Taxis, and motorbikes leaking oil onto the marble floor. At another I marveled at two metal safes, the size of small rooms, their doors swung open to show locks as intricate as the workings of a watch. The site had first been a church. Then it was bought by the Banco de Comercio in 1926, which installed safes where the altar had once been. Recently the building has been converted into a concert hall, and I sometimes listened to grave chamber music played there in the evenings.

I noticed similar progressions—from the sacred to the profane and then the melancholic—repeated elsewhere, even in the names of sugar mills. Cuba's first plantations were named after saints. Then neoclassical names like *La Ninfa*, the nymph, became popular. By the end of the 1800s planters christened their mills *Atrevido* (Audacious) and *Casualidad* (Chance), reflecting sugar's variable fortunes, and when the planters' own wealth waned, more desperate-sounding names like *Apuro* (Wit's End) and *Angustia* (Anguish) cropped up. One of Lobo's mills, founded just before the last war of independence, was called *Perseverancia*, or Perseverance. In the 1960s, such mills were renamed after revolutionary heroes or important socialist dates, and Lobo's Perseverancia was rechristened *Primero de Mayo*, the first of May, after Workers' Day. Before that, one of my cousins remembered playing at a ruined mill in Camagüey that was built in the 1950s but never operated. It was called *El Desengaño*, the Disappointment—a fitting Cuban epitaph.

Old Havana was scruffy and noisy, but Lobo enjoyed its bustle and dreaded the day when the migration of businesses to some "uptown" area might force Galbán Lobo to move too. From the second floor of *la casa* he could see cargo steamers and pleasure boats glide through the Havana bay, headed for the deeper blues of the open sea. Sometimes early in the morning, when the water was calm and the sun's rays bounced off the surface, flooding the city with light, rowing skiffs with four- and eight-man teams from the Tennis Club practiced in the bay.

During the sunniest hours of the day, many of the streets were shaded by colorful canopies, turning them into temporary shopping arcades. Then noise exceeded even the usual high Cuban decibels. Music blared from Victrola phonographs that played from the dark bar tucked inside the ubiquitous corner shop, the *bodega*. There was the sound of street sellers, the *pregón*. Some used a bell or whistle; many simply had a call, each sound a distinctive cry for the ice seller, the knife sharpener, the fruit vendor, the peanut salesman. *¡Maníí!* On street corners, passersby exchanged a few thousand words of casual conversation with each other. Traffic horns punctured the din. During one visit to her father's office, María Luisa remembered watching a driver stop his car in the middle of the street and block the traffic while he drank, with characteristic insouciance, a thimble of sweet, black coffee bought from a street stall. There were also smells, the thick odor and blue haze of frying pork fat from the Chinese restaurants, and the aroma of freshly made pastries from cafés such as the Europa. There, a genial Catalan baker served delicious pastries to his old city clientele of clerks, secretaries, and bankers, treating them all equally as royalty. The plain-looking dowager was a *su altesa*, your highness; young girls were all *princesas*; anyone with gray hair was a *distinguido*; men were counts, barons, and marquises.

The baker's patter at the Europa was all part of the tropical fantasy of a country where everyone, as the Condesa de Merlin remarked, was either "a master or a slave." And who wanted to be a slave—especially when there were so many Cuban kings and queens? To name a few, there were Ramón Fonst Segundo, fencing gold medalist at the 1900 Olympics, known as El Nunca Segundo, the Never-Second; José Raúl Capablanca, King of Chess and world champion from 1921 to 1927; Kid Chocolate, twice world featherweight boxing champion; and several and various kings of baseball and queens of *son*. Even Havana's beggars, or especially its beggars, shared this penchant for grandiosity. In Lobo's day there were the Emperador, the Emperor, who wore a braided jacket of the Austrian court, bristling with medals; another who called herself the Marquesa, a mulatta with rouged cheeks and ornate hats from the 1900s; and, most famously, the Caballero de París, the Gentleman of Paris, a quixotic figure who wore a black waist-length cape clasped at the throat of a soiled white shirt, faded black trousers, and broken shoes.

The Caballero de París first appeared on Havana's streets in the 1920s and paced them for the next fifty years. With his shoulder-length hair and Christ-like beard, he walked through the Dance of the Millions, the fall of Machado, the prosperity of the two decades that followed, and then the epoch-changing event of the revolution itself. Nobody knew why he walked, although it was thought it was because he suffered a broken heart, which made him a popular symbol of great love gone wrong. The Caballero de París neither drank nor smoked, was well spoken, unfailingly polite, and especially gallant with ladies. He once honored my mother with a rose and read her a poem, which was his calling card and for which she thanked him politely. He refused charity and said he slept in a "divine castle"—the boulevard of the Prado, whose bronze lion statues were his subjects. "I am the *King of This World* because the world is always at my feet," this gentlest of madmen once said:

María Esperanza on her wedding day, 1932.

I don't look at my dirty shoes. I look about at the ground, the pavement. Everything is below me. Above is the sky, from which I came
and where I will go. . . . Those who criticize or look down on me do
not know and will never know what lies in the depths of my heart.
Such Pharisees ignore the immense glory, the deep emotion that is
felt whenever I say: I am the *Caballero de París.*

Havana has always been an imperial city. While the Marquesa, the
Emperador, and the King of This World roamed the streets of Old Havana, in an office one floor above them worked Julio Lobo, the world's
King of Sugar, presiding over a vast domain described to him daily by his
electronic heralds of telex and telephone.

BY 1934, while Cuba was still in the throes of a terrible recession, Lobo
had been married for two years. María Esperanza Montalvo, his wife, was

a great beauty, with a petite figure, bow-shaped lips, dark curly hair, and fair skin. She came from a distinguished family that had its roots in Cuba's colonial aristocracy; the Condesa de Merlin was a great-aunt. They had met in the summer of 1931, during the annual festivities of the Havana rowing regatta, and had had a whirlwind romance. Lobo proposed in November, and they had married the following January.

They made a glamorous couple at the wedding: she had a good name and good looks, and Lobo had good prospects. Yet Heriberto had congratulated his son in a strangely formal letter that alternately praised María Esperanza for her evident beauty while gently warning his son about the responsibility he was taking on. María Esperanza had been raised at home by a governess and had led a sheltered life. Lobo, meanwhile, moved in a bustling commercial world. It may be that he saw in his bride some of her astonishing ancestor's glittering charm. As well as writing a popular memoir and marrying one of Napoleon's generals, the Condesa had presided over a celebrated Paris salon, where she gathered artists and statesmen like Lord Palmerston, Victor Hugo, and Rossini. Yet where the Condesa was outspoken—"lively and passionate, even to excess, I never saw any need to repress my emotions, much less hide them," she once admitted—María Esperanza was shy and reserved. Temperamentally, even in their early days of marriage, Lobo and María Esperanza were worlds apart.

The newlyweds moved into the middle house on Eleventh and Fourth streets that Heriberto had built next to his and Virginia's home. Their first daughter, Leonor, was born the following year, named after Lobo's deceased elder sister. María Luisa, their second child, was born in April 1934, the year after. María Esperanza remained at home, filling the largely decorative role of a woman of good breeding, while Lobo poured his more worldly ambitions into *la casa*. Home life increasingly took the backseat.

Only a year had passed since Lobo had almost been put against a wall and shot after the fall of Machado. The humility that Lobo had felt a few years before that, when he had offered his resignation to Heriberto, had also passed. Lobo now felt impatient. He sought to go beyond the huge sale of sugar he had made to Tate & Lyle in 1927, which had garlanded him with early success and prestige. Even in the midst of a global Depression, he wanted to take on the world. His opportunity came in 1934 with a remarkable feat of market manipulation. Lobo never commented on how he cornered the New York sugar market that December. It was, he would merely say later, the only "perfect squeeze that was ever pulled."

Corners, a trading tactic as old as markets themselves, are tense games that usually fail. Their aim is to acquire enough of a stock or a commodity to force—or "squeeze"—up its price and so catch out anyone who had sold it short in anticipation of buying it back later at a cheaper price. When a commodity is effectively cornered, the operator can demand any price he wishes from the short-sellers, who are legally required to cover their positions. As the saying goes:

He who sells what isn't his'n
Must buy it back or go to pris'n.

The main "longs" in this operation—the investors who owned physical sugar, hoping its price would rise—were two Cubans, Lobo and Marcelino García, a broker and former planter who had survived a brush with bankruptcy in the 1920s and since rebuilt his fortune, becoming head of Cuba's Sugar Institute, the government agency responsible for managing the crop. The two main "shorts"—the investors who had forward sold sugar, betting that its price would eventually fall—were Charlie Hayden, founder of the Boston-based investment bank Hayden, Stone, and William Douglas, long-standing president of the Punta Alegre sugar mill. Both were pillars of the U.S. business establishment. Hayden was a bow-tied businessman who worked with clipped efficiency and lived by the motto "time is money." Meanwhile, Punta Alegre was the prize asset in a John D. Rockefeller Jr.–led consortium that owned 318,000 acres of Cuban sugarcane. Hayden, and the company that Douglas headed, were as Yankee as they came.

Lobo's squeeze hinged on an unusual combination of circumstances. In May, as part of Roosevelt's "good neighbor policy," the United States had cut its tariff on sugar imports and introduced quotas instead. This had two benefits for Depression-ravaged Cuba. As a protected market, Cuba enjoyed U.S. sugar prices that were generally higher than in the rest of the world. The quota also assured Cuba a home for much of its sugar. The problem was that Washington rather than Havana determined the size of the Cuban quota and, as the United States was its main market, in effect also the size of Cuba's sugar crop, the remainder being sold on volatile world markets. That is partly why in 1960, Cuba's revolutionary government would denounce the quota as "economic servitude." Indeed, by then, as Lobo noted, the quota was used more often to subsidize and protect domestic U.S. sugar producers than to reward reliable foreign suppliers like Cuba. Still, in 1934, only a few months after it had been established, a group of Cubans saw a way to bend the new agreement to their advantage. Strategy was planned in Havana and then executed in New York from rooms on the twenty-third floor of 99 Wall Street, Lobo's office.

It was a brilliantly subtle plan. Under the quota's rules, Cuba had to sell to the United States its required amount of sugar or forfeit market share. To fulfill that obligation, in October Cuba sold the year's remaining quota to U.S. buyers for 2.18 cents per pound. It seemed like an innocent move, but the result was trading mayhem. Anyone who had sold Cuban sugar short on the futures market now had a serious problem. They could not cover their short position, as there was literally no physical Cuban sugar for them to buy back. It had already been sold.

The squeeze convulsed the New York market. The sugar price threatened to go through the roof. The president of the New York exchange resigned. The shorts, missing 35,000 tons of sugar, complained that they had been trapped. The longs, mostly Cubans, said the trap was of their own making. Trading was suspended. Investigations were opened and a Senate hearing convened. Senator Arthur Vandenberg, representing the beet interests of Michigan, asked whether Cuba had used the terms of the quota to manipulate the market—and in a way it had. The Cubans in turn suggested that the North American short-sellers were trying to force down the price of their sugar, which was also broadly true. It was all part of the usual to and fro of U.S.-Cuban relations.

In theory the Cubans could have asked whatever price they wished from the shorts, who had to pay up and buy the sugar from them or face default and go to jail. "The [short] seller either delivers or fails to deliver. There is no mid-ground," argued an attorney for the Cuban longs. "There is no reason for any excuse." In the end the American business establishment closed ranks, and the Cuban longs were forced to sell to the Yankee shorts for 2.38 cents a pound. Nobody went to jail. The Cubans complained vociferously about this show of favoritism. Even so, they netted an estimated profit of some $150,000 for themselves, and the island, at the expense of U.S. investors.

Much Cuban writing is a lament about how the island is forever at the mercy of speculative foreigners. But speculation is a double-edged sword, and when Lobo, the man who later boasted "I am the market," wielded that sword, often it cut in Cuba's favor. His ploy also showed that Cubans could play the speculative game just as sharply as their U.S. peers.

It was from this moment that *la casa* began to pull away from the commercial opposition with Lobo leading the way; Heriberto, now sixty-four years old, occupied a lofty supervisory role and offered only broad guidance. For the next two decades, much like his father before him, Lobo strove to keep himself disengaged from Cuba's disorderly political life, often violent but also pluralistic and often democratic, while he pursued a dream of wealth for himself and, sometimes, the island as well.

I REACHED LOBO'S OFFICE after a ten-minute walk. From the outside, it looked the same as it had fifty years ago. There was the same impassive gray stone, the same covered balcony with its belle époque balustrade protruding over the same narrow sidewalk that skirted the building and which I'd seen in an old photograph. Inside, everything was in turmoil; fourteen state-owned firms were moving out, as the building was due to be renovated as part of the restoration drive of Old Havana that is led by Eusebio Leal, the town historian. Lobo's old office would soon serve as a teachers' annex for the gleaming marble-and-glass library and lecture theater that had been built opposite, on the site of Havana's oldest university.

A stocky man with tremendous energy, Leal is responsible for almost single-handedly saving the old city. At the time of the revolution, it was estimated that only a sixth of the three thousand or so buildings in Old Havana were in good condition. Plans had even been submitted in the late 1950s by the U.S.-based Catalan architect and town planner José Luis Sert to raze much of the old town, turn its graceful squares into parking lots, replace colonial buildings with Le Corbusier–style skyscrapers, and link the whole lot to an artificial island off the Malecón that would have casinos, hotels, and malls. Instead the revolution happened, saving Old Havana from this fate, and it was left to slip into further disrepair. The city stood in the sunshine, slowly crumbling, until 1982, when UNESCO designated Old Havana a World Heritage site. Then, in 1994, after the Cuban economy went into freefall with the end of Soviet subsidies, Leal's office was given the power to restore buildings and turn them into tourist-related hotels, restaurants, and shops, with the profits reinvested in social projects. Such work has made Leal a controversial figure. He enjoys ministerial rank in Cuba, a great deal of autonomy and international prestige, and is sometimes mentioned as a possible post-Castro president. Yet he is also respected in Miami for his deep historical knowledge and obvious love of Havana—even if critics say that Leal has turned its restored parts into a Potemkin village for foreign visitors.

I talked with Leal on the street corner by Lobo's former office, and he recognized Lobo as a lover of the old city and spoke warmly of him. Oddly, Leal seemed to admire Lobo's speculative ability too. "Lobo liked to have thousands of tons of sugar in his hand," he commented, clenching his fist tight. "Then he would let it loose on the market to move it and get the result he wanted." Leal then opened his hand and pushed his palm into the air in front of his chest, almost like a tai chi gesture, the force of all that sugar being released onto an invisible world market long ago.

This was praise of sorts from a historian and high-ranking Communist official, especially as the speculator is a figure so often depicted as a cause of the country's woes—and not just latterly by the revolutionary government. In 1828, the Reverend Abiel Abbot compared the speculative merchant to a parasitical vine that strangles Cuba's noble ceiba tree. The Condesa de Merlin also commented on the high rates of interest which merchants charged Cuban planters to finance the sugar crop during the colonial years. At 2.5 percent a month, she wrote, "the exorbitant interest doubles the debt, payments at first difficult quickly become impossible, and soon the merchant owns an amount equal to the value of the whole property." Fidel Castro's government, of course, has routinely criticized all forms of financial speculation. In 1966, Castro spoke of "those persons [who] have a peso sign in the head and want the people also to have a peso sign in the head and in the heart. And if we want a people that gets rid of the peso sign in the mind and the heart, then we must also have men who free their thoughts of the peso sign."

The irony is that speculation has always been central to Cuban history and the Cuban character. Cuba's European discoverer, Columbus, was a speculator bent on discovering a new route to the Indies in a quest financed by venture capital supplied by the king and queen of Spain. During the colonial years, the city was a bazaar that sprang to life each time the Spanish fleet sailed into port: one of the first streets to be laid from the Plaza de Armas was called *Mercaderes*, or Merchants. Economically, Cuba came of age after the British capture of Havana, a time of Adam Smith and David Ricardo. And during the Republic, strategically located near the Panama Canal, Cuba stood at the crossroads of all the shipping of the Western Hemisphere, importing most of what it consumed and exporting millions of tons of sugar in return. Indeed, it is because of this long history that Cubans, both inside and outside the island, still sometimes refer to themselves as the "Jews of the Caribbean." By this cheeky adage, Cubans mean that they consider themselves commercially sharper than everyone else. It is unsurprising, therefore, that Leal would tacitly recognize speculation as part of the fabric of the old city that he loved, and that Lobo felt so comfortable in the Cuban milieu.

When Lobo wrote to Gerry Asher, one of his principal traders in New York, that he was always "seeking, prying and executing on information. Our business, as you know, [is] based on good, exact and fast information—the secret [is] how to interpret that news rapidly," he was merely echoing the practices of Cuban speculators down the years and other speculators everywhere. In the nineteenth century, the planter and trader Tomás Terry used to note down in a little black book the daily exports and imports of Cienfuegos so he could divine the trading positions of his competitors.

Speculators also have a natural enthusiasm for any technology that brings markets closer to the centers of the financial world, be that the telephone or the radio, railways or air flight. That is why Cuba has always been a communications center. Pan American Airways began its life early in the twentieth century on the Havana–Key West route, and the first submarine telephone cable linking the United States to another country was laid across the Florida Straits to Havana in April 1921. When President Harding finished a brief call to his Cuban counterpart President Menocal that marked the occasion, Sosthenes Behn, the president of the Cuban Telephone Company, declared that the cable was only a first step in creating a communications hub in Havana that would span South and North America. A few years later, Behn's holding company, International Telephone & Telegraph, bought AT&T's international operations and built up large businesses throughout Europe and the Americas.

Cubans also have a particular fondness for speculative wagers. Before Castro, Cubans bet on cockfights, the lottery, jai alai, horse races, baseball, and every sort of device the casinos could think of. It is only a short step from gambling to high finance. "It is worth recording," wrote the American historian Leland Jenks of the Dance of the Millions, "that there developed in Cuba between 1917 and 1920, under indigenous control, most of the phenomena of speculation, industrial combination, price fixing, bank manipulation, pyramiding of credits and over-capitalization which we are accustomed to regard as the peculiar gift of the high civilized Anglo-Saxons." This was despite the fact that the Havana stock market never amounted to much, with only eighty members and sixty listed companies, and no more than a handful of stocks ever traded. Even so, as Jenks wrote, Cubans have "an astonishing aptitude for the most advanced refinements of high finance."

It may be that this "astonishing aptitude" stems from a Cuban abundance of the irreverent and anarchic spirit which is so central to speculation. Like the commercial fairs in medieval Europe, which it grew out of, the speculative spirit delights in subverting the established order. That is why great speculative moments are sometimes described as "carnivals of speculation."

The gulf between Cuba's vibrant merchant past and its commercially sterile present is huge, as is the paradox. Although a nation of naturally savvy entrepreneurs, Cuba has been subject to a half-century experiment in socialism that has ground most of the economy into the dust. Of course, the U.S. embargo has exacted a toll. When I spoke with Leal of this, he had compared the island to a huge sugar mill with the embargo a bung jammed into the chimney. "The blockade has to be released, otherwise the mill will be filled with smoke and fire," he said. Yet there is also the heavier economic cost exacted by what ordinary Cubans call the "internal embargo." This is the thicket of bureaucracy and the government's traditional antipathy to individual enterprise that can turn even shopping for groceries into a surreal excursion. "Pssst," someone had whispered to me from a dark Havana doorway in the early 1990s, as if he were a pimp or a drug dealer. "Want to buy some cabbage?"

Restrictions have subsequently been relaxed somewhat, and Cubans have quickly demonstrated their entrepreneurial capacities whenever the government has let them; in private farming, say, or operating small restaurants. In 2008, Cubans were allowed to stay at hotels previously reserved for tourists—so long as they had the dollars to pay the bill—and buy cell phones (although not toasters). Restrictions may well be lifted further. Even so, the possibility that a private citizen might be allowed again to own a mobile phone or toaster *company* remains, for now, a long way off.

THE FRONT DOORS of the old Galbán Lobo office on Obispo were barred and sealed, and entry was around the back through a parking lot on O'Reilly. A guard sitting at a plastic desk inside the back door said he was sorry that the building was so dirty. With that faint apology, he waved me through.

Inside, there was the usual disrepair. The windows were cracked, and

Galbán Lobo mural, Old Havana.

office doors with handwritten signs like *Supervisor* and *Economics Department* had been jammed shut, nails hammered into the locks. A paper sign
stapled onto one wall had the single word *School* written in faint pencil
above a rough arrow pointing down a long corridor. The last time Lobo
had seen the office after his fateful interview with Che Guevara, the rooms
had been taped up and loose papers covered the floor. Now it was in a
similar state, as the state firms that occupied the building packed their
boxes and moved on.

"The place is a labyrinth," apologized one office worker with short hair
and green eyes who offered to show me around. "All the offices have been
boxed up by these partitions to make more space," he explained, thumping
a drywall in a cramped room. Even so, I could still make out the basic
layout of the old office; three floors of rooms arranged like figures of eight

around two inner courtyards. One of these, a colonial patio overgrown with plants, had an old well in the center and a statuette of San Ignacio set in a mossy niche above a studded wooden door; this was the former main entrance. Downstairs around the second, larger courtyard was the sugar mural that Lobo had commissioned to illustrate the harvest, and which office managers, clerks, and secretaries would have walked past every day. It began on one side with a barefoot worker wearing a straw hat, stooped over in a plowed field, planting seeds. Subsequent panels showed cane cutters, the cane then loaded into a wagon, oxen pulling the wagon to a mill, and a mechanic with a greasing can who stood next to a huge boiler. The sugar then spilled out of vast chutes into jute bags held by bare-chested men with thickly muscled arms and calm, classically Greek faces. The final scene showed an official holding a clipboard and sitting on a bollard at a quay, a ship behind him. It could have been Lobo.

Lobo's own office was on the first floor. Downstairs would have been a central switchboard, where women wearing headphones took calls and plugged phone wires into flashing equipment. Around it there would have been rooms filled with neat rows of clerks' desks, each topped by a sturdy black typewriter and a bakelite phone, and a sugar laboratory that looked like an old-fashioned doctor's surgery with labeled glass bottles on shelves above a wooden workbench. Phones rang, telexes chattered, and typewriters clacked amid the daily hubbub. "A fat blond man is summoned into one office by an urgent voice," wrote a Cuban journalist in 1937 in a profile of a day at Galbán Lobo. "An American comes out of the other with the step of a victor. Two other ruddy Americans go in. Someone gives a final order. Another one protests." The voices came from the trading room. "There is commotion. The whole place seems like a cyclone," the journalist concluded, drawing a scene of colorful confusion instantly recognizable to anyone who has seen the floor of the New York Stock Exchange or the trading pits of the Chicago commodity market.

It takes a man of rare qualities to rise above such a fray. But at his trading desk, Lobo floated above the market noise even as he sat in the thick of it, feeling its vibrations and flows, his mind the gnomic center of a trading operation that leaned with and sometimes directed the market traffic. Lobo was constantly immersed in information. To the right of his desk sat a personal telephone operator. Over her head, stretching along the wall, ran a blackboard on which international sugar prices were chalked, erased, and revised. In front of Lobo stretched two rows of facing desks, each occupied by an assistant who could supply detailed information about a specific aspect of the business. At Lobo's left hand was a ticker that spat out news from the New York exchange, and beyond that another telex that kept Lobo in touch with his New York representative, Olavarría & Co., and his other agents around the world. The markets whirled around him. By his own admission, he stood ready to buy or sell, at almost any hour of the day, any quantity of sugar that was offered or solicited by anyone, anywhere. Even so, Lobo contained his extreme mental activity within a physical stillness that many commented on. "The difficulty," Lobo confided to one competitor, Maurice Varsano, a French sugar merchant, "is that our business is one where all the excitement and nerves should take place inside, and not with frantic movement."

Although the speculative business is filled with confusing jargon—from longs and shorts to bulls and bears, straddles, butterflies, and strikes—Lobo's essential skill, like that of any trader, was simple: to make accurate judgments about what the market was going to do next. This is more than just thinking about whether markets will go up or down; it is about handling uncertainty. In financial circles, this is known as "risk." As Keynes argued, the speculator "is not so much a prophet (though it may be a belief in his own gifts of prophecy that tempts him into the business) as a *risk-bearer*. If he happens to be a prophet also, he will become extremely, indeed preposterously, rich." Lobo was certainly a risk-taker, yet always denied that any special ability—such as miraculous foresight—lay behind his success. Arturo Mañas, the powerful head of Cuba's Sugar Institute in the 1950s, put it succinctly. Lobo's achievements, he once wrote, are "not due to clairvoyance or some ability to see into the future but rather that he worked harder than the rest."

Lobo had a legendary appetite for work. Brokering in those days was often a leisurely activity begun at ten o'clock, with a long break for lunch. By contrast, Lobo's days began at dawn. An office boy arrived at his house at 6:30 each morning, carrying a clutch of decoded cables that had been sent overnight from Lobo's agents in Europe, the Middle East, and Asia. Lobo worked his way through the messages over breakfast, wrote his replies, and the office boy would return to Galbán Lobo to code the telexes and send them off. Lobo then drove his daughters to school, dressed in his usual white linen trousers and starched white guayabera, and continued to his office in Old Havana. When he arrived at about eight o'clock, replies from his morning cables waited for him. "In that way, I gained a huge advantage over my competitors, who got into their Wall Street offices at 10am," Lobo said.

At his peak, Lobo handled almost half of Cuba's sales to the United States, half of Puerto Rico's, and some 60 percent of the Philippines' sugar. Some believed the sheer size of this operation gave him a dangerous ability to rig market prices to his own benefit and to the industry's harm. It was all part of the mythic market power that Leal had commented on. Lobo's response to such talk was always to shrug. "No man can control a commodity as big as this. That's absurd."

Still, Lobo's massive position in the sugar market did make him a dominant and often forbidding figure. "He was used to getting what he wanted," the U.S. historian Roland Ely told me. Now in his nineties, Ely has a hangdog face and lidded eyes and is one of the few people still alive who knew Lobo's work life before the revolution. They first met in New York in 1951 when Ely was cataloguing the business correspondence of Moses Taylor, a nineteenth-century merchant who amassed one of the United States' largest fortunes, largely from trading sugar with Tomás Terry, the "Cuban Croesus." Intrigued by Ely's work, Lobo invited him to stay in Havana, making available his library of Cuban history books— Ely said it was one of the most extensive he had seen—and opening doors for the historian on the island, including to the moldering Terry archive in Cienfuegos. Ely's subsequent book *Cuando Reinaba Su Majestad El Azúcar*, "When Sugar Reigned in All Its Glory," is considered a fundamental piece of Cuban scholarship. "Lobo had an outsized ego, you know," Ely commented to me.

This ego often made Lobo unpopular with his peers, as did his almost

Napoleonic refusal to flinch from the prospect of conflict. "The sugar b[usines]s has mostly been handled by gentlemen and we don't propose to keep such racketeers in the b[usines]s as Lobo," George Braga from Rionda's Cuban Trading had vainly blustered in early 1940, when drinking had dulled Braga's edge amid the Sugar Exchange's cutthroat operations. Yet that "gentlemanliness" was often just a byword for a cozy Cuban world of mutual back-scratching that Lobo often upset. In 1944, Lobo publicly denounced an illegal sugar sale that another speculator, Francisco Blanco, had hoped to broker with Ecuador, forcing its cancellation and so beginning the two men's lifelong rivalry.

Speculators are also by their very nature outsiders—observing dispassionately from the sidelines, waiting for the propitious moment to strike. Indeed, Ely described how Lobo viewed business as an almost intellectual exercise, like a game of chess. "If you get it right, Lobo used to tell me, you got the other man into checkmate," Ely said. "That was where the fun was."

Still, if Lobo could be ruthless, nobody doubted his honesty. In one example, Lobo brokered a deal in September 1945 that swapped twenty thousand tons of sugar for Argentine candle wax, used to make soap. Although executed by Lobo, the terms of the deal were arranged by the Commerce Ministry. A huge scandal erupted when the details were revealed, and opposition politician Eddy Chibás (personal motto: "Shame against money") lambasted the government on his regular Sunday radio broadcast. But to Lobo, Chibás paid a backhanded compliment. "I generally believe the worst about *lobos*, the wolves, of this world," Chibás said during a detailed analysis of the affair on his show. "But despite a detailed examination, I find no reason to censure Galbán Lobo." Lobo may have played the game hard, but he played it fair.

Lobo's success was all the more remarkable in that he alone was largely responsible for it. Unlike many other privately owned businesses in the Hispanic world, or indeed his hero Napoleon, Lobo had very few members of his family in senior positions. "Papa always told me to never employ a nearby relative in a position with a lot of responsibility," Lobo once commented. By the late 1930s Heriberto was semiretired and Jacobo,

Lobo's younger brother, always played a minor role at *la casa*. Instead, Lobo relied on a tiny core team amid the four hundred or so staff that worked at the office. Most important was Carlotta Steegers, a prim nineteen-year-old assistant whom Lobo hired after an interview in 1939 at which her aunt had been present as chaperone. Carlotta had flaming red hair, a temper to match, and was agoraphobic—which is why the right-hand woman of the richest man in Cuba stayed behind in Havana after the revolution. Carlotta was unflinchingly loyal and one of the few people who could call Lobo an insolent idiot to his face. He enjoyed such raillery and trusted Carlotta so implicitly that she had power of attorney over all his affairs. "Carlotta could have left me standing in the street in just my underpants if she wanted to," he once observed.

Lobo's New York assistant, Margarita González, was almost as powerful. She handled all his American affairs and teasingly (and tellingly) referred to him in their correspondence as Caesar, while María Esperanza was dubbed Marie Antoinette. Enrique León, a shrewd man, meanwhile provided Lobo with political advice and legal counsel ("a lawyer should be like a priest," Lobo told León). They first met in the 1940s when León was acting as a young lawyer for the other side during a sugar deal. Admiring León's sharp mind, Lobo hired him as soon as the negotiations closed—although the manner in which he financed León's move to Havana from his home in Oriente is telling. León, short of funds, asked Lobo for a loan while he set himself up in Havana. Lobo agreed willingly— but then checked himself. "What if you die and can't pay back the office?" Lobo asked. León said he would take out a life insurance policy payable to Galbán Lobo in the case of such an eventuality. Lobo agreed; León never regretted the decision. Other than these three figures, the trading operation at Galbán Lobo was essentially a one-man operation.

It made for a punishing schedule, prefiguring the frantic life of a modern city worker. Each day, Lobo read and replied to some six hundred cables. He rarely stopped for an elaborate lunch, preferring milk and crackers or a simple meal delivered to his desk. "On the New York Sugar Exchange," he once explained mildly, "trading would not stop if I took a two-hour siesta. And even when New York is closed, sugar is traded almost every hour

María Esperanza, c. 1945.

somewhere in the world. So I try to be available." For Lobo, markets were continuous not only through time but also through space. "When a Cuban mill owner needs money to pay bills, I'll buy his next year's crop today. If a U.S. soft drink manufacturer is afraid prices will go up, I'll sell him sugar now, for delivery at any time." Yet he still found time to exercise regularly, unusual for those years. He fenced, boxed, and even sunbathed. He also organized his growing Napoleon collection, read copiously, expanded the spread of Galbán Lobo's businesses, and took his daughters on excursions around Havana and to his mills. The sole exception to Lobo's activity was María Esperanza, as they had become increasingly estranged.

"She was the most beautiful woman in Cuba when I married her," Lobo once told his son-in-law. But they'd hardly known each other after a mere six-month courtship, and there had been problems and incompatibilities from the start. While Lobo worked and traveled abroad on business—to the United States, Europe, South America, and around the Caribbean—María Esperanza attended to her boudoir at home, increasingly sullen and bored. "She was so pretty, but so selfish," remembered Fichu Menocal, one of the few members of Cuba's old social register to remain in Havana after the revolution. Some compared her cruelly to the Queen in *Snow White*, who asks the mirror: "Who is the fairest in the land?" Yet María Esperanza's mirror-gazing was less vanity than a narcissism that masked a wounded innocence. Lobo left magazines like *Time* and *Life* for María Esperanza to read in the hope that it might broaden her horizons. She preferred light novels about the tsarina's court or the life of the Chinese emperor's concubines. Leonor remembered how María Esperanza lost her temper if Leonor or her sister sat down while wearing linen, because it rumpled their clothes. "In those years, amid a world of caring grandparents, there were certain moments of pain," María Luisa similarly recalled. María Esperanza's loneliness grew only more acute as her husband began to conduct ever more elaborate love affairs, and she weathered the humiliation in the role of long-suffering wife in which she increasingly cast herself. "Please explain to Madame Reine that it is very difficult for me to call her now," Lobo had beseeched his New York assistant in one Christmas cable sent from Havana. Madame Reine was Lobo's first big love affair; they had met in Paris before the war. "Tell her that I think of her continually . . . that I love her more than ever," he added.

WHEN A MISTRESS MOVES IN, it has been said, a new job opportunity is always created. For Lobo, however, that job was his work. For all his gallivanting, he remained first and foremost a financier. He continued to take calculated trading risks, most of which succeeded, although some went spectacularly wrong.

One of Lobo's worst moments happened in September 1939. In Europe, Hitler was in power in Germany, Mussolini in Italy, and General Francisco Franco had assumed the presidency in Spain after the three-year civil war. In Cuba, Batista still ruled from behind the throne. Although a strong man, Batista was far from being the dictator that he would later become, and his "control" of the country was in reality a delicate balancing act; Cuba was disrupted regularly by sporadic shootings and strikes that continued after the fall of Machado. Batista clamped down on the unrest, but compared to the butchery of Rafael Trujillo, who was engaged in a blood-soaked reign in the Dominican Republic, he looked almost populist. To the U.S. press, Batista frequently denied that he was either a socialist or a fascist—although photographs that showed him standing in full dress uniform during military parades under the hot Caribbean sun were discouraging.

Lobo was in Havana on September 3, when Britain and France declared war on Germany. He didn't think the war would go as smoothly for the Nazis as it did in Poland, which they had overrun in just five weeks. He believed the sugar price, trading at 3.2 cents a pound, had to rise—just as it had during and immediately after World War I, when Cuba had cavorted through the Dance of the Millions. Onward to riches! Lobo started to buy.

Instead, the sugar price slipped. By the early spring of 1940, it had fallen to around 2.8 cents, a loss of 40 points. Lobo stood his ground. On April 9, the same day that Germany invaded Denmark and Norway, he cabled Charles Taussig, the president of the American Molasses Company, who knew both Lobo and Cuba well. (Taussig had been a member of Roosevelt's Brains Trust of advisers and had coauthored a study of the island for the president seven years earlier.) Taussig wanted Lobo's views on the sugar market.

"Re yr wire of this morning," Lobo cabled back. "Present prices are low in peace time. They are absurdly low in case of war. If people would only reflect for five minutes they would be buying . . . like mad."

For a while, Lobo's prediction seemed right. The sugar price edged up. On May 14, it reached a year's high of almost 3 cents. Then it started to drop as a major German offensive made rapid progress across France. Lobo watched aghast as Nazi infantry and tanks passed through "Belgium, Holland and France like a knife through butter." It soon became clear there would be no major disruption to Europe's beet sugar crop that year, and therefore no spike in the sugar price either. By the end of May, sugar had fallen to 2.7 cents. When the Germans entered Paris on June 14, it slipped again. By mid-August, it had dropped to 2.6 cents.

Lobo's position was huge, over 300,000 tons, and he had lost a fortune. If he had bought all that sugar at the prevailing price when war broke out the September before, he faced losses of $4 million, nearly $60 million in today's money. *La casa* would be bankrupted. Lobo was in the New York office when he telephoned his father in Havana to tell him the news. Heriberto advised him to put the family's belongings under his sister Helena's name, as at least then there would be something left "for the family to eat."

When the conversation ended, Lobo, then forty-one years old, put down the phone and stood at the window of his office, twenty-three stories above Wall Street. It was late at night. "Death is nothing," said Napoleon. "But to live defeated and inglorious is to die daily." Lobo wondered if he should just throw himself out onto the empty streets below. Most of the stories of millionaires bankrupted by the 1929 stock market crash who jumped to their deaths are apocryphal, but some failed speculators did take their lives. Later that year, Jesse Livermore, one of Wall Street's most famous stock market speculators, would blow his brains out in the cloakroom at the Sherry-Netherland, the same hotel where Lobo sometimes stayed when in New York.

Lobo, though, turned away from the window and left the office. Out of the building, he turned right and walked four blocks to the Wall Street subway on Broadway, planning to catch the train to his hotel on Madison Avenue and Fifty-eighth Street. Instead he paused outside Trinity Church, a century-old neo-Gothic church built of softly colored sandstone that still stands at the head of Wall Street next to the subway station.

Lobo went into the church, walked down the diamond-patterned aisle, and sat among the empty pews. He stared for a while at the high arched ceilings, the stained-glass windows, and began to pray. He forwent the usual Our Fathers and Hail Marys for a direct conversation with God.

"Lord, why are you punishing me like this?" he recalled asking. "I have never done anyone any harm. I've been a good son, a good father, a good brother" (though not, as Lobo omitted, a good husband). "I've not knowingly hurt anyone, I've been a hard and honest worker, and while you may have reasons to punish me, why the rest of the family too?" In his diaries, Lobo remembered that he continued like this for a while, talking with God.

Then he stood up, walked out of the church, descended into the bowels of the subway, and caught the train uptown. When he arrived at his hotel, a string of messages waited for him in reception. The cables were from Jean Lion, a Parisian sugar broker Lobo knew via his girlfriend Madame Reine. (Lion, incidentally, had recently married the singer and dancer Josephine Baker.) The French government, Lobo read, needed prompt delivery of 300,000 tons of refined white sugar, the same size as his position.

Victory belongs to the persevering. Lobo sprang into action. He started to swap the raw Cuban sugar that he held for the refined white sugar that the French government sought. "Thanks to good fortune and the grace of God, everything ended well. But it was a very dangerous moment for the house," Lobo later remembered in his memoirs. "It was also the only time in my life when I felt truly lost."

Lobo wrote that last sentence in his seventies, as he reviewed his life from exile in Madrid. It seems odd that someone who had suffered a homemade bomb exploding in his face, been put against the wall to be shot, and seen the bulk of his fortune confiscated after the revolution, should call that almost hidden moment in a dark office on Wall Street the *only* time when he felt all was lost. As Lobo recalled, it was only then, after making a market miscalculation that was his fault and nobody else's, that he felt a true sense of desolation.

It is a telling revelation. Although Lobo's obvious worry about the future of *la casa* is a mark of his concern for others and the continuity of their lives above his own, his despair at being proved wrong by more powerful and implacable historical forces is a sign of how strongly he believed in his own abilities. Lobo, after all, was a man "used to getting what he wanted," as Ely said. That was true even if it meant facing death, as Lobo soon would again, when his stubborn unwillingness to accommodate himself to others provoked a hail of bullets in a Havana drive-by shooting. Such violence was the Janus face of Cuba's and of Lobo's coming golden age.

Seven

THE EMERALD WAY

Among the skirts of Turquino
The road of emeralds, oh!
Invites us to take our ease;
The love struck campesino
Among the skirts of Turquino
Sings and loves as he may please.

—José Martí

After Lobo's brush with disaster betting against the Germans, most of Cuba had a quiet Second World War, although the country joined the Allied war spirit with enthusiasm. My grandmother composed a song, "Fire over England," and mailed it to Winston Churchill. His office replied: "Enjoyed the music, especially the spirit in which it was written." Several hundred Cubans enlisted in the U.S. Army, and the government executed a German spy: Heinz Lüning, known as the "Canary" because he kept birds in his apartment to mask the sound of his radio transmissions, was the only spy to be shot in Latin America during the war. German submarines could be seen from the Havana waterfront prowling the sea, and as part of the war effort a blackout was ordered in all coastal towns. Havana's lights stayed off only for a week, the German subs continued to sink ships, and sometimes the Malecón was plunged ankle deep in oil from the tankers torpedoed off the northern coast. Shortages and rationing increased. The tourist trade collapsed, and Britain—Cuba's largest market for tobacco—banned Cuban cigar imports as an unnecessary luxury. Even so, conflict in Europe found Cuba where it always was when the rest of the world was gripped by war: ready to make a profit.

Sugar prices rose, as did production. The 1944 crop hit 4.3 million tons, the largest since 1930, and fetched $330 million, the highest since 1924. Cuban good times promised to reach the same dizzying heights they had in the 1920s. Furthermore, the country was on the brink of a twelve-year period of democratic rule. Batista resigned from the army in 1939 to run for president—he never wore a military uniform again, *el mulato lindo*, the pretty mulatto, as he was known, preferring immaculate white linen suits instead. The next year he won the elections, supported by the Communist Party. Batista, so far removed from the dictator he later became, then called for a constituent assembly. The result was a new constitution, seen throughout the Americas as a model of progressive legislation where workers, for example, were guaranteed paid vacations. Grau, the old revolutionary leader, won the next election in 1944 and Batista, contrary to expectations, left quietly for Daytona Beach, Florida, where he lived in baronial style to sit out "a pleasant exile in some of the New World's toniest suites," as *Time* magazine put it.

Cuba lived through much of the war years in a halcyon haze. Grau promised everyone "a pot of gold and a rocking chair." My grandfather's store flourished on San Rafael Street, near Galliano, a street corner known in Havana for its *piropos*—the unsolicited compliments, comments, and tributes that Cuban men made to female beauty, not always welcomed but often. More innocently, my mother went to school at the Convent of the Sacred Heart, where the nuns forbade their charges from watching *Gone with the Wind* because of the morning-after scene in which a ravished Scarlett O'Hara wriggled in bed with sensuous delight, having been carried off the night before in the arms of her husband, Rhett Butler.

Lobo and María Esperanza moved into a new house in Miramar, a comfortable and modern mansion with a large garden built in a revival colonial style. Their daughters were away during the school year at Rydall, a small boarding school in Pennsylvania, and thence Ethel Walker in Connecticut, where they had been sent to get a proper education, as Lobo put it. Lobo and María Esperanza went to the best parties, his wealth and her position ensured entrée everywhere, and the couple lacked for nothing—although Lobo preferred to live simply. "I have no yacht," he said. "Frugality is a virtue rather than a vice."

Meanwhile, at *la casa*, Lobo changed with the times. To date he had only worked as a financial speculator, buying and trading sugar. Now he started to purchase mills. It was a huge strategic shift, given his disastrous first attempt as a sugar producer at Agabama, when the cane rollers had collapsed in the middle of the grinding season and he had lost most of the harvest. In 1943 he bought Pilón, a midsize mill in the far east of the island in Oriente Province. The next year he bought Tinguaro. A one-hour drive from the beach at Varadero, and three hours from Havana, Tinguaro lies in the red-earth sugar plains of Matanzas and soon became Lobo's favorite mill, his country house. Other plantations followed quickly: San Cristóbal in 1944, Fidencia and Unión in 1945, Caracas in 1946, Niquero in 1948, Pilar and Tánamo in 1951. None of them was large but together they made a massive operation. By the end of the 1950s, Lobo's mills together produced over half a million tons of sugar, almost 9 percent of the Cuban harvest. The crop they milled each year was worth some $50 million.

Becoming an *hacendado*, or mill owner, brought the social cachet and sense of aristocracy still attached to land ownership from the colonial years. Roland Ely, steeped in the history of that era, attached great importance to this. "Lobo only ever bought mills because he wanted to belong to the old school club," he told me—although it is hard to believe this was the case. Lobo had married into the oldest of Cuban families, the Montalvos, while his brother had married a Menocal, a relative of the third president of the Republic. His sister meanwhile had married Mario Montoro, son of the old Autonomist and a respected politician after independence. Lobo's lawyer León suggested a simpler reason. Lobo bought mills "because there was money to be made."

Many Cuban plantations were still owned by foreign banks after the 1930s bust, and were often run poorly and unprofitably from New York. "You could pick up mills cheaply in those days," León remembered. Lobo also needed to channel his energies into new arenas. Because of the war, Cuba presold its whole 1944 crop to the United States, and fixed prices elsewhere limited the scope for Lobo's speculations. International diversification provided one release. Buying sugar mills was another. Lobo would now not only sell other planters' sugar, warehouse it, and arrange for their cargos to be shipped abroad, he would produce it too.

Rural Cuba was also largely at peace with itself. Living conditions outside the major cities were often miserable and still the subject of periodic exposés by the Cuban press. Yet the violent strikes and labor problems of 1933 had passed, thanks to the growing prosperity and also to legislation enacted after the Depression. "Everything was legally organized, there was a structure to follow," León remembered. "There were unions, the Ministry of Labor was involved. Worker relations were generally cordial, even friendly. Disputes were treated as a constant process of negotiation. . . . It was almost a formal process." So formulaic did this process become that the government also fixed the date the harvest began and controlled the amount of international sales, domestic production quotas, the local price of cane, the amount of worker holidays, and their salaries too. Although Castro's government usually depicts prerevolutionary Cuba as a place of savage and exploitative capitalism, the last time the industry was genuinely liberal was in the 1920s, and by the 1940s large parts of the economy were state-run. It was a stable system, but also a stagnant one.

The sugar industry settled into the ordered routine of a sugarcrat's prosperous middle age. The annual cycle—first the *zafra*, then the *tiempo muerto* or dead season—was as regular as breathing. First came the inhalation every December, when mill owners once again borrowed funds to pay the workers to cut and mill the cane. In the countryside, families began to purchase meat, rice, new clothes, and shoes. Traveling salesmen ventured out of Havana and crowded the second-class hotels in rural towns. The railroads took on extra helpers, as did the ports. Lights began to appear about the countryside as rural Cubans once again had enough money to buy kerosene. Everything quickly assumed an air of prosperity as credit flowed around the island once more. Then came the exhalation a few months later when the harvest ended and the kerosene lamps inside the countryside's thatched *bohíos* flickered out.

Lobo accommodated himself to this regularity and his work continued much as before. As an *hacendado*, he now described himself as 90 percent sugar producer—and also 90 percent financial operator. Routine management of his mills was delegated to adept administrators, poached from competitors when need be. ("How much does Rionda pay you?" he asked Tomás Martínez, chief engineer at the Manatí, Cuba's fourth-largest mill. "$25,000? I'll pay you $35,000." Martínez joined Lobo's team.) Beginning on Monday morning, Lobo still financed and traded sugar through the week at Galbán Lobo. It was only after markets closed on Friday afternoon that his life changed gear. He climbed aboard an ingenious cot strapped into the back of a car, slept overnight while he was driven through the Cuban countryside, and woke up at one of his mills the next day.

The frequency of these unannounced visits set Lobo apart from the tradition of absentee planters, so coruscated by the Condesa de Merlin, who spent their days idly in Havana; or the mill owner that the former slave Esteban Montejo remembered riding past in a carriage "with his wife and smart friends through the cane fields, waving a handkerchief, but that was as near as he ever got to us." Lobo did not travel to his mills as a tourist. "One of the things I learnt is that you cannot manage a mill by remote control," he said. Lobo tromped through the *batey*, issued instructions, and stopped to talk with workers whom he called by name and who knew him as Julio in turn.

This lack of pretension was one of Lobo's most appealing features, and he fostered the same spirit among his daughters. Not for them the closeted existence of their mother, a throwback to the sheltered lives of the

Leonor, María Esperanza, and María Luisa, c. 1945.

colonial years, when women of good breeding passed their time applying a powdered eggshell cosmetic called *cascarilla*. When Leonor and María Luisa went to the yacht club, Lobo insisted, they would "travel on the bus," Route 32.

Such instructions show that Lobo was an engaged parent, even down to mundane details such as the state of his daughters' teeth, sometimes sending peremptory handwritten notes to their dentist. However, Lobo also brought home the divide-and-rule strategy he followed at work. His two young daughters did not then know of his love affairs and mistresses, so he played the innocent victim to María Esperanza's temper. Perhaps as a consequence, a deep rivalry developed between Leonor and María Luisa for their father's affections. María Luisa remembered that as children, whichever sister behaved best would have the honor, "the great honor," of

Cuban landscape, by Esteban Chartrand.

lighting their father's cigar, "and putting on, as a ring, the golden paper cigar band."

Nevertheless, he was a doting father. In the mornings, Lobo woke his daughters to hear the "pop" of cactus flowers opening in the garden that he claimed he could hear. In the evenings, he sat with them in the garden to paint skyscapes of Cuba's tangerine twilight on the back of old cigar boxes. "Let's see if we can't do something that doesn't come out entirely kitsch," he would tell María Luisa. "This evening light is so difficult. Chartrand was so right!" On weekends when in town, they scrambled together around the leafy Bosque de la Habana, a wild and half-tended city park by the Almendares River. On school holidays, Lobo took his daughters to the famous beaches at Varadero or to his sugar mills. On such jaunts, they traveled without their mother or governess through the same Cuban landscapes that Esteban Chartrand had eulogized in his sentimental nineteenth-century oils of *bohíos*, small streams, and vehement Cuban sunsets.

María Luisa remembered these trips as "more romantic than any adventure on the Orient Express." They caught a scheduled train from the

Havana railway station at dusk, bounced and rattled through the night, and arrived at dawn, stopping unexpectedly in the middle of a cane field. From there they rode on horseback to the *batey*. After they arrived, Lobo gave the girls simple instructions. Go wherever you will, but never so far that you lose sight of the smoke from the chimney. While Lobo attended to sugar, Leonor and María Luisa swam in the river and rode on horseback through the rolling scenery of the Cuban countryside, which has the intimate qualities of every island. Instead of the mythic scale of the mainland—all those unexplored savannahs, giant mountains, and plains—Cuba's landscape, much like England's, has a softness won from long agricultural use. There is also the surrounding sea, which lends a special quality to the light—luminous and ever-changing—and palm trees, their trunks rising slender, fresh, and tall. Leonor and María Luisa chased each other among green fields glutted with sap, played hide-and-seek with the other young girls at the mill amid the sheds, cane-crushers, and boiling pans, and tobogganed down steep hills of sugar on jute sacks that they later used to slide down the marble steps of the central staircase at their grandparents' house in Havana.

Even island scenery has its epic moments, though, and the biggest exception to Cuba's tameness is the wilderness of the Sierra Maestra mountain range, which spreads for a hundred miles along the anvil-shaped easternmost tip of the island. The area still has a faraway feeling. Dominated by Cuba's highest mountain, the 1,972-meter Pico Turquino, it was also then a place where primary rain forest, too inaccessible to cut down, survived. With only a few small towns and villages, it was inhabited by simple *guajiros*—the illiterate peasant farmers whose beaten straw hats, gnarled bare feet, and almost unintelligible Spanish made them folkloric icons, and sometimes the butt of disparaging jokes. The Sierra was the wildest part of Cuba's "Wild East," nearer to Port-au-Prince than Havana, a distance that made it a crucible of Cuban rebellion. It was here that Fidel Castro ran aground on the *Granma* when he invaded the island from Mexico with eighty men. It was also where José Martí had landed sixty-one years before, after dispatching a farewell note to his son.

Lobo's daughters were intrigued by the black orchids said to grow on

Turquino's upper slopes and the fossilized seashells Lobo told them could be found there. "Is that proof Cuba was once Atlantis?" they asked him, and Lobo had smiled. So when Leonor, enticed by such stories, said she wanted to climb to the top as a reward for good school grades, Lobo had acquiesced. It was 1946; Lobo was then forty-seven years old, Leonor thirteen, and María Luisa twelve. Their trek to Cuba's tallest point demanded more adventurous qualities than did their gentler adventures in the island's old sugar lands. It was also, literally, the high point of a life-changing summer for all their lives. If they reached the summit, Leonor and María Luisa would be the first Cuban women to do so.

They arrived at Pilón on July 2 at the start of the school holidays, after an arduous three-day trip from Havana that ended with a short plane hop to Lobo's mill. Although it was the dry season, and a jeep could have made it down the dusty track from the local town of Manzanillo, the road was blocked. Lobo had argued bitterly with a planter named Delio Núñez, who ran Pilón's neighboring mill, the Santa Isabel. They had once been coinvestors in Pilón, but had quarreled over everything. They almost resorted to a duel—still common in Cuba then, especially around the Sierra, where differences were settled with machetes at dawn. Instead, at Lobo's suggestion they wrote sealed bids for each other's share of the mill on separate pieces of paper. Lobo's higher offer won, and Núñez in a fit of pique subsequently forbade Lobo from using the road that ran through his land. So now Lobo flew over the Santa Isabel instead, a neat parry, as the plane doubled as a small air service delivering mail to some of the region's remotest spots. It was a typical example of Lobo's commercial adroitness, for which he was increasingly renowned. Back in Havana, when Lobo had attended three separate wakes at the same funeral parlor in one day, the owner had joked with Lobo as he left after paying his last respects: "Julio, business is not always this good, you know."

The girls' sprits were still flying high when the single-propeller plane taxied to a halt at the end of Pilón's short airstrip. As they climbed down, Lobo told the girls to ask the mill doctor, Dr. Manuel Sánchez, if one of his daughters would like to accompany them on their adventure. Sánchez, a widower with eight children, was well known in the area as an accomplished and kindly doctor with an amateur interest in archaeology and Cuban history—he had discovered the spot where the "father" of the nation, Carlos Manuel de Céspedes, had been ambushed and killed by Spanish troops seventy-two years before. A reedy-looking man with distinguished white hair and glasses, Sánchez later helped organize an expedition that carried a life-size bust of Martí to Turquino's peak. He was also a local politician, having stood as a congressional candidate for Grau's party in the latest election. Sánchez lost, despite winning more votes than the rival Liberal Party candidate, Delio Núñez, the neighbor with whom Lobo had quarreled.

Leonor and María Luisa tromped across Pilón's sandy *batey*. They wore trousers, unlike most young ladies of that time, and were puffed up with self-importance, thinking the doctor would consider their request an honor. The Sánchez house was set back from the mill in a lush, wooded garden, and as the girls approached the front door a figure watched them from a tree house in the upper branches of a stately algarrobo tree that shaded the porch. She was wild-looking, Leonor remembered, with a stringy frame, tousled hair, and a defiant face. It was Celia Sánchez, peering out of the branches. Then twenty-six years old, Celia later became a close friend of María Luisa, and worked with her on social programs funded by Lobo to help indigent cane cutters around Pilón. Later, Celia helped set up the revolutionary network in the Sierra that supported Fidel Castro and his band of guerrillas while they hid from Batista's forces in the mountains. Celia soon became Castro's confidante, personal secretary, and rumored lover. Compassionate, like her father, Celia was also the one person who could tell Fidel that he was wrong or simply foolish. As Carlotta Steegers was to Lobo, so Celia Sánchez was to Castro. Celia remained close to the Lobos throughout the revolution, especially María Luisa, despite their political differences.

Dr. Sánchez came to the door and greeted Lobo's daughters. They extended their invitation. Contrary to what the girls had expected, he took affront. "You can tell Mr. Lobo no, thank you," the doctor replied. "My daughters are not *marimacho* tomboys who go climbing around hills. And certainly not in trousers." Ten years later, when Celia was in the Sierra with Castro, Leonor would sometimes joke with María Luisa: "I wonder what Dr. Sánchez makes of Celia now that she is climbing around the mountains with combat trousers on!" By then, though, Celia's proud father was riddled with cancer. Too sick to work, he refused to accept the wages that Lobo insisted he be paid, so arrangements had to be made to transfer his salary to Celia instead.

Leonor and María Luisa walked back from the house to find their father deep in conversation with the plantation's general manager. Pilón was in the middle of a strike, and the manager had some grave advice for the group. "Julio, it is not safe here for you and your daughters," he said. "This is not like Tinguaro, the people here are not the same, and they do not know you so well. Stay in the residency if you like, but I recommend that you do not leave on your expedition."

Lobo ignored the warning. He was too headstrong to stop—he had come this far and he had promised Leonor the trip. Late the following night, Lobo and his two daughters sneaked out of the mill residence. They skirted the *batey*, dodging from tree to telegraph pole to tree in the moonlight, until they reached the wharf. There they climbed into a waiting launch that ferried them across a bay that sparkled with phosphorescence to a beach at the base of Turquino, a rocky cove called Bella Pluma. They splashed ashore through the shallows, and when dawn broke they began their climb. There was no time for rest; Lobo wanted to return quickly to Pilón to settle the strike.

At first they passed through palm and coconut groves. Wild melons grew by the path and the sea spray mixed with the damp smells of the forest. The vegetation thickened as they climbed, and the scenery turned prehistoric. Huge fern fronds, more than a meter long, dripped with water. They saw hummingbirds the size of insects, and huge insects the size of small birds ("green, with ugly yellow eyes," Leonor remembered). They stopped for a brief lunch at midday, eating freshwater shrimp caught in a rock pool. When they continued, a guide in front cleared the way with his machete, Lobo and the two girls struggled up the steep path behind, and three porters brought up the rear. A thick mist fell about them.

That night they camped at Alto de Cordero, a thin ridge 1,215 meters above sea level, shivering around a sputtering fire after a rainstorm drenched their clothes. They woke at dawn and Lobo and María Luisa, exhausted, decided to break off the climb. Leonor was more resolute. After a long discussion with her father, "harder even than the climb itself," she set off after a light breakfast with three porters and a guide to try to complete the last several hundred meters. Lobo and María Luisa meanwhile returned down the mountain to the beach.

The way up was often blocked by thick stands of the *tibisí* plant and the small column had to hack improvised paths through the jungle to get around their spiny walls. The air grew thinner as the mist thickened, and Leonor caught occasional glimpses of the peak, "laughing," she felt, "at our pretensions." At the Paso de las Angustias, the Pass of Anguish, the track narrowed to an arm's length across and deep chasms fell away a thousand meters on either side. Clouds streamed over the precipice, particles of water vapor flickering in the dull light. On the final approach the slopes became almost vertical. After a hard scramble, Leonor reached the top. Instead of breaking out onto a plateau lit with blazing sunshine, everything she saw was green: the lichen on the rocks, the ferns, the emerald carpet that covered the ground, the green raspberries that rambled among the rocks, the stunted trees, the bromeliads that grew on their branches, and the drops of water on the plants that caught the misty light. Minute streams crisscrossed the plateau like the veins of a leaf, and it was cold. Leonor shivered.

Elated to be the first Cuban woman to reach the island's highest spot, she ran to the small cairn that marked the peak and opened the sealed casket at its foot. It contained a Cuban flag, and a stoppered bottle containing a note left by a scientific expedition the year before. "As lovers of liberty we proclaim our support for the triumph of Democracy in its struggle against the enslaving forces of the world," its message declared, the familiar exhortation. The note closed with a final paragraph asking its reader to mail the letter to the Cuban Potholing Society at 11 Villegas Street in Havana.

So much future antagonism is contained in that plucky foray. Leonor went on to write a version of the adventure that was anthologized in school primers and became required reading for Cuban fourth-graders. Antonio Núñez Jiménez, the young geography professor who had led the potholers' expedition and would later head Castro's agrarian reform, invited Leonor to give a series of educational talks at Havana's Liceo about the climb. María Luisa squirmed in the audience. She hadn't made it to the top, and "my father called her a quitter," claims Leonor. "And he hated quitters." The girls were barely teenagers, but the Pico Turquino ascent was an early seed of a mutual antagonism that continued to the end of their lives. "They are two characters, wholly opposed," Lobo commented to their grandmother shortly afterward.

Eight

SUN, SEA, AND SHOOTINGS

> *To say the name Lobo is to speak of money-changing,*
> *speculation and black markets. Why should the*
> *government mourn the fate of such a man?*

—NÉSTOR PIÑANGO, Cuban politician, August 1946

> *Cuba would be a happier place with many more Lobos*
> *and far fewer Piñangos.*

—UNION OF SUGAR WORKERS, Tinguaro sugar mill

Lobo returned to Havana with his daughters in high spirits after the trip. On August 1, Heriberto and Virginia celebrated their golden wedding anniversary. They hosted a large party at home in Vedado, and Lobo gave them a set of twenty-four gold dinner plates from Tiffany's. He also settled the strike at Pilón, having agreed to a pay raise. Then he set his eye on a new prize, the sugar mill Caracas.

As well as its name, the mill had a number of evocative associations for Caracas-born Lobo. It had once belonged to Tomás Terry, like Lobo a Venezuelan-born merchant-planter who had made his fortune after arriving in Cuba. It was now owned by First National Boston, the same bank that Lobo had done battle with during his "perfect squeeze" on the

New York sugar exchange twelve years before. Caracas would be Lobo's largest mill, almost twice the size of nearby Agabama, although with a grinding capacity of 4,400 tons it only ranked nationally as midsize. It was also badly run. Lobo would pay $1.6 million for Caracas and estimated that he would make almost all of that back from the extra sugar it could produce the following year. It would be a sweet deal.

Lobo signed the deeds with Enrique León at First National Boston's office in Havana early in the evening on August 6. León left afterward to take his wife out to dinner to celebrate their own wedding anniversary, and then to see a late movie, one of the Hollywood gangster films then so popular in Cuba. Lobo meanwhile returned to his office with Carlotta to tidy up loose ends. Lobo was at his desk, thinking of the party he would give at the mill to celebrate its purchase, when the phone rang. On the line was Alberto Inocente Álvarez, Grau's minister of state.

"What are you still doing in the office so late?" asked Álvarez.

"I don't know why that seems strange to you—I am often here until later," Lobo replied, surprised by the call. It was just past 7 p.m.

"Well, take care. I just want to warn you *they* are going to kidnap you," the minister said.

They referred to the trigger-happy *bonches*, or bunches, the political militias that had fought against Machado in 1933, supported Grau's reelection in 1944, and since degenerated into gangs of armed thugs. Like Grau, these "student revolutionaries" of old were now more often interested in lucre than liberty. Led by men with picturesque names such as El Oriental, El Colorado, and El Extraño, the strange one, they "marauded through the dark streets and the musty ministries of Old Havana," Guillermo Cabrera Infante wrote, "killing each other over ideologies more obscure than the streets themselves." Their violence did not color all of Cuban life; the *bonches* had never targeted a wealthy businessman like Lobo before. Their victims, instead, were associates of the old Machado regime, who had been protected during the administrations controlled by Batista. Under Grau, the *bonches* now meted out punishment themselves. Grau condoned these political thugs and provided many with government sinecures, which fed public disillusionment with his presidency. After all, voters had elected the old revolutionary to office with high expectations of honest government under conditions of peace and prosperity. But Grau's administration had become an orgy of extortion and theft. In one celebrated scandal the year before, on St. Dismas's Day, which honors the patron saint of thieves, a robber stole a twenty-three-carat diamond from the base of a statue in the central lobby of the well-guarded Capitolio building. The perpetrators were never found, and the diamond reappeared mysteriously on Grau's desk a year later. When a journalist asked the president how it arrived there, Grau had replied: "Anonymously."

Lobo thanked Álvarez for calling, put the phone down, and turned to Carlotta. He told her that he wasn't worried about the men that were supposedly going to kidnap him. "They know they won't get a cent from me." But he was worried about his family. At the same time, Lobo did not want to call home and alarm anybody needlessly. "I have to act," he said.

They set off from the office in his car, a black Studebaker parked nearby. Lobo drove down the Malecón, went up Linea and dropped off Carlotta in Vedado on the corner of Twenty-third and Twenty-second streets. As he drove away from her apartment building, the headlamps of a car following behind glared in his eyes. Lobo adjusted the rearview mirror and thought no more of it. Then he crossed the Almendares River, heading west, and dropped down to Eighteenth Street, making good time to his home, which lay on the other side of Fifth Avenue, Miramar's main strip.

Despite the minister's warning, Lobo later recalled that he felt in a buoyant mood. It was a beautiful summer night, a gentle breeze was blowing in from the sea, and he drove with the car windows open, enjoying the cool after the heat of the day. He discounted the possibility that anything serious might happen; everything else was going so well. The Pico Turquino trip had been a success. His parents had celebrated their fiftieth wedding anniversary. He felt elated by the deal he had just signed.

He stopped briefly to post a letter to a girlfriend in Mexico and thought again of the party he would give at the mill to celebrate its purchase.

He drove down Eighteenth Street and heard the eight o'clock bells ring from Miramar's clock tower on Fifth Avenue, a few blocks away. As he passed the corner of Ninth Avenue, the car that had been trailing him suddenly accelerated down the middle of the street and drew close to his rear bumper. The first pistol shot came through the back window, whistled past Lobo's head, and punched a hole through the windshield. The second shot hit Lobo's rear door, the third ricocheted off the front doorframe and buried itself in the dashboard. Then the attackers pulled alongside, firing from close range. The next shots hit Lobo in the head, right leg, and left knee. Lobo's car swerved to the side of the road, bumped over the curb, skidded on the grass of a trim lawn, and crashed into a telegraph pole. The lights of the nearest house flickered and went out. Inside, Alberto Alejo, a twenty-four-year-old doctor, was having dinner with his wife. Alejo later told the newspaper reporters who swarmed around the scene how he ran to his front door to find out what was the matter, saw a black car on his front lawn, steam rising from the crumpled hood, and rushed to see if there were any survivors from the crash. "I am Julio Lobo," groaned the folded body inside the car. "I am wounded, call my family." Then Lobo blacked out, and his body slumped forward against the car horn on the steering wheel. It had broken in the crash and only made a plaintive *thweet*.

Alejo called for an ambulance and rang the police. It was the forty-third *bonches* shooting that year and the Havana press, which listened for crime traffic on radio frequencies used by the police, quickly relayed the news that Lobo, the famous speculator, might be dead.

Five blocks away, at Lobo's home, Leonor was brushing her hair, listening to a popular radio show, *Tamakún*, the nomadic avenger, when the announcer suddenly broke off the program. "We interrupt this broadcast to bring you the extraordinary news, the *noticia luctuosa*, that Julio Lobo has been shot and killed." Leonor ran to her mother's room. María Esperanza, who had also heard the news, was frantically packing a small bag.

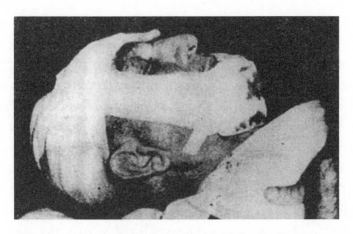

Front-page newspaper photograph of Lobo after the shooting.

She called an aunt to come and stay with her daughters and rushed off to Camp Columbia's military hospital. Meanwhile, in central Havana, León was leaving the cinema with his wife when he saw the newspaper hoardings on the pavement outside. León dismissed the lurid headlines as sheer sensationalism, as he had been with Lobo only a few hours before. "You might be wrong," remarked his wife, Rosario Rexach, a literary scholar with an eye for detail. "Look at the date. These aren't the evening papers that were being printed this afternoon when you were with Julio. They are tomorrow's."

The front pages of the newspapers that the rest of Havana woke up to the next day had all the grimy realism of a scene captured by Weegee, the Polish-American news photographer then famous for his stark black-and-white pictures of New York City crime. One photograph showed Lobo's head wrapped in bandages stained in blood, his eyes closed. In another, Lobo lay in the back of an ambulance, surrounded by medics. Others showed the metallic dimples of gunshots in the car body alongside panoramas of the scene drawn over with white markings and arrows, as in a police file. Cuba had absorbed not only the method of North American gangland executions, but their gory aesthetic too.

Havana was filled with speculation over who had tried to kill Lobo, and no two theories were the same. The other shootings that year had all been obviously political. That alone made Lobo's unusual. Shooting no. 42 had taken place only a few weeks before, when assassins had peppered a former chief of police under Machado with bullets while he read a newspaper on his front porch. They left behind a black-humored note, "Justice comes late, but it comes." It was the telltale sign-off of the Union of Insurrectional Revolutionaries (UIR), one of the *bonches* that operated with impunity from within Havana's university. Constitutionally off-limits to the police, the two-hundred-year-old university provided an almost Greek backdrop to the brutal goings-on inside. The entrance to the campus at the top of San Lázaro Street was a magnificent sweep of 163 white stone steps, dominated by a statue of the alma mater dressed in Greek robes. At the top, Doric columns flanked the schools of science, philosophy, law, and engineering. Inside, almost every day someone was killed in a political turf war. Fidel Castro, an active *pistolero* and UIR member, had joined the university as a law student the year before and later remembered it as even "more dangerous than all the time I fought against Batista from the Sierra Maestra."

The ambulance took Lobo to the nearest hospital at Camp Columbia. Carlos Prío, the prime minister, hurried across town from the Presidential Palace. When Prío arrived at the hospital, he pushed his way through the crowd of journalists downstairs and went up to Lobo's room on the third floor. Lobo was lying on a hospital bed and had regained consciousness. He had even dictated a brief will after the military doctors had patched him up, roughly sewing a large chunk of his skull back onto his head. Lobo later recalled their conversation in his diary.

"Who did you think did it?" Prío asked, standing by Lobo's bedside.

"I don't know," Lobo replied. "Why don't you ask Inocente? He seems to know. He called me up before to warn me. Inocente seemed worried— although not worried enough to send an armed guard."

Prío bent over Lobo's bed and whispered quietly in his ear, as he didn't want the doctors and nurses milling around the room to hear. "Inocente called and told me the same."

"That makes it all the worse," Lobo grunted back. "Two ministers who knew something was about to happen, but didn't do anything to stop it and don't even know who the perpetrators were."

Such cynical unknowingness was typical of Grau's administration.

A colonel then burst into the room and approached Lobo's bed. "In the name of General Pérez Gamera [the acting head of the army], you can stay here as long as you need until you are fully restored to health," the colonel barked. Turning to the rest of the people in the room, he added in a loud voice, "Mr. Lobo, you can be sure that you will be fully protected by the Army while you stay here." But it was a pantomime performance of military authority, because the colonel then came closer to the bed, bent over Lobo's head just as Prío had done, and whispered in his ear, "But if I were you, I would leave immediately as the people who shot you are nearby."

Doctors whisked Lobo away from the military hospital to the Anglo-American, a private clinic in Vedado. There Octavio Montoro, the brother of his sister's husband and a well-known doctor, took charge. The following night, Montoro spelled out Lobo's position. A bullet was still lodged in his head and had to be removed. "If we operate you may end up blind, aphasic, or an idiot. And if we don't operate you will die for sure," he explained.

"What are you waiting for?" Lobo replied.

While the doctors scrubbed down, Lobo turned to the head nurse and said that he wanted to confess. Although he was ambivalent about religion, "I was born a Catholic," Lobo explained, "and before they operate I want to be at peace with God."

A priest was summoned, and Lobo spoke while lying on his back on the hospital litter, staring at the ceiling.

"Father, I've lost a lot of blood, the wounds make it hard to concentrate, and I have forgotten how to confess," he remembered saying. It had been fourteen years since Lobo had last told a priest of his sins, and that had been on the eve of his wedding to María Esperanza.

"I just want to say that other than killing and stealing I have broken all the other commandments, many times. Absolve me, Father, I cannot remain conscious anymore."

The hospital orderlies gathered to wheel Lobo into the operating theater while the priest intoned the absolution in Latin. Then he made the sign of the cross, and Lobo closed his eyes.

HAVANA SPECULATED WHILE the surgeons operated. Who had tried to kill Lobo, and why? Many believed it was because he had refused to pay extortion money to one of the *bonches*. It was a natural assumption, but one that Lobo denied from the start. "I don't have any problems with anybody," he had told reporters at the hospital on the night of the shooting. "This act of aggression is unexpected."

Others supposed the attempted killing was a general warning to Cuba's gilded commercial class. Postwar shortages were high, black markets rife, and ordinary Cubans struggled with the high cost of food. If a man like Lobo "the wolf" was rich, it was easy to believe he was shot because his wealth was ill-gained; that was the dark side of Lobo's public renown. *Hoy*, the Communist newspaper, ran the headline "CUBAN BLACK MARKET KING SHOT." Néstor Piñango, a minor politician and sometime journalist, wrote in *Prensa Libre*: "To say the name Lobo is to speak of money-changing, speculation and black markets. Why should the government mourn the fate of such a man?" *Bohemia* then commented that Piñango's statement merely echoed what everybody else said under their breath. Among the few newspapers that condemned the attack, *Diario de la Marina*, the voice of the establishment, ran a story about three other businessmen who had fled to New York, fearing for their own lives. "I feared such terrible conditions would come," Lawrence Berenson, an American lawyer with long experience in Cuba, cabled Lobo a week later. "Perhaps you understand why I have not wanted to come to Cuba these past two years."

Indeed, subsequent events seemed to confirm that the Lobo shooting *was* part of a broader social vendetta. Piñango revealed that he had found a note at the scene of Lobo's crime which explained the murder attempt. On a piece of paper headed *Committee of Public Health*, someone had scribbled the name "Julio Lobo" and next to it a list of basic necessities, such as beans, butter, and cooking oil, each labeled with question marks. When no other newspaper reported the note, casting doubt on its authenticity, Piñango insisted he had found it inside Lobo's damaged car.

Then, on August 9, three days after Lobo's assassination attempt, Antonio Valdés, a prominent lawyer, narrowly escaped a drive-by shooting as he left his house. His attackers sent a message to the newspapers, signed *The 13*. "We are not hoodlums," it read, "but we cannot remain passive in the face of such official inertia. Our wives and children are suffering from speculation. We are going to liquidate all the barons of the black market." A few days later, the sixteen-year-old son of Joaquín Martínez, a senator and lawyer, was also shot while driving his father's car. Fearing for their lives after the trio of shootings, Havana's haut monde shivered in their Miramar and Vedado homes.

Ironically, it was the workers' union from Tinguaro that rallied to the defense of Cuba's cowed captains of industry. "Mr. Lobo may not be an angel, he has no halo, and makes no boasts about his honesty," the union replied to Piñango's charge in *Prensa Libre*. Lobo "invests, he works quietly and assiduously." He makes cheap credit available to his employees and builds extra school and hospital rooms, they continued. "This mill never enjoyed as much investment when it belonged to an American company as it does now, under Mr. Lobo, the 'wolf,'" the union wrote. By contrast, "what has Mr. Piñango done for Cuba? Nothing that we know of . . . Cuba would be a much happier place with many more Julio Lobos and far fewer Piñangos."

The unionists' letter injected richer subtleties and truths into the speculation that had gripped Havana. Great wealth might imply great crime. That was the experience of many during Grau's presidency (as the notorious political career of his education minister had shown: José Manuel Alemán stole millions—allies said ten, enemies fifty—some of which he used to build Miami's Key Biscayne). But gross criminality and corruption were not always to blame. In fact, it soon transpired that the Valdés and Martínez shootings which followed Lobo's attempted killing had nothing to do with a supposed *bonche*-led social vendetta against the black market speculations of the Cuban well-to-do. Instead, they formed part of an elaborate crime of passion. Furthermore, by a process of tendentious logic, it was assumed that Lobo's shooting was somehow linked to this sad love affair as well.

The saga's complexities are worthy of a radio soap opera. Enrique Sánchez del Monte, a recently divorced planter from Oriente, had gone mad with jealousy when he learned that his ex-wife was enjoying a high social life in Havana and that Lobo was reputed to be one of her lovers. Unhinged, Sánchez tried to join a monastery. Rejected for lacking any vocation, he turned his thoughts to revenge.

He hired a Havana hood known as El Manquito, who had gained a revolutionary reputation in the fight against Machado and since been rewarded with various sinecures at the Education Ministry. Manquito handed out these jobs to friends on commission. He also ran a series of rackets from within the university, including a garage that remodeled and repainted stolen cars. The mobster charged Sánchez $3,000 to kill each of his ex-wife's divorce lawyers—first Valdés, and then Martínez—and a further $6,000 to finally murder his ex-wife herself.

The plan unraveled when the police caught one of Manquito's gang members and he confessed. Newspapers subsequently reported that the police now thought the .38-caliber pistol used in the Martínez shooting might have been the same gun used against Lobo. Furthermore, police believed that Manquito might even have been responsible for the theft of the Capitolio diamond. That added a touch of Pink Panther glamour to the whole affair, while also suggesting that Lobo, the "King of the Black Market," the "Cuban Tsar of Speculation," had somehow been involved in the unsolved diamond robbery as well.

So much could be made to seem to connect, to explain something else. Many years later, in a musty storage deposit in downtown Miami, I found a bloodstained letter among Lobo's papers. He had jammed it in his suit pockets before he raced downstairs with Carlotta to his car, so I reasoned it must have been important. I unfolded the letter under a strip light and looked at the brown stains made by Lobo's dried blood, thick around the creases. I examined the signature at the bottom and the date at top, a week before the shooting took place. It all reeked of so much potential significance that even now I somehow believe the handwritten note might be a clue. But it was only an innocent message. "Will you write us confidentially what your objections are?" the registrar at his daughters' school in Pennsylvania had asked Lobo, a concerned parent. "It would seem in fairness that we should know."

Who tried to kill Lobo that summer remains a mystery. There was never a proper investigation into why two men armed with .38 revolvers tried to kill Lobo that night. It is possible that Inocente Álvarez, who made the warning phone call, might have told Lobo later how he knew something was about to happen. If he did, Lobo never recorded the answer. Many years later Lobo told León, ominously, "that everyone who tried to kill me is now dead." Yet León believed Lobo was only expressing a ghoulish probability, playing the story tough, as he did when he told embroidered versions of the tale to his wide-eyed grandchildren. After all, an escape from a gangland shooting lends itself to forgivable hyperbole.

Lobo left Havana on September 3 for the Mayo Clinic in Minnesota. He was accompanied by María Esperanza—their marriage now on its last legs—his daughters, and a military doctor. He was almost completely paralyzed from the waist down, and could only move one of his toes. It would take six months before he could walk again. Even so, Lobo remained active from the hospital bed. It was as if the assassination attempt goaded him into action. By sheer force of will he *would* move again; the shooting would *not* stop him from his work and his life.

First, Lobo quarreled with the Cuban doctors over their fees; to the anesthesiologist, he offered $300 instead of the $500 that was billed; to another doctor, $2,000 instead of $3,000; and for the surgeon who had led the trepanning operation on his skull, $10,000 instead of $25,000. Lobo had checked with his brother-in-law Montoro on what similar treatments would have cost in the United States, and perhaps the Cuban doctors had overcharged. Still, Lobo's tightfistedness, reported in the Cuban press, won him little admiration at home.

That was only practice, however. Next, also from his hospital bed, Lobo sold the Galbán Lobo provisions business—the same one he had worked at when he first joined *la casa* almost two decades earlier, hawking beans, flour, and chickpeas. Some took the sale as indirect proof that Lobo had been speculating in foodstuffs after all, ramping up the price of butter and cooking oil, as Piñango suggested. But Lobo had little fondness for the operation; he described the period he worked in it as "very disagreeable years." The basic food products it sold at fixed prices were also rationed, so although it was a profitable operation, it was also controversial and complicated, a constant headache. Furthermore, by the end of the war, it had shrunk relative to Lobo's huge and growing sugar operations. Selling it looks wise rather than like a tacit admission of guilt.

Physical pain continued to spur Lobo on, even as he convalesced. He was frustrated at being invalided, so his mind had to travel in different ways. Six months after the shooting, he limbered up for his biggest fight of all: a corporate raid on one of the island's largest firms, the Cuba Company. Founded just before the turn of the century, it owned much of Cuba's eastern rail network and two mills, and had large amounts of cash on its balance sheet, although it had not paid a dividend since the mid-1920s. It was run by sleepy North American directors who rarely visited the island and enjoyed their undemanding posts on the company's board in New York. At the end of the year, the Galbán Lobo office formed a consortium that began quietly buying its shares on the New York Stock Exchange. The following year, it filed a proxy notice to shareholders saying that the consortium wanted to take over the firm. The aim was to restructure the company and release its cash. Today the move would be recognized as a classic hostile takeover. Then it was an unprecedented piece of corporate buccaneering. What made it all the more remarkable is that Lobo orchestrated the operation from a hospital in North America while he could still barely stand. Fragments of lead remained embedded in his body, by his right knee and in his head, and he suffered fierce, crushing headaches.

The takeover attempt was ultimately unsuccessful. After a general meeting that dragged on for two weeks, until then the longest in U.S. corporate history, the Galbán Lobo office only gained control of 45 percent of Cuba Company, and later sold this stake. Even so, the raid ultimately led to control of the firm being transferred to Havana, with a Cuban board appointed in 1948. The incident shows again how confident Cuban financiers felt when they took on their North American peers. In finance, if not in politics, Cuba was less a neocolonial satrapy of the United States, as so often depicted, than simply the Latin American economy most closely integrated with the mainland.

A further irony is that even as the attempted takeover of Cuba Company was taking place, a young Fidel Castro had broken onto the national political stage with a speech at the University of Havana in which he first talked of ideas that would later become favorite themes. Castro spoke of the nationalist revolution that Grau had promised Cuba. But it was a "betrayed revolution," Castro said, that had left "the country's wealth in foreign hands." Lobo, by contrast, was doing something about such Yankee imperialism, albeit in ways that Castro and other hotheaded students might not give due weight or understand. "Some people have made the country great with the sword, others with the pen. I have done so by creating wealth," as Lobo liked to say.

Yet by the end of 1947, even the thrill of a big corporate dustup had faded for Lobo. He wrote from New York to his mother in Havana the next spring that work left him with a flat taste in his mouth. It "used to be a source of diversion and pleasure for me, and I was starting to feel enthusiastic again about fresh projects; no longer." He added that he felt like an uprooted tree "which can't be transplanted without fear of damaging its roots." He said that he could not make plans, was unsure what to do, that he needed to think things through. Lobo had always liked to travel, be that around Cuba on holidays with his daughters or on business trips around South America, Europe, and the United States, and he relished the adventure, visiting new countries with a curious eye. During one trip to Haiti in 1941, he noticed over lunch with President Élie Lescot that all the cutlery around the table had been taken "from various hotels in New York like the Astor, the Waldorf and others." Yet now, normally so alive to the unusual and the picturesque, Lobo wrote that he was "tired of hotel life, of living out of a suitcase, of not having a home or family around me." He wanted to return to Cuba but felt unsure that it was safe to do so. He felt "banished from my country, with no plans of return."

Other than a few fleeting visits, Lobo stayed away from Cuba for two years. He only properly returned to Havana after the elections in 1948, Cuba's last free vote to date, won by Carlos Prío, Grau's former prime minister, who had visited Lobo in the hospital on the night of the shooting. Even so, when Lobo arrived in Havana he traveled home from the airport in a bulletproof car with an armed guard. For someone used to mixing freely in Cuban daily life, who even insisted that his daughters "went to the club by bus," it was a potent symbol of the divorce between the island and its commercial class. Ultimately, the divide would cost them dearly.

MY OWN FAMILY also removed themselves from the hurly-burly of Cuban life during this period, and also for reasons of health. Around the time that Lobo was shot, my grandfather was stricken with tuberculosis. His doctor recommended a long period of convalescence in a North American sanatorium. My grandmother borrowed money from her father and in the winter of 1944, she, my mother, her brother, her sister, and my grandfather left Cuba for an eighteen-month stay at a nursing home by Lake Placid, New York, a traditional rest cure for tuberculosis sufferers.

My mother's recollections of that time—everyone wrapped in thick coats, snow on the rooftops, with white hills and bare trees in the background—seem incongruous compared with the more tropical memories of her childhood. My maternal grandfather, a gentle and studious man, said it was the happiest time in his life. Wrapped in blankets, with the snow-covered hills of New York State in view through his bedroom win-

My grandparents, Lake Placid, 1948.

dow, he reread his favorite book, *The Magic Mountain*, Thomas Mann's description of the intellectual development of Hans Castorp, a young German tuberculosis sufferer, in a Swiss sanatorium during the second decade of the twentieth century. At the end of the novel, Castorp discharges himself from the "half-a-lung club" and descends to the "flatlands" of Europe, where he dies among millions of other anonymous conscripts during World War I. I cannot help but wonder if my grandfather, suffering from tuberculosis like the hero of Mann's novel, felt any sense of doom when he returned to the flat sugar plains of Cuba.

My grandfather's forebears, men such as Colonel Enrique Loret de Mola, had once risked all in Cuba's political struggles. By contrast, everybody in Havana now wrinkled their noses when anyone mentioned politics, while politicians were viewed as "non-U," in Nancy Mitford's phrase, or violent and corrupt—often all three. "They're all the same" was the common and disheartening refrain heard across the island. Removed from political life, like so many of his peers, my grandfather worked at the store and raised his family. His greatest consolations lay in the music of Beethoven, rare books of Buddhist thought, and the writings of the Catholic philosopher Miguel de Unamuno. I have his copy of *The Tragic Sense of Life*, Unamuno's meditation on the quixotic human desire for immortality, the longing for everything—homes, families, even countries and ways of life—to remain the same. It is also the same edition that my grandfather read many years later while in exile, when his feelings of impermanence were strongest, and the margins are filled with notes and whole pages of text are underlined.

Lobo also sought out fresh consolations after his return to Havana. There were his growing Napoleon collection and his love affairs, which became ever more complicated and varied. Lobo's work remained as important as before, and the biggest deals were yet to come. Yet even these triumphs were now tempered by a sense of evanescence.

The following October, he and María Esperanza divorced. She had long known about his affairs; formal separation was only a matter of time, and it was easier with their two daughters abroad at school. They reached a settlement and sold their place in Miramar. María Esperanza set up a new house, and Lobo moved back to his parents' in Vedado and sought to regather himself at his childhood home. Instead, he found only more sadness and death. Less than a year later, his mother died. Imperious Virginia, who had seemed almost immortal in her family's eyes when she had smashed an umbrella over Cipriano Castro's head, had been unwell for several months, slipping in and out of a coma, no longer recognizing the familiar faces around her bed.

"Fortunately she suffered nothing, and went out like a candle," Lobo wrote to María Luisa in Pennsylvania. "We were all by her side when she died, and afterwards her face rejuvenated itself. She seemed only thirty years old. You've no idea how marked the change was. She became a young woman again."

The Lobo family. Heriberto, Virginia, Helena, and her husband, Mario Montoro, are in the middle. Lobo is second from the left at the back, next to María Esperanza. Jacobo stands on the far right. Leonor and María Luisa sit in the middle at the front.

Six weeks later, Lobo's spry eighty-year-old father collapsed, felled literally by a broken heart. Heriberto had been married to Virginia for fifty-five years. Death caught him on a glorious December morning as he dressed for battle at the office, like a good general, with his boots on. Heriberto regained consciousness one last time after he was found on the floor of his bedroom. When placed on his bed, Heriberto addressed his last thoughts and words to the worried faces gathered around him. "*¿Qué pasa?*" he asked—What is the matter? One unfortunate answer came two months later on St. Valentine's Day, when Lobo's younger brother, Jacobo, committed suicide with a bullet to his head. Some said it was because of drugs or alcohol; others, love; some that his business affairs had turned sour.

It happened early in the morning, and the single shot woke Lobo, whose bedroom was across the hallway from Jacobo's. Since his divorce and Jacobo's recent separation from his own wife, Estela Menocal, the two brothers had lived together as bachelors at their parents' old house on the corner of Eleventh and Fourth. They were the antithesis of each other and made for odd housemates. While Lobo worked and studied, Jacobo drank and socialized. Jacobo was often rash at work; it was said that his two mills, Amazonas and Limones, were failing. While Lobo kept himself trim, Jacobo's waistline was a balloon. Yet any jealousy flowed both ways. Jacobo was *simpático,* he had *un don de la gente,* a gift for people. So although it was his elder brother who enjoyed business success, it was Jacobo who held the floor at parties. Living together, they had grown close again, and any former rivalries had dissolved. After Jacobo's death, Lobo put the squeeze on his brother's business partners, and when he had finished, Jacobo's sons had inherited $1 million between them.

Lobo found himself suddenly alone. Sharp physical pain and the recurring operations that he had to endure were frequent reminders of his own near-death experience. "The truth is I have been unlucky lately," he wrote to María Luisa after an unfortunate fall. "Gun shots, a broken skull, broken ribs, sinusitis, operations on my spine, headaches, stomach cramps, a bust sacroiliac, and now a broken leg. I've had my full quota in the past few years, hopefully those that come will be happier and more tranquil."

Lobo's condition mirrored that of his country; prosperous and hopeful, but battered. The Prío government was better than Grau's. Debonair and charming, the "President of Cordiality" surrounded himself with able technocrats, the sugar price was high at over 5 cents a pound, the economy growing, and the press was free. *¡Qué Suerte Tiene El Cubano!,* how lucky Cubans are, ran a popular Bacardi rum advertising slogan that summed up the national mood. But El Presidente Cordial, the man who told Lobo on the night of the shooting that he didn't know who had tried to kill him, could not or would not end Cuban gangsterism and corruption. While Prío took delight in La Chata, his luxurious farm outside Havana that was fitted out with what has been called the understatement of a Busby Berkeley production, Cubans felt that the corruption of Grau's years was repeating itself.

Prío's presidency came to a premature end, hastened—if only indirectly—by a charismatic rival, Eddy Chibás. An emotional man who always dressed in white, Chibás was also genuinely honorable, the heir to a huge fortune, and totally uninterested in money. Widely seen as the man most likely to win the 1952 election, his favorite image was the broom—to sweep away corruption. His favorite word was *aldabonazo*—the sharp knock or wake-up call. His political prescription was to throw corrupt politicians in jail. And his greatest weapon was the radio. Cuba literally stopped every Sunday at 8 p.m. to listen to Chibás's increasingly hysterical broadcasts on the CMQ station. His show on August 5, 1951, ended in a typically ringing style, with a description of Cubans as a Chosen People, defeated by original sin.

"Geographical position, rich soils and the intelligence of its inhabitants mean that Cuba is destined to play a magnificent role in history, but it must work to achieve it," Chibás harangued. "The historical destiny of Cuba, on the other hand, has been frustrated until now by the corruption and blindness of its rulers.... People of Cuba, arise and walk!" he screamed. "People of Cuba, awake! This is my last call!" Then Chibás shot himself in the stomach. Rushed to the hospital, he died of internal bleeding eleven days later.

Probably an accident more than a suicide, the probable reason for Chibás's self-immolation was his inability to provide proof of corruption charges he had made against one of Prío's ministers. Chibás was also Cuba's great hope, and his death created a political vacuum. Into it stepped Batista. The former president, still popular with the military and rural vote, had returned from Florida hoping to make a comeback in the forthcoming election. But his campaign sputtered, and a December poll showed him trailing in third place. Faced with the prospect of losing the vote, and encouraged by disaffected army officers who believed that Prío was planning a coup—although there was no evidence of this—Batista literally took the country by surprise.

At around 3 a.m. on March 10, 1952, Batista drove up to the main gate of the Camp Columbia army base in a Buick with his co-conspirators.

He was waved through by the captain of the guard, who was a party to the plot. Once inside, they arrested the chiefs of staff. Tanks were dispatched to the Presidential Palace; Prío drove off to seek support from loyal regiments outside Havana, but found that they had changed sides. The whole affair took only a few hours. Cubans woke that morning to martial music on the radio and found out that Prío was no longer president, that Batista was again their ruler, and there would be no election in June—although one was promised soon. The former stenographer declared: "The people and I are dictators."

Prío went into exile with his family after taking refuge in the Mexican embassy. "They say that I was a terrible President of Cuba," he remarked later. "That may be true. But I was the best President Cuba ever had." Fifteen years later in Miami, Prío shot himself, as Chibás had done. Nobody had noticed that he was feeling depressed; Prío was cordial until the last.

Like Cuba itself, Lobo was left without a compass. He had no parents to turn to and no wife. His brother had shot himself, and his elder sister Leonor had died many years before. His only other remaining close relative was Helena, his younger sister. His daughters were away at school and he wrote frequent and tender letters to both in his cramped hand, often late at night. He reassured them, made plans for their holidays (trips to a music festival in Europe, fishing jaunts around his mills in Oriente), and visited them whenever he traveled to New York for work. He was philosophical but missed their company dreadfully. "My life alone is no pleasure," he admitted to María Luisa in one letter.

In Havana, Lobo returned home after work and rattled around the three adjacent houses at Eleventh and Fourth streets. He had lived in one, Jacobo in the second, his parents in the third. Now, except for his own rooms, they were empty. In the evening he sometimes sat with a glass of scotch by the swimming pool in the garden, under the shade of a mango tree. Lobo said he did some of his best thinking there. If Leonor or María Luisa were in town during the holidays, they joined him for a drink. Lobo punctuated the conversation with poetry. Shelley's "Ozymandias" was one of his favorites.

". . . Look on my works, ye Mighty, and despair!"
Nothing beside remains. Round the decay
Of that colossal wreck, boundless and bare
The lone and level sands stretch far away.

Within a decade, Lobo's mighty works would also disappear. Fifty years after that, Castro's socialist revolution would seem like an Ozymandian dream too.

Nine

IMPERIAL AFFAIRS

⸺

Fortune is a woman and the more she does for me
the more I demand from her.

—NAPOLEON BONAPARTE

The cartoon says it all. With one hand, Lobo holds above his head a giant globe labeled "The World of Sugar." He is lithe, almost naked in swimming trunks that are patterned with small dollar signs, and would look like an Atlas were it not for the smoking cigar that hangs from the corner of a rather sour-looking mouth. Conrad Massaguer—noted cartoonist and illustrator, founder of the glossy magazine *Social*, and brother-in-law of Jacobo Lobo's widow—drew similarly jokey portraits of Cuba's other sugarcrats. He had sketched Manuel Aspuru, a playboy *hacendado* and friend of Lobo's, saluting from a paper sailboat in a stylish captain's uniform. He also executed a Charles Addams–style rendering of Arturo Mañas, head of the Sugar Institute, who looks positively devilish as he ladles another spoonful into an American coffee cup while asking, "More sugar, Sir?" But the Lobo lampoon is the most outlandish of them all. It pokes fun at the virility of a man who drew his inspiration from Napoleon and held the world's sugar market in the palm of his hand.

Lobo as Atlas.

The 1950s marked the zenith of Lobo's power, although they were uncertain years too, as they were for the Republic. Few Cubans immediately mourned the passing of the corruption of the Grau and Prío presidencies. Yet Batista's coup did call into question the image that the country had of itself as an "oasis of liberty" in the Caribbean. There was its exalted 1940 constitution, its irresistible sensual pleasures, and its high cultural life. Middle-class Cubans could also boast about the air-conditioners and TV sets that put them on a par with Americans. But now they also had a shabby military dictatorship more worthy of a banana republic than a country aspiring to join the modern world. Chibás's last message to them had been "Wake Up!" Instead they had remained asleep. The month after the coup, *Time* ran a front-page picture of a smiling Batista with the caption "Cuba's Batista: he got past Democracy's sentries." Although Batista always appeared confident in the capitol, for the next six and a half years there was never a moment when Cuba could be said to be at peace.

Lobo questioned his life. He reminisced in letters to his daughters about those moments as a carefree student when he had been "completely broke, and I can assure you that these were always the happiest days of my life—perhaps because I had nothing to lose." It was a remarkable change for a man who had so purposefully pursued fortune all his life, even if Lobo's new mood was in keeping with the times. In *The Quest for Wealth*, a history of man's acquisitiveness published in 1956, the economist Robert Heilbroner argued that money-making was no longer generally esteemed due to the experience of the Great Depression. Previous generations had celebrated men who transformed the world. In Cuba there had been sugar barons like Rionda; in the United States, tycoons like Henry Clay Frick with his coal, Cornelius Vanderbilt with his steel and railroads, and Henry Osborne Havemeyer, the "Sultan of Sugar," with his refining interests on the East Coast. These men lent respectability to their new wealth by buying art, often indiscriminately. "Railroads are the Rembrandts of investment," Frick once commented, for the value of railways—like that of Rembrandts—always went up.

Such industrialists were no longer flattered and admired. By the 1950s, the archetypal U.S. businessman had become the colorless if reliable figure satirized by Sloan Wilson in his novel *The Man in the Gray Flannel Suit*. The change in style was accompanied by a shift in corporate priorities too, with other motives such as stability, continuity, and responsibility toward the community predominating over the profit motive. "Opulence, the adulation of money-makers, and the wish for great wealth have given way, in part at least, to a new set of values: the camouflage of wealth, the contempt of 'mere' money-makers. And even a certain disdain or disinterest in the goal of wealth itself," Heilbroner wrote.

In Cuba, a short plane hop from the United States, such attitudes chimed with prevailing social democratic ideals and, increasingly, Lobo's beliefs too. "Money not only does not bring happiness, sometimes it destroys it, and I sometimes even think it is no less than the devil's invention," Lobo wrote to María Luisa in May 1950. "The only way money can bring happiness is if it is used to do good and to help the lot of the less fortunate . . . That's why I take such a great interest in the problems and well-being of the people at the mills, their education, their health."

Although sincerely believed, Lobo was not always as disinterested about his wealth or as philanthropic as he sometimes imagined. He continued to reject many of the luxurious fripperies of a Cuban *hacendado*: "I have no yacht." Nonetheless, the 1950s were also years when Lobo, like the American robber barons of the previous generation, expanded his collection of European art, mostly old masters, haggling with dealers over the price of a Goya self-portrait or a watercolor of Napoleon's quarters at St. Helena. It was also a decade when Lobo pursued some of his most disruptive and ambitious business schemes. There was certainly a Napoleonic quality about Lobo's offer to buy the whole Cuban sugar crop in 1952 and again in 1953, as there was in his Napoleon-like womanizing and the size of his Napoleon collection itself.

As an English schoolboy, I knew that Napoleon was short, sometimes tucked his right hand inside his tunic, rode a horse, suffered a dreadful retreat from Moscow, and was decisively beaten by British troops led by the Duke of Wellington at Waterloo. Later I absorbed the knowledge that Napoleon ended his life in exile, although for years the thought vaguely persisted that St. Helena was an island somewhere in the Mediterranean instead of deep in the South Atlantic. It was there, in his damp and cramped quarters at Longwood, that Napoleon dictated his memoirs, reinventing himself as a liberal emperor—and one of history's great victims. "My fame lacked only one thing—misfortune," Napoleon once said. "I have worn the Imperial Crown of France, Italy's crown of iron; and now England has given me one that is greater and more glorious still—that worn by the Savior of the World—a crown of thorns."

There are many Napoleons. There is the lonely Napoleon of high office, and the vicissitudes he suffered in exile. There is the Romantic hero of Balzac and Stendhal, who rose from obscure beginnings to scale great heights. There is the despot, interested only in power, the military hero on a horse, the warlord surrounded by the whiff of grapeshot, who was admired by self-aggrandizing leaders such as Cipriano Castro and later Batista. And there is the empire builder, the man who left behind in France a system of administration and civil reforms that still endures. This is the Napoleon that so many successful businessmen style themselves upon. Thus there have been Napoleons of Steel, of Railroads, of Finance, of Sugar, and even one of Crime.

I went to the museum in Havana that now houses most of Lobo's Napoleon collection. Built in 1928, it is a four-story Florentine-style mansion near the university, built in gray stone. It once belonged to Orestes Ferrara, a Neapolitan-born Cuban politician, and now has the hushed and gloomy feel of a mausoleum. When I visited, the windows' heavy wooden shutters were closed, and the polished stone floors gleamed with only faint, ambient light. In the lower rooms, there was a sparse collection of sabers, regimental shakos, Napoleon's "bed pot," some furniture, and in a glass cabinet one of the emperor's molars that my mother remembers seeing in Lobo's house sixty years ago, which caused her to shudder with squeamish delight. More notable objects were on the second floor: in one cabinet, locks of the emperor's hair; in the corner of a dark room, a bureau that belonged to Napoleon's minister of police and was used by Lobo as his desk; and in another, the baptismal service with which Napoleon had baptized his son, the king of Rome, and Lobo his first grandchild, Victoria Ryan—although with cane juice rather than water, which he passed over her lips "so that she never forgot the taste."

Doubtless Lobo saw himself reflected in Napoleon's character. Unlike some more comic Napoleon enthusiasts, though, he did not reenact old battles with tin soldiers spread over a green baize cloth; nor did he strut around the room wearing one of the emperor's old hats, as the British diplomat Lord Curzon supposedly did. "An infinite capacity for taking pains," "an intuitive sense," "an indomitable will to power," and "firmness of action" are some of the qualities attributed to the emperor. Compare that with this description of Lobo by Rosario Rexach, the wife of his lawyer León. Lobo, she said, "had an extraordinary ability to create, but

to create one has to believe firmly in what one is doing . . . When he em-
barked on a course of action, he applied all his energies until he achieved
it. He went direct to his objective. Often he achieved it. Sometimes he
failed. But he had an uncommon courage to accept the consequences of
his actions. He never complained when a project failed. And he was always prepared to start again."

John Loeb, a prominent Wall Street banker who knew Cuba well,
once described Lobo as "an unusual man, whose most memorable quality
for me was his Napoleon complex. . . . Julio was not the easiest man to
deal with." Yet in an interestingly partial appreciation of his hero, it is
significant that Lobo singled out these qualities above all others: "In addition to his abilities as a soldier, statesman, financier, civilizer, organizer,
and man of great vision, [Napoleon] was a good son, good brother and
good father. . . . He was never cruel with the vanquished, ruthless with
the disposed, nor prejudiced with racial minorities." Lobo once said he
wanted his Napoleon collection to be a "laurel to the Emperor," which
alone suggests he saw his collection as a monument of appreciation rather
than one of emulation. Like many collectors, Lobo's need to admire was
greater than the need to be admired.

Money is the collector's usual constraint, and as Lobo's wealth grew
so did the collection. Initially, Lobo stored his Napoleon documents and
relics in a haphazard fashion around the house in Miramar. After the
divorce from María Esperanza, when he moved back to Eleventh and
Fourth streets, the collection expanded until it covered several floors of
two of the houses, with Lobo living in a rooftop apartment in the third.
By the time of the revolution, it had grown into the largest collection of
Napoleonica outside France, with over 200,000 documents and 15,000
objects, managed by a staff of five full-time professional librarians led by
an aristocratic bibliophile, María Teresa Freyre. Lobo dispatched his assistants to France for lessons in Napoleonic history, and then to England
for the Wellingtonian view. Back in Havana, they used a special cataloguing system commissioned by Lobo and designed by Josy Muller, a curator
from Belgium's Musées Royaux d'Art et d'Histoire. If Lobo wanted to
consult a rare document or book, an assistant would bring it to the library,

Lobo's Napoleon–bedecked sitting room. Havana, 1958.

a room exclusively for his own use. Lobo would read in an easy chair, his head tilted into the book, straining in a circle of light, searching among the pages. "It was a sacred place for Julio," remembered Audrey Mancebo, the library's second-in-charge. "I often wondered how many of his ideas were born that way."

Lobo's collection was the extravagance of a true collector. It was obsessive and unnecessary, yet by definition all great private collections are so. In 1959, when Lobo privately published a volume of letters between Napoleon and the Comte de Mollien, his minister of finance, General Charles de Gaulle, another difficult man with a sense of destiny, wrote from Paris to thank Lobo for "this priceless contribution to the study of the Imperial Age."

Today, most of Lobo's Napoleonic books are kept on the top floor of the museum. Ringed by a breezy terrace, it is the only bright room in the old house. Wooden shelves run down both sides, bursting with leather-bound books, some with the initials "JL" gold-embossed on their spines. When I asked one of the attendants if I could open a book, just to have a peek, she said no, reflexively, although perhaps the supervisor might be able to help. I climbed down the marble steps, knocked on the cracked window of an office on the ground floor that overlooked the garden, and a thin woman with the beleaguered look of a minor civil servant came out. We sat in the shade of an arbor overflowing with pink and orange bougainvillea, and she politely explained, with a resigned sense of the absurd, that *tristemente*, sadly, nobody was allowed to consult the books, not even professional Napoleon researchers. It was the common story of modern Cuba. That which should be possible is forbidden. Everything else is illegal.

It would be fascinating to know more about what Lobo thought about Napoleon—especially as his hero was responsible for the industrial development of beet sugar after the English blockade reduced Caribbean sugar supplies to France. The shortages were such that imperial dignitaries were known to suspend a piece of sugar on a string from the ceiling, with each member of the family allowed to dip it into their cup only briefly. Sadly, only scraps of Lobo's views survive. He jotted down asides in the margins of the histories, memoirs, and biographies that he collected, scribbling *FALSO* next to statements he disagreed with. (Here, as in much else, Lobo had made up his mind.) But most of these thoughts are now sealed off in the museum's bookshelves—or lost in semidarkness in the subterranean archives of Cuba's National Library. The other day, an archivist announced with great fanfare that he had found a complete ten-volume edition of rare Egyptian drawings that Napoleon had commissioned, part of the study of Egyptology that he invented, and that had once formed part of Lobo's collection but had since moldered in a library basement for fifty years.

One of Lobo's few surviving extended disquisitions concerns the emperor's death mask, kept on a velvet cushion in a glass cabinet on the second floor of the museum. It is a scholarly article and tells a story curious for the macabre object itself, the long controversy that surrounded its maker, and how it arrived in Cuba.

Napoleon's last physician, Francesco Antommarchi, was by the emperor's bedside with several other members of the court when he died on the afternoon of May 5, 1821. At 5:51 p.m., the thirty-two-year-old Corsican-born doctor pronounced Napoleon officially dead and closed his open eyes. Napoleon's body was laid out in the billiard room on a trestle table, and the following day Antommarchi performed an autopsy. He opened the cavity of the chest and removed the organs; Madame Bertrand, the wife of the Marshal of France, asked to keep the emperor's heart, but her request was refused. Antommarchi then shaved Napoleon's head and took precise measurements of the skull. The circumference was 22½ inches, an average size, despite most descriptions that agreed Napoleon's head was disproportionately large for his body. "If we were to catalogue that in its most prosaic form, we would say that his head measured a hat size number 7," as Lobo wrote.

Although Napoleon's death had been foreseen for weeks, nobody had taken the precaution of gathering the chemicals necessary to embalm the great man's body, let alone the plaster required to make a death mask. So that night an enterprising Englishman, Dr. Francis Burton, rowed out to a nearby island to collect some gypsum deposits. He roasted and crushed the crystals into a fine white powder, and on the afternoon of the following day made two molds, one of Napoleon's face, the second of the back of his head and ears. The next day, Burton took positive casts and left them to dry. On his return, he discovered to his fury that Madame Bertrand, having failed to secure Napoleon's heart, had packed the face mask in her bags and now refused to part with it. No more is known about the cast of the back of Napoleon's head; according to some reports, Burton smashed it on the floor in anger at the theft. Madame Bertrand meanwhile took her mask to France.

Burton spent seven years trying to recover the property, but Madame Bertrand kept it with her. Antommarchi took a copy during a visit to her house in 1822 and, when Burton died six years later, made a limited edition in bronze and plaster, put forth his right as the author of the original, distributed several copies among Napoleon's descendants, and left for the Americas with three others wrapped carefully in his bags.

He made for Santiago de Cuba, where a community of French plant-

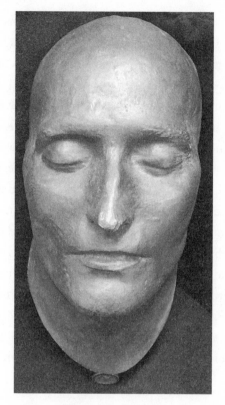

Napoleon death mask.

ers had settled after Haitian independence, including Antommarchi's first cousin, Antonio, who owned a coffee farm thirty miles outside the city. Antommarchi arrived in November 1837 and set up what promised to be a thriving medical practice on the corner of Gallo and Toro streets. An operation on the cataracts of the Marquesa de las Delicias de Tempú was a notable early success. Unfortunately, the city was gripped by yellow fever at the time and Antommarchi had no natural immunity to the disease. He died just five months later, in the house of the Spanish governor, Brigadier General Juan de Moya y Morejón. The old soldier was Antommarchi's closest friend in Cuba, despite the fact that he had lost an eye to Napoleon's troops during the siege of Zaragoza.

Three Napoleon death masks radiate out from this point. Antommarchi had bequeathed two copies to friends in Santiago, one of which eventually found its way to Lobo's collection. He gave a third to Dr. Wilson, a North American physician. Of the other imperial souvenirs that Antommarchi brought to Cuba, such as the silver dinner service, the locks of hair he shaved from the emperor's head, and the other body parts he kept, nothing is known. They may still be in Cuba today.

Antommarchi was buried quickly because of the heat, and when his body proved too big to fit into General Moya's private tomb, the Marqués de Tempú provided his own, "in gratitude for the operation on his mother's eyes." Antommarchi's remains were later transferred to the Santa Ifigenia cemetery in Santiago where they now rest, mingled with the remains of the Tempús and alongside better-known figures from Cuban history, including the grave of José Martí himself. It is a mournful postscript to the story that a French plan to erect a large structure in the Santiago cemetery to honor the emperor's physician came to naught. Still, as Napoleon once said: "It is the cause and not the death that makes the martyr."

THE IMAGE OF LOBO researching an article about Napoleon's death mask in his private library in a pool of light is a lonely one. Werner Muensterberger, a psychoanalyst who has made a study of collectors, has even called collecting a reaction to "the trauma of aloneness." Lobo was certainly a loner by temperament, and the constant physical pain that he suffered after the shooting, plus the end of his marriage shortly after, would only have increased this natural instinct to retire into himself. The ex libris that Lobo's assistants pasted into his books even showed a picture, drawn by Lobo, of a Byronic-looking squire in a checked dressing gown, reading in a wingback chair. Above runs a legend in Gothic letters: *Nunca menos solo que cuando estoy solo*, never less lonely than when I am alone.

Obsessive collectors are also frequently bachelors, which may be why Lobo collected women too. His divorce from María Esperanza marked the beginning of what Margarita González, Lobo's assistant in New York,

Lobo's ex libris.

referred to as his "playboy years," even if Lobo only partly matched the required profile of a playboy. He had a good wardrobe, if not good looks. He had languages, manners honed into reflexes, wit, a sense of humor, connections, wealth, and intelligence—both bookish and worldly. Extra points: he had a reputation for dangerousness. This transformed the artery that could be seen faintly pulsing in a soft patch at the back of his skull, where a bullet had plowed through bone, into a roguish attraction. Unlike the shy and withdrawn María Esperanza, the women Lobo courted were also fiery and strong-willed, somewhat like Napoleon's first wife herself, the worldly Josephine, second daughter of a Martinique sugar planter, whose memoir was the last book Napoleon ever read. "I really loved her," the emperor announced suddenly to his court one day, six weeks before he died, perhaps remembering Josephine's indolent Caribbean walk, musical voice, and large eyes—if not her teeth, blackened by a child-hood of chewing sugarcane. "She had something, I don't quite know what. . . . She was a real woman. She had the sweetest little backside in the world."

Josephine was the woman who broke Napoleon's heart, and after their divorce—because she could not bear him an heir—the emperor took up with a string of actresses, even sharing one with his conqueror the Duke of Wellington. (Mademoiselle George later observed indiscreetly that the Iron Duke, as a lover, was "*le plus fort,*" perhaps in revenge for Napoleon's once describing the act of love as "an exchange of perspirations.") So Lobo had actresses in common with Napoleon too. Movie stars often visited Cuba during the golden age of Hollywood, and although Lobo was only tangentially part of this world, gossip columnist Hedda Hopper was a close friend and mentioned him often in her newspaper columns. Unlike Napoleon, however, Lobo was no misogynist. He remembered his former lovers to the end, remaining firm friends, often corresponding with them until his last years. One of the most famous was the Hollywood icon Joan Fontaine.

Fontaine is best remembered for her lead role in Alfred Hitchcock's celebrated 1940 version of Daphne du Maurier's gothic novel *Rebecca.* She plays the cowed second wife of a rich Englishman, Max de Winter, portrayed in clipped style by Laurence Olivier. The drama takes place in a seaside Cornish mansion haunted by the memory of de Winter's first wife, Rebecca, who died in a mysterious boating accident. As is so often the case, Fontaine's demure screen image belied the actress's true personality.

Du Maurier had written the book while living in Egypt with her husband, desperately missing her home by the Cornish sea, a place of rocks, dark nights, and smugglers' coves. Du Maurier wrote that the homesickness she felt in Egypt was "like a pain under the heart continually." Hitchcock captures this dreamy longing in the watery unconsciousness of a crashing sea, and in the flickering light that plays across Fontaine's face. In *Rebecca,* she wrings her hands, rarely raises her eyes, and speaks in a voice that alternates between a monotone and a quavering tentativeness. Fontaine later struggled to escape the typecasting. It was only in later years, with her patrician beauty and sharp intelligence, that reviewers praised Fontaine for her "majestic stride and presence, robust humor and sense of the dramatic," as one critic noted in a 1979 comeback performance of *The Lion in Winter*, a review that Lobo clipped when he was a lion in winter himself.

Lobo and Fontaine first met during the winter of 1951 in a psychologically cramped setting worthy of any Hitchcock film: a hotel elevator. Lobo was in London with his daughters to open a branch of the Galbán Lobo office. Fontaine was in England to film *Ivanhoe*, playing the part of Lady Rowena, opposite Elizabeth Taylor. Unbeknownst to each other, they were staying at the same hotel, Claridge's. After dinner in the hotel restaurant, Lobo and his two teenage daughters went up to their rooms, Fontaine stepping inside the lift as the doors closed behind them. Lobo took no notice, burying his nose deeper into a newspaper as the bell pinged at each floor. Leonor remembers how she and María Luisa meanwhile elbowed each other in the ribs, tittering behind their hands. When the Lobos got out at their floor, Fontaine continued on to her suite on a floor above. "What was all that fuss about?" Lobo asked the girls, putting his newspaper aside when they reached their rooms. "You were being preposterous."

"But Daddy!" they chorused, flushed with the excitement of having stood so close to a Hollywood star. "That was *Joan Fontaine*, and you didn't even notice."

"I see," replied Lobo, who hadn't. He thought for a moment, and lifted up the phone.

"I would like to leave a message for Miss Joan Fontaine," he told the hotel operator. "A mutual friend of ours insisted that I call her when I passed through London."

The girls were aghast at the fabrication. But a few minutes later the phone rang with Fontaine on the line. Lobo's eyes lit up and they arranged to meet in the lobby for a drink.

The girls teased their father the next day. Many years later Lobo told Fontaine that the evening "was one of the outstanding moments in my life"—he always knew how to pay a beautiful woman a compliment.

At the time he only commented that the London sky was very beautiful at night.

Lobo's charm is apparent in the relationship he struck up with Fontaine's mother, Lillian. A formidable woman, often estranged from her two daughters, Joan Fontaine and the actress Olivia de Havilland, Lillian developed a deep fondness for Lobo over a correspondence that spanned twenty years. The affection was mutual. Lobo sent her rare books, such as *The Art of Worldly Wisdom* by the Spanish friar Baltasar Gracián, and the sayings of the Greek philosopher Epictetus. ("I am certain both will become part of your bedside literature," he wrote. After his shooting, Lobo was nothing if not stoic.) He also sent music, including an original score by Camille Saint-Saëns ("rather unusual; I trust you will like it"), recordings of Haydn and Bach, with Lobo often gently teasing Lillian in the accompanying letters. In one he asks if she had received a recording of the Cuban zarzuela "Cecilia Valdés" and then says music doesn't really move him, quoting Lorenzo's speech in *The Merchant of Venice* about the dangers of "the man that hath no music in himself." Lobo joked: "So beware! I really must be a bad character!" Neither Lillian nor Joan Fontaine ever found him so.

I telephoned Joan Fontaine in Los Angeles, having written a few weeks before. I had been warned that she refused most interview requests and lived in near seclusion, preferring a quiet life and gardening. Speaking about Lobo was clearly an exception. Fontaine greeted my call with a firm, bright voice.

"Oh, I am so glad you called. I've been thinking so much about him since you wrote. I adored Julio—he was the best friend I ever had."

There was a whistle of air and static on the line as we talked.

"Wasn't he driving the car when he was shot?" remembered Fontaine. "I think he was." *Sushh*, whispered the telephone. "And didn't he fall on the car horn when he was wounded? I think that is right too."

Lobo eventually proposed to Fontaine. "I couldn't—it would have been like marrying my father," she told me. "Julio was like my adviser, he was always there during the hardest times of my life."

To his credit, Lobo easily made the transition from suitor to friend. In later years, he called Fontaine a person among his "first row," and valued her above all for her companionship, even though he also thought her *loca*, a bit crazy. "As you know, early in the 1950s I very much wanted to marry you," Lobo wrote to Fontaine in his eighties. "I suppose that now, looking back, I understand why you got cold feet at the last moment. I think that perhaps you did the right thing."

Perhaps Lobo was deluded to think Fontaine would ever have agreed to marry him. He may also only have been trying it on, floating the suggestion out of curiosity to see how she reacted. Still, it is striking how frank Lobo and Fontaine are with each other in the letters that they exchanged in the last years of his life, and how tender. "Like you, I am a loner and relish solitude and actually require it," she wrote in 1981 when, for a moment, it appeared that Lobo might move to the United States to be nearer his old flame during the last two years of his life.

"I am so glad you were touched by my letter for I meant every word of it," Fontaine wrote. "My apartment is on a floor with an elevator so your visits here could be easily managed. And I have a large leather arm chair with a foot stool by my library fire that would fit you! I am hungry for good conversation and never had better ones than with you."

They had much in common: an interest in books, in archaeology, and a similarly turbulent family life. Fontaine had a lifelong rivalry with her sister, Olivia de Havilland, an enmity that had a special resonance for Lobo, given the antagonism his two daughters felt for each other. "The sadness which envelopes my heart is very great because the two girls do not talk to each other," he wrote to Fontaine in 1977. Perhaps because of this, Lobo was one of the few people to bridge the Fontaine–de Havilland rift. Although his letters to de Havilland never approached the same warmth as those to Fontaine, he corresponded often and took a medical interest in her son, who suffered from Hodgkin's disease, Lobo sending her clippings of the latest treatments.

Fontaine learned about Lobo's death long after the fact. "I only found out when his secretary wrote to me," she told me. "But the letter was translated from the Spanish and there was no sense in it that he had gone." Fontaine paused, the gurgle of our phone connection filling the silence. "I miss him so much."

Fontaine's initial brightness had faded, and I didn't have the heart to ask this nonagenarian former Hollywood icon why she hadn't mentioned Lobo in her memoir, *No Bed of Roses*, an omission that had hurt him.

Fontaine closed bravely. "Is there anything more I can tell you? I hope that I have been of help. There are so many emotions going through me right now. Goodbye. Oh dear," she said, and put down the phone.

THE CONVERSATION I HAD with Fontaine made me think of Tinguaro, Lobo's Shangri-la. She had often stayed there alongside the writers, painters, diplomats, artists, and English lords Lobo invited to the mill. The singer Maurice Chevalier came, as did the *New Yorker* cartoonist Charles Addams, Ginger Rogers, Merle Oberon, and Cesar Romero, best known for his role as the Joker in the *Batman* television series but whose other claim to fame was as José Martí's illegitimate grandson. The only people rarely present were Cuban politicians. Esther Williams remembered the plantation fondly in her memoir, *The Million Dollar Mermaid*.

> Years ago, when I was still at MGM, Ben [Williams's then-husband] and I had gone on a junket to Cuba with Cesar Romero and a group of wealthy MGM investors. Julio Lobo . . . had been our host. . . . He had a magnificent villa. . . . There had been some magnificent parties, and Julio had extended an effusive, open-ended invitation to come whenever I wanted.

Lobo's hospitality grew out of the traditional generosity exhibited by all Cuban *hacendados*. Baron von Humboldt, the nineteenth-century German naturalist who knew high society in Europe and the Americas, observed that "hospitality, which generally diminishes as civilization advances, is still practiced in Cuba with the same profusion as it is in the most distant Spanish American lands." Of that profusion, there is this

An Afternoon at Tinguaro, *by Hipólito Caviedes.*

description by a traveling Bostonian businessman of one particularly opulent nineteenth-century plantation. "The luxuriousness of the residence
is known throughout the island. Its stables have space for fifty horses. The
house, of one floor, has internal patios that cover a huge area; it could
accommodate at least one hundred people. . . . You arrive at its roman
baths, of exquisite marble, by an avenue of bamboos that form an arching
roof seventy feet high. . . . It seems like a fairy tale. . . . In the morning,
gin flowed from a fountain in the garden, and in the afternoon there
burbled a flow of Cologne, to the delight of the guests."

While welcoming, Lobo disdained such showiness. In 1950, when he
offered a joint coming-out party for his daughters with four hundred
guests, María Luisa wrote to her father saying she had found a beautiful
dress in New York for $600. Lobo sent a curt reply: "You know I am mod-
est in my habits and way of life and that I hate ostentation, a sign of bad
taste and the 'nouveau riche,'" and he recommended that she find a
cheaper dress in Havana. Rather than amid brazen luxury, Lobo's guests
at Tinguaro slept in a modest if well-appointed *casa de vivienda,* a stag-

gered row of clapboard buildings, with air-conditioned rooms and white porches joined by stone paths that curved through well-tended lawns. During the day, they rode on horses through the grounds or socialized around the pool. In the evening, a local orchestra composed of plantation workers played during dinner. Fireflies danced in the bushes, and the mill puffed and groaned in the background with a comforting hum. Hipólito Caviedes, the Spanish artist who painted the mural at the Galbán Lobo office in Havana, remembered—and drew—a typical afternoon:

> When Hollywood stars visit . . . their beauty is a wonderful compliment to the surrounding countryside. Joan Fontaine is an island apart, with her enchanting intelligence. Esther, the Venus of the day, bounces off the springboard and splashes the less athletic around the pool. . . . Carlos chooses a recording of violin music while discoursing on "hi-fidelity" versus "hi-*infidelity*." Someone else cuts the hair of the Italian ambassador, while he reads the score of a Bach sonata. . . . While all this goes on, Julio periodically receives enigmatic messages from the office written on blue or yellow slips of paper: glucose, lactose, polarization, the state of sugar production at 4.30pm.

Even in swimming trunks, Lobo was always at work, reading dispatches, taking phone calls, compartmentalizing his attention so that he could read a telegram, play the sugar market, or act as gracious host at the same time. It was this constant activity, plus the horn of the plantation train, the smoke from the mill's chimneys, the sweet smell of molasses, the sound of the carts bringing cane from the field, and the factory whistle, which announced the change of shifts during the height of the *zafra*, that saved Tinguaro from a *Dolce Vita* decadence. Lobo wanted Tinguaro to be a Shangri-la for all, including the families that worked there. The American bankers who sold Lobo the mill in 1944 had told him that Tinguaro's "land was bad, the cane was bad, the mill was bad—but worst of all were the people." Lobo set out to prove them wrong. Everybody at Tinguaro knew him as Julio, from Lola the maid or El Chino the Communist carpenter to the bishop of Matanzas, who inaugurated the chapel named after his mother's saint's day, Eduvigis.

Tinguaro's swimming pool.

Lobo built a clinic, a small library, a primary school, and provided scholarships for promising students. When Havana's Malecón was remodeled, he also bought the seafront's discarded belle époque streetlamps and stationed them on street corners throughout the *batey*. He refurbished houses, paved street sidewalks, and modernized the mill as much as Cuban labor laws allowed. A tunnel was dug to transport the milled bagasse cane stalks more easily to the furnaces that powered the grinders, and the machines were painted a smart orange so that leaks and grease could be noticed quickly and cleared. "A sugar factory should be as clean and as hygienic as any other food processing plant, such as one that makes condensed milk," Lobo wrote. When he took ownership, Tinguaro milled around twenty thousand tons of sugar a year. Twenty years later, it produced three times that amount.

"We spent a lovely weekend at Tinguaro during the May day holiday," Lobo wrote to María Luisa in 1950, wishing that she could have been there too. While some guests sang, others painted, and "everyone did their thing, except for me, who played at being master of ceremonies." When

María Luisa did go to Tinguaro, my mother sometimes went with her too. There she swam in the pool, flirted with Havana's young Turks, and drank cocktails with the rest of Cuba's *jeunesse dorée*. One of the pictures in her albums shows her sitting cross-legged on the diving board, wearing shorts and a loose shirt, beaming, obviously happy. Another shows a group of six friends crouched in the shallows of the swimming pool, the midday sun bouncing off the water, all smiling, some wearing sunglasses, arms around one another's shoulders, drinks in their hands raised in a toast.

"Was it possible for the spirits of the young people present to give themselves over to pastimes other than those suggested by the pleasing objects before them? No, it was impossible." The question is asked and answered by Cuba's first novelist, Cirilo Villaverde, during a description of a Havana ball in 1830. More than a century later, the glittering young things of Cuban society still did what they had always done: the right thing, with the right people, at the right time, and in the right places, be that the Country Club and the Yacht Club for the Christmas and New Year parties, lunches in Havana at the Floridita, or summer sojourns at Varadero or a *finca* like Lobo's. It seems frivolous now only because of what happened later. But at the time, if the Hollywood stars who visited Cuba so often did the same, emulating their life, who could gainsay them?

LOBO'S PARTIES AT TINGUARO, however much fun, or his affairs, however gallant, were still diversions from his work life. Indeed, while Lobo was courting Fontaine, the largest sugar harvest in Cuban history was being reaped. Its size was due to good weather and large cane sowings during the first days of the Korean War. The bumper 1952 crop promised an island-wide bonanza. Yet as before, many also worried that the surfeit of Cuban sugar would depress world prices. Just as Machado's government had done twenty years before, Batista's government stepped into the breach. In an attempt to keep prices high, it decided to keep back 1.8 million tons in reserve and restrict Cuba's next harvest as well.

The plan was vigorously attacked by Lobo, among others. For the traders, Havana broker Lamborn & Co. wrote in July 1952: "Restriction is not the only or best response in a world of growing population and expanding markets. . . . The effects could be felt for years." As for the producers, Alejandro Suero Falla, the president of Cuba's second-largest sugar company, wrote that August: "The Cuban people should not accept the resolution, as it will affect the whole economy, today and tomorrow." Such men's reasons were long familiar. If Cuba restricted its harvest, other producers would simply increase theirs. The world price would still fall, only Cuba would suffer most and the island would repeat the same mistake it had made during the Great Depression, when the Chadbourne Plan that Lobo had criticized so fiercely had failed, as would this one.

Lobo, now a major planter in his own right, had a different vision of Cuban sugar. He envisaged a modernized industry that used tractors and trucks instead of cane-laden oxcarts, each year grinding out an outsized crop of low-cost sugar that it would then slap onto the market. Although prices might fall, Lobo believed higher volumes would compensate. Cuba, uniquely well suited to growing sugarcane, would then emerge victorious from the ensuing price war, and dominate the world market as never before. Instead Cuba had retreated and the opposite had happened. The Cuban crop had barely increased over the past twenty-five years, and no new mills had been built since 1928. Meanwhile, world consumption had doubled. To Lobo, this meant that upstart nations with modern methods had taken a bigger and bigger piece of the fast-growing pie. Worse, Cuba had let them do it.

Lobo knew that to achieve his ideas would require a complete sea change in Cuban attitudes. One third of the Cuban labor force was directly employed in sugar, and their pay was linked to what was known as the annual average price of sugar, or *promedio*. If the *promedio* was low, everyone earned less. Lobo's emphasis on the volume of the harvest rather than its price therefore threatened everyone, from the man with a machete to the man with a mill. That was why Eusebio Mujal, head of the Cuban Trade Union Federation, called Lobo Cuba's public enemy number one. Cuba's sixty thousand small sugar farmers, called *colonos*, felt much the same. And at official levels, opposition to the kind of mechanization Lobo proposed was such that when he imported an experimental cane-cutting machine, it remained in a customs warehouse for five years and was eventually returned to Louisiana after the authorities refused it entry.

The country was in a bind. In 1955, the National Bank warned that Cuba needed to produce more sugar—seven million tons—if it wanted to maintain living standards from ten years ago. Cubans were therefore doomed if they embraced Lobo's suggestions, and doomed if they didn't. Diversification away from sugar was one alternative, and Cubans might have been happy to see the sugar industry modernized if displaced workers could get jobs elsewhere. Unfortunately, such jobs did not exist. Meanwhile the industry was governed by labor laws that had been necessary and humane in the 1930s, but twenty years later had boxed it into a corner. International quotas also restricted some foreign markets. The system had reached its limits and was only rescued when prices rose thanks to unpredictable circumstances elsewhere, such as the Korean War or the Suez crisis. This, though, was a lottery.

Lobo continued to cajole and protest. "One has to modernize or disappear," he argued. Yet no government, neither Grau's nor Prío's before, nor Batista's afterward, was prepared to defy the political power of the sugar laborers or the *colonos*. And it was the Cuban state that ultimately ran the industry, not the mill owners. Sometimes that even meant abetting speculation on international markets. This was the seamier underside of ostensibly enlightened government involvement that Heriberto had seen firsthand twenty years before when Colonel Tarafa had asked him for advice on a speculative position. In fact, it was now thought that one reason for Batista's restrictions was again to profit a speculator close to the president.

The magazine *Bohemia* revealed an interesting detail about Batista's sugar policy that related to Francisco Blanco, Lobo's longtime adversary. Born in Oriente, Blanco was a well-known speculator and capable *hacendado* who maintained good political connections. He had been close to Prío, who years before had allegedly bailed Blanco out of a losing short position when the sugar price was rising. To stave off his potential ruin, the government had rescued Blanco by selling him 815,000 tons of sugar on the cheap from its own reserves so that he could close his position without bankrupting other Havana sugar brokers, counterparties to the trade. When Prío went into exile after the 1952 coup, Blanco cozied up to Batista.

How interesting, *Bohemia* pointed out in an article, that Blanco, whose nephew managed Batista's sugar mill Washington, had paid $24 million to Dr. Jorge Barroso, head of the Sugar Board. How interesting too that almost every morning Blanco visited Amadeo López Castro, the government's representative at the committee on sugar sales. Was it as a result of this, perhaps, that a Cuban sugar selling agency had been set up, which was now dominated by Blanco? Others believed so. "Of Blanco," Lobo later wrote intemperately, "nothing surprises me because he was a crook." Raúl Cepero Bonilla, a respected economics correspondent, went further. He suggested the restrictions were solely designed to bail Blanco out of a huge speculative position. To cover it, Blanco needed prices to rise. Instead, they were continuing to fall, and Blanco faced a large margin call he could not afford to pay.

Blanco turned to Lobo for help, visiting him at the Galbán Lobo office with two officials from the Sugar Institute. Lobo obliged, buying 387,000 tons of sugar, worth some $30 million, that Blanco would otherwise have dumped on the market. It was not out of charity. Lobo believed Blanco was "an S.O.B. of the first order," and acted only to prop up prices and so save his own and others' positions. More remarkably, Lobo next approached the government. He offered to buy the surplus 1.8 million tons that Batista had planned to stockpile and keep back from the market. The Sugar Board refused. "We don't deal with speculators," said Barroso, despite his links with Blanco, one of the country's biggest.

Undeterred, Lobo tried an even more ambitious ploy. Later that same year, on December 10, he visited Batista at Kuquine, the president's luxurious *finca* outside Havana. They had first met almost exactly ten years ago when Lobo had attended a large banquet at the Waldorf Astoria in honor of the then newly elected president—a different man. That had been the "good Batista" of the 1930s and '40s, a nimble and imaginative politician, with two Communist ministers in his cabinet, who transformed Cuba into a country with a large social safety net. This was the second, "bad" Batista of the 1950s who had emerged after the coup. Gone were the reputed sixteen-hour workdays of his first presidency. Instead Batista played canasta, watched horror films, and obsessed over minor details such as the correct tying of a tie or the punctuation of a letter. He was also less intent on winning popular support and, because his presidency came on the heels of Grau's and Prío's eight years of corruption, at first he did not need it. But opposition was growing quickly, and, soon, like all dictators, Batista would face a succession crisis, one that he resolved, as dictators so often do, by postponing elections and his scheduled departure from office. As in so many corrupt sultanates, his most creative schemes also involved growing his fortune and those of associates and friends.

Batista received Lobo in splendor. In his private office there was a large painting of the president as a sergeant, a solid gold telephone, along with busts of Churchill, Gandhi, Stalin, Rommel, Joan of Arc, and the president himself. There were also the telescope Napoleon used on St. Helena, two pistols the emperor had used at Austerlitz, and, open on a lectern by the doorway, an 1822 edition of the *Vie politique et militaire de Napoléon* by Antoine-Vincent Arnault.

Lobo made the president his offer. He asked Batista to drop next year's restrictions, adding that he would buy any sugar that Cuba produced over and above the three million tons destined to meet the U.S. quota and Cuba's own needs. In effect, Lobo was saying, let the Cuban sugar crop rip and *he* would absorb it as a substitute world market. (Pleasing irony: Che Guevara would assert seven years later that Cuba, after it lost the U.S. quota, should become "master of the world market, able to dictate prices," close to Lobo's aim then.)

Batista asked Lobo what price he had in mind. Lobo offered three cents a pound, slightly less than the prevailing world price, with the only provision that he would take all profits if the sugar price rose above that level, tax free.

It would be a huge position, over three million tons, Lobo estimated, worth some $225 million, or $2 billion now. The risks were tremendous. If Cuba produced as much sugar as it could, world prices could plummet— and Lobo would lose a fortune. But from his London agents, Lobo believed that Britain, after thirteen years of postwar sugar rationing, was poised to lift restrictions, and that extra demand from the sweet-toothed English would support the market. Mujal, head of the workers' union and present at the meeting, thought otherwise. He told Batista that Churchill would tighten further the British belt, and Lobo's plan was thus doomed to fail. That would ruin Lobo and possibly Cuba. Batista refused the offer, although events soon proved Lobo's prediction right. On February 5, 1953, Churchill began to lift Britain's sugar rations, and there was a rush on stores as schoolchildren emptied their piggy banks and men in pin-striped suits queued to buy boiled sweets during their lunch breaks in the City of London.

Barroso, head of the sugar board, worked hard to mask the failures of Batista's sugar policy. He praised the decision to restrict exports, claiming it "had staved off the collapse of the Cuban economy and the sugar industry." For this fealty, Barroso was rewarded with a ministerial post. Yet Cuban abnegation did little to help prices. By the end of 1953, sugar traded at 3.1 cents per pound, much as it had a year ago and only slightly above Lobo's offer. Producers elsewhere meanwhile ground their sugar merrily, just as Lobo and others had predicted they would. Baron Paul Kronacher, a Belgian producer and occasional visitor at Tinguaro, built a huge sugar mill in the Congo, while one enterprising Cuban *hacendado*, Jesus Azqueta, developed a mill in Venezuela, in part to circumvent Batista's restrictions. Lobo could have done the same but believed it "undignified," even if good business, to compete from abroad against Cuba, the country to which he owed his fortune. Prices continued to fall, as did the Cuban crop: by 1955 it had dropped a third to 4.5 million tons, while world production rose to fill the gap Cuba had left.

His grand stratagems thwarted, Lobo returned to his entertainments at Tinguaro, his love affairs, and the Napoleon library at his Vedado home. He was in a philosophic mood, yet ready to hatch new plans. In the middle of 1953, he founded a new enterprise, Banco Financiero. He also started to buy mills again, beginning negotiations to buy his twelfth, Araújo in Matanzas, while also consolidating control at another, Unión.

It was the same pattern as after the Second World War, when restric-

Banco Financiero. Havana, c. 1958.

tions had limited Lobo's scope for market speculation and he had chan-
neled his energies elsewhere. The difference this time was his health, which
was failing. He suffered a mild heart attack in the spring of 1953 and a
more serious stroke that summer. Batista's presidency also suffered its first
serious blow that summer after Castro launched a rebel attack on the
Moncada military barracks in Santiago. The raid failed, and Castro was
captured and sentenced to prison. But Batista, believing his position secure, granted an amnesty in May 1955 and Castro left for Mexico shortly
after, where he met Che Guevara for the first time. Together they made
plans to launch an invasion of Cuba in December the following year
under the banner of the 26 July movement, the date of the Moncada
attack.

   Lobo meanwhile convalesced in Havana after his heart attack. "I know
now the time has come to relax and slow down," he wrote to Lillian Fon-

taine that summer. "I was traveling on the highway of life at a breathtaking speed and in so doing could neither heed nor appreciate the landscape. Now I can take my blinkers off and leisurely enjoy the vista. . . . I am glad and relieved. That is my compensation."

Lobo had been reading Ralph Waldo Emerson, the New England transcendental philosopher, patron of Walt Whitman and friend of Thoreau. In his essay "Compensation," Emerson had developed the idea of a spiritual ledger, with debits and credits, and had advised the reader: "If you are wise, you will dread a prosperity which only loads you with more. . . . For every benefit which you receive, a tax is levied. He is great who confers the most benefits. He is base who receives favors and renders none."

As Lobo lay in bed, reading Emerson and ruminating about his future, rumors began to spread that he was about to give away his fortune and meditate on life as a monk in Tibet.

"The idea might seem fantastic to a public that only knows Lobo for his implacable business sense," gossiped one society writer. But "it would not be the first time that a man, known for being hard, ambitious and implacable in the business jungle, should decide to end his days with an act of contrition in a place that is fitting for meditation on the human condition and the uselessness and difficulties of finding happiness through wealth."

It was also closer to the truth than many imagined. "The life I had been living could hardly be called life, looking at it retrospectively," Lobo had written to his new love interest, Varvara Hasselbalch, a Danish aristocrat, on October 15. "I hope that my chances will be better this time and that it will enable me to live life to the fullest."

It was only a passing fancy. Even as he recuperated, Lobo admitted to a growing restlessness and continued to act on it—just as he had in 1947 when he had orchestrated the hostile takeover attempt of Cuba Company from a hospital bed in the United States. It was as if the sugar business that ran in his veins made rest impossible. Constant physical pain also goaded him on.

"I've been in pain for so long now that I don't think I remember a day in the past seven odd years, when I was machine gunned, that I have not suffered physical pain of some nature or another," he wrote to Lillian Fontaine later that year.

"I know that pain can either destroy a person or build up his moral substance to something akin to granite. Probably I have achieved certain goals and ambitions because my good friend *pain* was always with me. I really think I should miss him if he were to desert me today."

In January 1954, Lobo closed negotiations to buy the mill Araújo, signing the deeds from inside an oxygen tent. A telephone by his bedside kept him in touch with the daily ups and downs of the international sugar market. It made for a ghoulish scene: the stricken millionaire, supposedly at death's door, unable to desist from his schemes. On February 14, Leonor wrote her father a fitting ditty, "To the Proud Owner of Central Araújo on Valentine's Day":

> In the oxygen tent he buys his mills,
> While taking his cardiograms and pills.
> He swears to retire when he feels "the oppression,"
> But market maneuvering is *still* the obsession . . .

Lobo lightened the mood further with gallows humor in a letter to Varvara, in which he detailed his plans and invited her to come stay in Cuba. "As Jonah said to the whale," he wrote, "you can't keep a good man down."

VARVARA HASSELBALCH, the great-granddaughter of the Russian princess Varvara Sergeievna, arrived in Havana on March 25, 1954. She had met Lobo two years before at a dinner party in New York. A photographer who worked in Africa and Europe, she had been decorated during the Second World War for her bravery as a frontline ambulance driver. She was also twenty years younger than Lobo and, standing well over six feet in her high heels, several inches taller. Of all the guests that night, though, "Lobo was by far the most fascinating," she told me. It was Lobo's sense of humor that attracted her, she said, his cannon-black eyes, and his intel-ligence. "He always had something turning in his mind, some idea or other. That was what made him so captivating."

I had gone to see her in Copenhagen on a bleak January afternoon when a sharp north wind had emptied the city's streets. Snow scudded over the threshold as Varvara opened the door of her apartment on the second floor of a solid stone building. Eighty-six years old, she wore gold lamé trousers, shiny silver pumps, and a white T-shirt with "CUBA" sten-ciled across the front. "It's in honor of you, my dear," she explained with aplomb, ushering me inside.

With her flamboyant dress sense, smoker's voice, and ribald sense of humor, Varvara is sometimes referred to in her native Denmark as the coun-try's "Dame Edna," after the cross-dressing comedienne and satirist. Her rooms were an Aladdin's cave of exotic souvenirs. Books, papers, gold ash-trays, and kitsch gadgets were piled on side tables. Portraits of Russian an-cestors hung on the walls, as well as the head of a deer with a tiara perched on its antlers, while a mannequin stood in one corner wearing a burka. I followed Varvara as she made for the kitchen, pushing a walker as though it were a lawnmower, clearing an open trail of red carpet through the impe-rial bric-a-brac. She settled at a table under a garden umbrella, fairy lights and plastic flowers threaded among its frets, and pushed a button. The lights twinkled and birdsong warbled from speakers hidden around the room. "Ahh, my little Tivoli," she said with a triumphant sigh.

Varvara had found a somber mood prevailing when she arrived in Cuba in 1954. It was eight months after the Moncada attack, and an airport official rifled through her luggage; smuggled guns, he told her, had been discovered the week before. Lobo met her outside immigration dressed in his usual white linen trousers, guayabera, and black bow tie. In the car on the way into town, he said: "I'm glad you finally came, it has been so long I had almost given up hope." His voice was softer and kinder than she remembered. Elsewhere, though, Varvara sensed threat amid the luxury and beauty.

In Havana, she was struck by the heat, by the coolness of the white marble floors at Lobo's house, by the Vlaminck, Turner, and Utrillo paint-

Varvara's photograph of Tinguaro's batey, 1954.

ings that hung on the walls of her bedroom, and by the two maids dressed in starched white pinafores who packed her clothes and suitcase away. She delighted in the blue of the swimming pool amid the lush greens and bright red flowers of the garden. She also shivered at the iron grilles on the windows and the heavy front door that had closed behind her with a clunk.

Lobo took her on a tour of his mills. At the beach at Tánamo, Varvara shied away "like a coward" from swimming, worried that the wire netting stretched across the mouth of the bay would let in sharks and barracudas from the open sea. At Pilón, Varvara went horseback riding one evening with María Luisa. She was bewitched by the twilight, the inky silhouettes of palm trees that reminded her of the ruins of a Greek temple, the fields of harvested cane golden with fallen leaves, the rugged hills in the distance, and the sight of a hawk hovering over a clump of trees. Then night fell, it began to rain, she sang to keep her spirits up, and the shadow of a boy ran past, screaming as if in pain and then laughing at her from the faintly illuminated doorway of a hut.

At Tinguaro she felt that same sense of unease shading into peril. One day, Lobo suggested that she take some pictures of the mill, explaining that he had an important meeting to attend. Varvara photographed the *batey*, the two chimneys of the mill, the chapel dedicated to Lobo's mother, and the old lamps from the Malecón. Walking back to the guesthouse, she saw a battered limousine pull up in a cloud of dust. Two men dressed in shabby guayaberas and black trousers got out in a hurry. They left soon after in an even faster rush.

"What was all that about?" she asked, climbing the steps of the porch, where Lobo stood waiting for her in the shade.

"That was two of Batista's men," Lobo replied. "They picked up a check for thirty thousand dollars. We got off cheap."

Varvara left Cuba soon after on a scheduled return flight to Portugal. Lobo had asked her to marry him before leaving. Free-spirited Varvara had prevaricated. Stopping over at New York, she met with Belle Baruch, a childhood friend and daughter of the legendary Wall Street investor Bernard Baruch. Belle was worried about her future.

"Let's drive over and visit Father," she told Varvara when she picked her up at the airport.

A self-made millionaire, Baruch had created his first fortune speculating in sugar stocks on Wall Street in the first decades of the century. He spent of much of his later life as "Adviser to the Presidents," most recently Roosevelt and Truman, and the familiar newspaper photographs of Baruch cogitating on a park bench across the street from the White House somehow reassured millions of Americans that the nation's leaders were being sensibly counseled. Baruch has been credited with originating the phrase "the Cold War," in 1947, and his independence of mind and spirit earned him the epithet "the Lone Wolf of Wall Street." Lobo would have approved, if not of the advice he subsequently gave Varvara.

John Foster Dulles, the U.S. secretary of state, was leaving when

Varvara arrived at Baruch's Long Island property. She found Baruch, eighty-four, in high spirits after his daily swim. While Baruch dried off in the sun, Belle began to tell him about Lobo. Baruch listened closely, turned serious, then put on his pince-nez and looked Varvara in the eye.

"A Cuban? Never! A millionaire on paper, maybe," he said.

"Feather," he called her. "You must promise me never to marry him. If it is an elderly millionaire you're looking for I have plenty of friends I know who would more than willingly marry you."

Belle was triumphant. "You'll just have to listen to Father."

Varvara was interested in Lobo, but not his money; she feared living in a gilded cage. At her apartment in Copenhagen, she showed me the five-page handwritten letter that Lobo had sent after she finally refused his marriage offer. ("Are you sure?" Lobo had cabled earlier. "Definitely," came her reply.) I commented that she was one of the few women to have refused his attentions, and Varvara punched the air, her hands losing themselves momentarily in the plastic flowers and fairy lights above her head.

ONE HIGH-SKIED APRIL DAY I went to visit Tinguaro, now a state-owned mill like all the others in Cuba. Cresting the hill in a rented car, I saw a lush grove amid the surrounding sugar fields, with two chimneys standing clear above the trees. I had dropped off a hitchhiking accountant a mile back at the crossroads after picking her up two hours earlier at the start of the drive. Pertly made up, with red lipstick and a crisp white shirt, she had contorted herself as she dropped a small bag into the backseat, then introduced herself as Gladys, thanked me for the lift, and unrolled a litany of soft curses about the interminable wait for the bus (called *La Madre*, the mother, as there was only one). There were also the poor pay at her job, the health of her mother she was now visiting, the state of the country, and her absent boyfriend.

Car windows rolled down, we drove through the back roads of Matanzas, past half-started industrial projects, now roofless and rusted lumps of iron by the side of the road, the single lane of tarmac kinking through shabby former sugar towns, where clumps of people stood on street corners in the shade beside shuttered shops. Their expressions seemed marked with a bitter lassitude that I had not seen elsewhere in Cuba. "What are they waiting for?" I asked. "To die of hunger," came Gladys's reply, a remark that triggered the memory of a cane cutter I'd picked up on another drive, a wiry and rangy-looking man with a gravelly voice, who had commented sourly when a boxy Lada had overtaken us on the highway, driven by what he took to be a party functionary: "See that man? He eats a lot of *meat*."

I had wanted to visit Tinguaro in the hope I would find some shard of Lobo's life that might help conjure up the past. What I had not expected was a day so joyously beautiful. The hum of the car wheels on the road, the warm breeze, and the tawny fields of uncut sugarcane soon lulled Gladys and me into silence. After she again twisted around in her seat to retrieve her bag and waved goodbye from the side of the road, I drove into the peaceful view of the old mill in front of me and pulled up through open gates into Tinguaro's *batey*. There the greenery, the warm midmorning light, and the birds singing in the ficus trees conjured up a sense of the beginning of things, a moment before the times of malice and misdeed.

I got down from the car, and what first caught my eye was a metal stirrup by the steps leading up to the *casa de vivienda* that Lobo's guests had once used to scrape mud off their shoes. There were also a delicate, knee-high hooped metal railing that circled the front lawn, an arched hedge that rose over a walkway, wildly overgrown and shaggy with leaves, and next to it one of the streetlamps that Lobo had brought from Havana's Malecón. Time and weather had done their work elsewhere, obliterating most other traces of the past. The trees that once shaded the house had long gone, blown down in a storm, as had the palms I had seen in my mother's pictures. The roofs of some of the other buildings in the *batey* had fallen in, and one wing of the guesthouse had burned down and been replaced by a well-tended vegetable plot.

Tinguaro felt deserted. Some boys jostled around an improvised basketball hoop they had pinned to a wall near the empty kidney-shaped swimming pool that Esther Williams had once dived into and where my mother had swum. It had looked so glamorous in old photographs but was no larger than the backyard pool of so many suburban American homes, and was empty of water, blue tiles ripped off the sides.

Manolo Suárez, a swarthy man in his fifties, accompanied me while I strolled down Tinguaro's main street, pushing a pedal bike. The chapel at the end was shut, as was the funeral parlor next door. We passed tidy workers' houses that lined cramped but leafy walkways, their beams sagging with age. Without prompting, Manolo commented that Lobo had been much liked at Tinguaro, that he had treated people well and helped them when they needed it. Manolo's only personal memory—a flash of glamour—was of a convertible car driving into the *batey* with Lobo sitting in the back. A local teacher added: "Yes, he was a good man; I remember everyone saying so when I was a small girl."

Tinguaro was Lobo's pet. He lavished attention and money on the mill and showed it off to others, like a prize cat. He ran it like a benevolent patriarch, or feudal lord, depending on your point of view. Yet he saw the weakness of such a system and thought of ways to improve it. In 1958, he sent a newspaper article from the United States to María Luisa. By then, she had left school and was working at Galbán Lobo to try to improve social conditions around Lobo's mills; Leonor was still in the United States, working in publishing after graduating from Radcliffe. The clipping that Lobo sent to María Luisa told the story of a company lumber town in Arkansas that had turned itself over to the inhabitants. Crossett, with a population of three thousand, had flourished, the article said, when its single company owner abandoned its patriarchal system and allowed workers to choose their schools, organize their own affairs, and buy their houses using subsidized credit. "Perhaps this is the solution to Tinguaro? Or something like it," Lobo had scribbled to María Luisa in an attached note.

Tinguaro's founders had been progressive men too. In 1799, Don Pedro Diago had complained of Cuban sugar mills' technical inferiority due to the negative influence of slavery. Four years later, he installed windpowered cane grinders, following the successful example of English plant-

María Luisa and her father.

ers in Barbados. When Don Pedro's experiment failed—"because when there was wind there was no cane to grind, and when there was cane there was no wind," as Lobo put it—he installed a steam engine instead, a ten-horsepower machine brought over from England. This was probably Cuba's first commercially successful steam-powered mill, although the Conde de Montalvo, María Esperanza's ancestor, had studied the idea a decade before. Other planters soon copied Don Pedro's example. "If only current generations of *hacendados* imitated the same spirit of progress that inspired those planters, instead of the extraordinary slackness that characterizes our class today," Lobo wrote disparagingly in 1958.

The mill at Tinguaro, the last of a two-hundred-year-long line of sugar mills at the site, has been dismantled now, the buildings stripped bare by trucks and cranes to salvage any reusable ironwork. All that is left are the chimneys that Varvara once photographed, stenciled with the faded slogan "THE MOST EFFICIENT OF ALL"—a cheap revolutionary irony—and some of the fretwork that held up the huge shed which once housed Lobo's orange-painted cane grinders. Even these steel beams have collapsed at one end, leaving the roof girders bent down to the ground like the skeleton of a huge dinosaur feeding out of a trough. As chance had it, a sole cloud hovered over one of the chimneys like a puff of smoke, giving the impression that the furnaces were still working, the *zafra* in full swing. It suggested a distant if improbable hope of regeneration. Lobo, who had called the operation he rebuilt at Tinguaro "a Phoenix, rising from its ashes," had felt a similar optimism several decades before.

Ten

AT THE ALTAR

*The Americans invented wash and wear, clothes you did
not need to iron. The guerillas invented* patria o muerte,
and you did not need to wash.

—Eladio Secades

t is in the last years of the Republic that the dissonances become
sharpest—between the Cuba that so many people suppose existed before Castro came down from the Sierra and the life that my family,
Lobo's family, and their friends remember. There is so much that feels as
though it needs to be said. Yet when I collect my thoughts they make an
awkward collection, as if each incident or image was elbowing the one
next to it in the ribs. There is no consistency. Instead, there is diversity.

There are the high-society parties in Havana, the men in black or
white tie, the women softly abundant in bosomy dresses with deep décol-
letages and bare shoulders. There are also the obligatory family lunches
every Sunday, the conservative social mores, the Catholicism, the deco-
rous attention to propriety. When my mother felt hot, she was advised
to "close her pores." If she went on a date, it was with a chaperone. Like
most middle- or upper-class Habaneras, my mother didn't ride on public
transport—unlike the Lobo daughters. She didn't play in public parks or

go to public schools—which were for poor people. Nor did she bathe at public beaches. Instead she went to Varadero, where the days passed in a languid routine. El Chino, the Chinaman, an itinerant portrait photographer, patrolled the white sand with his camera, wearing a pith helmet and commenting on how everyone had grown from the year before. In the evening, a record might be placed on the phonograph, the music floating out over the waves. At night a line was trailed out to sea and tied onshore to the clapper of a bell that rang out when a hooked fish started to run.

As for black Cuba, the only contact that my mother had was when María la Gorda, Fat Mary, her beloved nanny, took her by bus to a small house on the outskirts of Havana one evening. It was a dramatic if not untypical introduction for an upper-class white girl to the Santería liturgy— the drummed invocation of the spirit of African gods. Yet, even though she is in her spry mid-seventies, it is also one she can hardly remember now.

Far from the seedy downtown areas such as the Barrio Colón or the sex shows in the back streets of Chinatown, my mother's life, like that of her peers, revolved around family gatherings and social events held in private clubs such as the Havana Yacht Club, which refused to accept Batista because he was a corrupt politician and also mulatto, which made him a social pariah. In the suburbs of Vedado, Miramar, and the Country Club, she attended a busy round of dances, sporting events, extravagant coming-out parties, and even more lavish weddings, each one carefully described the next day in the social pages of the newspapers. At the pinnacle stood the *boda del gran mundo*, the high-society wedding—none more magnificent than the 1955 marriage of Norberto Azqueta Arrandiaga to Lian Fanjul y Gómez-Mena, which united three of Cuba's most powerful sugar families, the Fanjul-Riondas, the Gómez-Menas, and the Azquetas. "Their marriage will forever be inscribed in gold in the annals of our social history," gushed the *Diario de la Marina*'s social diarist. Below the *boda del gran mundo* ranged the lower social heights of the *boda elegante*, the elegant wedding, only slightly less magnificent; then the *boda íntima*, with diary coverage limited to a portrait of the bride and a description of her dress; and then the lowest category of all, the *boda*, with no qualifying adjective whatsoever. The church was just as fastidious. Cardinal Manuel Arteaga y Betancourt, Havana's archbishop, fumed about "the fashion of impudent dressing which has become more prevalent and indecent among women" and ordered that no woman attending a Cuban wedding could wear "a low-necked dress, short dress, or sleeveless dress." If they did, the priest would suspend the ceremony.

Set against such images, there is the Havana most popularly remembered: the opulent Mafia-infested gambling den–cum–brothel, its beauty a decadent façade behind which languished a people mired in want. This is the Havana of the Casa de Marina—Havana's fanciest bordello; of the "love motels" that my mother and her girlfriends would cruise by at night to see if any of their boyfriends' cars were parked outside; and of Meyer Lansky, the Mob King, padding around an air-conditioned suite above the casino at his hotel, the Riviera. It is also the Havana of the boozy good times of American tourists boxing with maracas in their hands as they staggered back to their hotel bedrooms at night; the humiliating comment that Errol Flynn scrawled across the menu of the Bodeguita del Medio, a bohemian bar in the old town, "Best place to get drunk"; and the luxury of the Hotel Nacional, rising from its rocky Vedado bluff above the Malecón. Lansky had revamped the Nacional's casino at Batista's invitation and called it the Parisien, although my aunt Carmen remembers the hotel in another way. She was the daughter of the American manager, and grew up in Suite 230, "the one with the wraparound balcony on the second floor." Her earliest memories are of getting caught among the legs of chefs and busy waiters carrying room service on silver trays, watching guests drink highballs in the Palm Court from behind the potted palms, and snooping on film stars when she hid in the closets in their rooms.

It is because of such high jinks that Carmen maintains she is the inspiration for Eloise, the naughty six-year-old girl of Kay Thompson's books, who grows up during the 1950s in New York's Plaza Hotel. Eloise "skibbled" through the Plaza's corridors, zoomed up and down its elevators, "sklonked" kneecaps, visited Paris and Moscow, where she saw that the Russians stood "in line for absolutely everything," and made other droll pronouncements, such as "getting bored is not allowed" and "sometimes I comb my hair with a fork." Carmen's story may or may not be true. Still, two of the few things that she brought out of Cuba when she left the island were a browning photo of Thompson sitting in an outdoor atrium of the hotel with herself and her father, and a letter, now sadly lost, thanking Carmen's father for the idea behind the Eloise books.

Descriptions of Cuban revolutionary fever sit incongruously next to such scenes. By the mid-1950s, Batista was on his back heels and the tradition of rival, rebel *bonches* had returned. Some operated secretly in the cities; others comprised groups of disaffected officers plotting in the army. At one point, there were even student rebels in the Presidential Palace itself. On March 13, 1957, the Revolutionary Directorate shot its way into Batista's office on the second floor. Their leader declared in a broadcast from the CMQ radio station, seized in a separate attack: "People of Havana! The Revolution is in progress. . . . The dictator has been executed in his den!" But in Batista's office all they found was a half-finished cup of coffee, steaming on his walnut desk; the president had escaped the attack, rising in an elevator to a sealed and guarded room on the third floor. *The* Revolution, *that* Revolution, was yet to come.

The problem in bringing all these disparate images into single focus is that Cuba was, as modern tourist literature might describe it, a *Land of Contrasts!* Rural conditions could be miserable, especially in Oriente, where María Luisa saw on trips around her father's sugar mills "the kids with swollen bellies, dirty eyes and bare feet." There was high unemployment during the dead season after the sugar harvest ended and cane cutters were laid off. Yet 1957 was also one of the best years the Cuban economy had ever enjoyed, thanks to the Suez crisis, which drove sugar prices to a high. Indeed, if misery and want alone could cause a revolution, then the "first great patriotic, democratic and socialist revolution of the continent . . . should have been first produced in Haiti, Colombia or even Chile," as veteran Communist Party chieftain Aníbal Escalante said in 1960. "Cuba was not one of the countries with the lowest standard of living of the masses in Latin America, but on the contrary one of those with the highest." It had more doctors per capita than France, Holland, Japan, even England.

The legacy of this prosperity can still be seen in Havana districts such as Miramar, beyond the shopping district of El Centro and the hotels, businesses, and all-night cafés that lined La Rampa, the broad avenue that rises from the Malecón into Vedado. Planted with large shade trees, Miramar still exudes a plush restfulness, with balconied houses set back from the streets amid generous gardens. Most impressive are such suburbs' size. Miramar alone runs for a hundred blocks. And beyond Miramar the white stucco houses keep on going, through the quiet streets of residential areas now called Siboney, Náutico, Flores, and Cubanacán.

In the mid-1950s, Havana became known as the "Paris of the Caribbean," the "Monte Carlo of the Americas," the greatest party town on earth. Its nightlife was compared to that of prewar Paris or Berlin. There were flawless suits and glittering casinos, hot dance music and seductive showgirls, guerrillas in the mountains and repressive policemen in the streets. The city's "gangster chic," as Mob historian T. J. English describes it, so redolent of the golden age of Hollywood, was part of Havana's glamour, and glamour generates myths, such as the valiant revolutionary during the last years of Batista who blew himself up after rushing a policeman. That, at any rate, was the scene that Don Michael Corleone saw from the back of his car when he came down to Havana in *The Godfather Part II* to try to secure his influence over the city's casinos. Yet *The Godfather Part II* is just a movie, and the scene is only a plausible invention, since there is no record of a revolutionary suicide-bomber.

Members of my grandparents' and mother's generations living in Havana at the time would have been perplexed by the portrayal of their city in such films. And yet the Batista government did fall almost as rapidly as these movies depicted it. Then all the parties with the men in black tie, the women in cocktail dresses, the debutantes in fluffy confections of white silk and linen and tulle; the extravagant shows at the Tropicana; the Mafia, their casinos, and the famous American actor drunk in a small bar in Old Havana were suddenly over, gone with the wind, and the traces and stories that they left behind grew into legends. How could they not?

Havana Country Club, New Year's Eve.
Leonor wears a dark dress in the middle; María Luisa is second from the right;
my mother second from the left.

A scene that bad was too good for any Hollywood screenwriter or revolutionary ideologue to ignore.

ONE DAY IN HAVANA, I went to a bougainvillea-shrouded street in Miramar to visit Guillermo Jiménez. A retired economist and journalist of distinction, Jiménez is also a decorated comandante who took a bullet in the fight against Batista fifty years ago. A wiry seventy-year-old, with a warm face, nervous hands, and a natty dress sense, Jiménez has the careful manner of someone who, like Cuba itself, has triumphed because he has survived. Unlike many, he looks forward to the future.

"Sometimes I get requests for interviews when there is some revolutionary anniversary or other," he told me as we sat in his study, a shady room at the front of the house. "I am glad to help, but we have to get on, to live in the present."

Such optimism about the future may be because Jiménez has spent so much time examining the past. When we met he had just completed the second of a planned four-volume economic history of prerevolutionary Cuba. The first describes its largest businesses; the second is a series of biographical sketches of their owners, the country's 551 richest and most influential men and women (mostly men). The research is meticulous, shorn of inference and ideology. "Its eloquence, if there is any, stems only from the force and aridity of facts, without any interpolation by the author," as Jiménez wrote in the preface. Indeed, with their crisp entries arranged in alphabetical order, the books have the utilitarian feel of a dictionary. They make "no concession to the reader," as Jiménez said. All of which makes the success they have since enjoyed in Havana, and in samizdat versions in Miami, more surprising.

The second volume was released on June 2, 2007, at a launch party held at the Palacio del Segundo Cabo, a three-story colonial building in Old Havana with a fountain set in an inner courtyard. There had been a violent rainstorm the night before, and the Cuban book institute was hopeful of a good turnout. Soon they worried the second floor of the building might collapse under the weight of the eager audience. Some there recalled the crush in 1991 that had followed the reissue of José Lezama Lima's baroque masterpiece *Paradiso*. Partly because of its homosexual references, the authorities had tacitly banned the novel after a limited print run in 1966. *Paradiso*'s rerelease two decades later was more of a rock concert than a book launch. People chanted "Paradise! Paradise! Paradise!"—a recovered Paradise—as the crowd ebbed and flowed from one floor of the building to another as rumor spread that copies would be sold upstairs, then downstairs, then outside. Although Jiménez's history book does not pretend to be literature, sixteen years later there was pushing and shoving again in the Palacio del Segundo Cabo among the lines that formed in front of the two tables stacked with copies of his book, and a huge uproar when someone said there were only 150 copies to go around. The head of the institute rushed off to get more, assuring the crowd that if these ran out there would be an immediate reprint, ready in a month.

Jiménez was characteristically modest about his book's reception and genuinely puzzled too. Amid the crowd, he saw men and women he had not spoken to for years; old friends from the revolutionary struggle in the mountains, the city, and the plains. There were also journalists and novelists. One asked Jiménez to dedicate a copy, and then turned to a young poet next to him to explain the importance of the book. Jiménez could not understand the interest in his work, and was reticent to try and explain it.

It may be that the book is simply an invaluable work of reference and, in a country of frequent shortages, Cubans out of force of habit leap on anything that is useful. But the greater part of the interest, I believe, is that the book offers its readers a chance to escape the relentless drizzle of a historical past that Cubans have suffered, day by day, speech by speech, like acid rain. Jiménez said his motivation for writing the book was that young Cubans knew neither the capitalism, nor its capitalists, that once formed part of Cuban history. But it is also true that many *older* Cubans have little memory or understanding of prerevolutionary Cuban capitalists either. Their obvious interest in Jiménez's book, it seemed to me, represented a hunger for something closer to a historical truth, and so also a step toward a reconciliation with Cuba's past. There, detailed on paper, were the long-held and moneyed adversaries of the revolution: great capitalists like Lobo, powerful clans like the Falla-Gutiérrez and Bacardí families, their business interests calmly noted and accurately presented for the first time. Jiménez's biographical sketches showed that behind the doctrine, source of so much division, there lay a people and humanity against which abstractions such as class struggle inevitably become remote, an observation as true of the men and women who once fought so bravely for the revolution as of those who subsequently fought against.

Leaf through the book and it becomes apparent that many of these 551 *propietarios* were not the rapacious exploiters of the proletariat they are often thought to have been. Or if they were, in socially mobile Cuba some of them came from that same proletariat they exploited. One example is Vicente Domínguez, a mulatto cane cutter who got his break as a mechanic at Lobo's first mill, Agabama. Domínguez later rented the mill from Lobo, with funds borrowed from Galbán Lobo, and was so successful that he went on to control five Cuban sugar mills, as well as another sugar interest in Haiti, later sold for $1 million. "Not bad for someone who did not know how to read or write," Lobo commented.

Batista's entry is the longest, running to almost ten pages, twice the length of any other. But then it has to be. The dictator controlled some seventy businesses, including a bank, at least four sugar mills, swaths of Havana real estate, construction firms, one television station, two newspapers, various radio stations and hotels, and, most impressive of all, much of Cuba's air and shipping networks, plus three quarters of its bus and road carriage companies. Perhaps it was because of his military past that Batista sought this strategic lock hold on Cuban transport.

Much of Batista's wealth derived from gambling rackets or public contracts, from which he and his associates took a generous skim off the top. There was the tunnel built under the Havana Bay which linked the city to the beaches at Varadero in the east and was financed in a controversial deal criticized in the newspapers. There were also the expansion of the Rancho Boyeros airport and the new hotels that sprouted up in Havana, cofinanced by the notoriously corrupt state development bank Bandes, from which Bastista took his cut. The ubiquity of Batista's businesses meant that getting ahead in Cuba, or even getting anything done, often required his involvement, and one unfortunate consequence of this was that it reduced civic duty to a simple philosophy: easier to pay off a public servant than to be one.

The only notable absence in Jiménez's tour of Cuba's prerevolutionary financial landscape is the Mafia, which kept a low profile, Lansky only ever appearing on his casino's books as a minor administrator of the Riviera's kitchens. Such shadowiness makes the Mob ripe for exaggeration, and it has become a postrevolutionary rite to conceive of Lansky, the "Mafia's Henry Kissinger," as a giant spider at the center of a web of corruption that controlled Havana, or indeed the whole country. The Mafia was certainly an important and corrupting force that coexisted with

Batista. Yet Cuba produced much else in the 1950s besides casinos—not least sugar, the activity on which all other activities hung and which brought in ten times the revenues that tourism ever did.

Still, tourism was then Cuba's fastest-growing industry. The number of hotel rooms in Havana doubled to 5,500 under a rule that allowed a casino to be added if more than $1 million was spent on a hotel. Pan American Airways made it easier to travel "down Havana way" by offering a $39 round-trip flight from Miami, advertised in newspapers up and down the east coast of the United States. A drive-on drive-off car ferry service opened between Florida and Havana, making the ninety-mile voyage in seven hours, at a cost of $23.50 per person round-trip. The boom was on.

Lobo could not but get involved, and Banco Financiero helped finance the construction of the Riviera and the Capri, both owned by the Mob. This did not make Lobo's bank a front for Mafia money, although it did count among its shareholders Amadeo Barletta, a burly, silver-haired Italo-Cuban born to a wealthy family in Calabria.

A successful businessman, Barletta had moved to the Dominican Republic from Italy in the 1920s, where he opened a car dealership and served as Italian consul. In 1935, he was accused of attempting to assassinate the dictator Rafael Trujillo and was only saved thanks to Mussolini's intercession. He had since settled in Havana, where he was known as the majority owner of the newspaper *El Mundo* and proprietor of the General Motors and Cadillac concessions, among other concerns. Suspected of Mafia links, although nothing was ever proved, Barletta was invited by Lobo into Banco Financiero as a minor shareholder in the hope that he would help broaden the bank's business beyond sugar. Their association ended in 1957.

Such intershading of interests and allegiances was inevitable. Although the drama is great, the stage was cramped, and Cuba was a small country marked by a dense and complex web of relationships that made it hard for anyone to claim to have never dealt with Batista, the Mob, the rebels, or often all three. In 1957, Lobo himself paid $25,000 to the Montecristi movement, a group allied to a military conspiracy against Batista. He paid a further $25,000 to Castro's rebels in the Sierra after they threatened to burn his cane fields—the time-honored guerrilla tactic. Lawrence Berenson, Lobo's old friend, was later taunted for knowing someone who had aided the rebels, although Lobo was far from being the only businessman to do so. Both Castros later singled out the Bacardís for their help in the Sierra. And the son of Lobo's oldest friend George Fowler, owner of the Narcisa, a mill in Las Villas, was actively engaged in Castro's 26 July movement. Anyway, if Lobo really had had Mafia connections, as some writers have since argued, it is doubtful so many senior government members, including Che Guevara, would later wear any previous association with him as a badge of their own professionalism. Raúl León Torres, a die-hard Communist who served as vice-minister of commerce and head of the Cuban National Bank, often boasted to Spanish officials in the 1970s that he had once worked with Lobo.

Instead, in Mafia-infested and corrupt Cuba—at least as conventionally remembered—Lobo made his money on his own terms, using his wits and guile. It was a point of pride. "I'd feel intellectually degraded if I ever obtained a success thanks to the help of some dishonest government functionary," he once told León. Such pig-headedness made Lobo unforgiving and stubborn, qualities that won him more critics than admirers. "But if he had not been like that he would not have created. He would have been paralyzed," as Rosario Rexach, León's wife, remembered him. "And every leader, before anything else, is a man of action." Indeed, it was this appetite for action that led Lobo to embark on one of his most stubbornly pursued and audacious deals. Only later would he view the $25 million purchase of the three Hershey sugar mills outside Havana as his Waterloo, the moment that he returned to in exile when times seemed bleakest, just as Napoleon returned to Waterloo during his most pessimistic moments on St. Helena. "There were many *comemierdas*, or assholes, in Cuba," Lobo wrote in one bitter letter from Spain. "Hershey showed I was the biggest of them all."

MILTON HERSHEY, the chocolate maker, was the soft-spoken son of a Mennonite family, an Anabaptist sect similar to the Amish. His Cuban

property, founded in 1916 to supply Hershey's growing American chocolate empire, consisted of three sugar mills, a refinery, and fifty thousand
acres of choice real estate about a half-hour drive outside Havana. It was
established along the same lines as Hersheyville, the utopian factory town
he built outside Philadelphia, with subsidized houses equipped with elec-
tricity and running water for the workers. Hershey's own house was an
elegant hacienda, with private rooms that opened on three sides to sweeping views of the Caribbean, the cane fields, and the refinery. Hershey
spent most of his later years living on the estate, plagued by insomnia,
grieving the death of his beloved wife, Kitty, whiling away the hours
scraping liver spots from the back of his hands with a penknife and treating the wounds with cocoa butter.

Lobo had first stalked the property in the mid-fifties when he tried
to take over Cuban Atlantic, the sugar company that had bought Hershey's mills in 1946 shortly after the old man died. Czarnikow-Rionda,
getting wind of Lobo's interest, tried to stall their competitor by leaking
a spoiler to the press. The article that appeared in the *Journal of Commerce* on February 3, 1956, claimed that if Lobo's bid was successful he
would control as much as half of Cuba's sugar production. Lobo could
then say to U.S. refiners, "Pay me my price for your sugar, or else." This
was indeed theoretically possible, due to the small size of "freefloat" sugar
then actively traded. Most of the 50 million tons the world produced each
year was consumed in protected home markets. Cuba, producing 5 million to 6 million tons, was the largest single exporter and accounted for
as much as half the freely traded market. Anyone who controlled Cuban
sugar could therefore control the world market. The Cuban Atlantic deal,
the article suggested, would be a classic Lobo market squeeze, only on a
global scale.

From New York, the day after the article appeared, Czarnikow-Rionda
warned Havana about possible repercussions. "Lobo's office has admitted
to us that their organization is quite upset and [Lobo] is naturally quite
wild," the cable read. "This is probably the first round." It was. Ten days
later, Lobo moved on Cuban Atlantic in the same way he had tried to
take over Cuba Company ten years before. He bought 300,000 of the

firm's shares on the open New York market, a 15 percent stake, and planned to gain other allies and so take over the rest at a shareholders' meeting in March.

It was a daring raid. Hostile takeovers were still rare then, although Lobo was more or less infamous for them. Hostile takeovers funded by debt were rarer still; they would become commonplace in the United States only in the mid-1980s, with the rise of Michael Milken, the junk bond king. Lobo was therefore ahead of the financial curve. Politically, though, he had miscalculated. Laurence Crosby, Cuban Atlantic's chairman, was close to Batista, who could be persuaded to oppose the deal. Crosby could also count on Lobo's old adversary Francisco Blanco to cast his 100,000 shares alongside the company's incumbent managers. Meanwhile two North American investors, the Bronfman family, which owned the Seagram distillery, and the Wall Street banker John Loeb, teamed up with Cuba's largest sugar concern, the Falla-Gutiérrez trust, and bought 25 percent of the company. Blocked and unable to gain control, Lobo backed out, sold his stake to Loeb, and watched with dismay as Blanco was elected to the board.

Still, Lobo made a handsome profit. Cuban Atlantic's share price had almost doubled to $14 during the battle, and Lobo pocketed some $2.5 million from the increase. His life offered other compensations too. One month after retiring from the battle, Lobo married again, this time to a mysterious international glamour girl who had the looks of a Valkyrie, Hilda Krueger.

A FULL-BODIED BLONDE with wide lips, high cheekbones, and a figure that stopped traffic, Krueger had first met Lobo in Havana eleven years earlier, while he was still married to María Esperanza. Krueger had come to Havana to give a lecture about La Malinche, the Native American mistress of Spanish conquistador Hernán Cortés, and to interview then-president Grau for a Mexican newspaper. Krueger telephoned Lobo in Havana after one of María Esperanza's cousins arranged the introduction. Out of courtesy, Lobo met Krueger for a drink at the Nacional. It was her birthday, and they celebrated. Lobo had been unable to forget Krueger ever since—notwithstanding his subsequent affairs with Fontaine, Varvara, and others. It was to Krueger that Lobo had stopped to send a love note while rushing home the evening he was shot.

Born in Cologne in 1912, Krueger is an intriguing character, more survivor than free spirit. She made her name in prewar Germany as a minor film star. An American diplomat described her then as "one of those bevy of girls that were called upon occasionally to furnish a little 'joy thru strength' to the Hitler-Goebbels combination by a night of frolicking à la Nero." In Berlin, Krueger also knew Jean Paul Getty, the American industrialist and a known Nazi sympathizer. When she emigrated to the United States after war broke out, FBI agents trailed her because of their supposed love affair.

The FBI gamely referred to Krueger as "Hitler's lover" and suspected her of being a spy. In New York, they tapped her phone calls and read every telegram sent or received, and most of her mail. In Los Angeles, one agent reported that he found a heavily marked-up biography of Mata Hari in her bags. Blackballed, Krueger was unable to find work in wartime Hollywood and so moved to Mexico, Getty arranging the visa. There she took up with Miguel Alemán, Mexico's minister of the interior, although Getty did not seem to mind the slight. He gave Krueger $5,000 to finance her film activities and asked her to marry him, saying that "he didn't care about his wife" and "couldn't wait to get a divorce to marry again." Krueger declined, finding Getty too prudish, too concerned about others' opinions, and having "a very feminine attitude." Soon after, she and Lobo became lovers. She moved to Havana and eventually issued an ultimatum that he marry her. Lobo agonized over the decision for months. Jealous and suspicious, he even hired private detectives to trail Krueger when she traveled abroad.

They eventually wed in a small civil ceremony on April 9, 1956, and Mrs. Hilda K. de Lobo began to make a new life for herself in Havana. For a while her name appeared in the slim blue book that Lobo used to note down menus and placements for dinners held at the house on Eleventh and Fourth streets. She sat at the head of the table facing Lobo on

July 24, again on January 8 the following year, and on January 22, two weeks later. Then Krueger's name suddenly dropped away, and Lobo's sister Helena sat again opposite her brother at the head of the table.

Separation had been only a matter of time. It was impossible for Krueger to build an independent life in Cuba. Tight-knit Havana society circled its wagons around María Esperanza, who had remarried to Manuel Ángel González del Valle, a well-connected real estate developer. Lobo meanwhile pursued his ventures, including a large real estate deal with the U.S. real estate tycoon Bill Zeckendorf. Amid such wheeling and dealing there was little room in his life for Krueger. "Hilda was very beautiful, very alive," remembered León. "In Havana she wanted to go out for dinner, to go to the Tropicana. All Julio wanted to do was go to his mills. That wasn't the life for a woman like Hilda. The marriage ended—because she got bored." Lobo saw it much the same way. "Yes it was a busy and interesting life," he later reflected with regret. "My emotional life with my two wives took a backseat, and there are times when chasing the things money can buy, one can lose sight of those things which money can't buy and are usually free."

Krueger left Havana in March 1957, less than a year after the wedding. She was relieved to be out of an increasingly unsettled country that reminded her of the Germany she had escaped two decades before. In December, Castro had landed in Cuba on the *Granma*; Lobo was eating dinner at home on the terrace when he took the call from Pilón's manager to tell him that there had been fighting around his mill. Furthermore, a few days before Krueger left, the Revolutionary Directorate had assaulted the Presidential Palace. Krueger also left $1 million richer, thanks to the prenuptial settlement she had insisted on. (In Copenhagen, Varvara's ambitious mother was furious. "You idiot," she told her daughter. "You should have done the same." Varvara was nonplussed.) Still, if Krueger had dug Lobo for a million, he nurtured no resentment. The separation was mutual; they remained friends for life, and less than six months after the divorce they lunched at the Sherry-Netherland in New York. The news of the day was the successful Russian launch of Sputnik, the first satellite in space. Lobo turned to León, also there, and asked in jest, "Enrique, do

Leonor on her father's arm. Havana, December 1957.

you think with all these technological advances my engagement ring to Krueger might become worthless as they will soon be making artificial diamonds just as big?"

"No," interjected Krueger in her German-accented English. "Because before that happens I will already have sold."

Even Lobo's market timing was rarely this good. As he wrote to Varvara the following year, "Most people do the wrong thing at the right time or the right thing at the wrong time." And, in Lobo's case, sometimes both.

BACK IN HAVANA, Lobo's thoughts returned to Hershey. This time he found Loeb a keen seller. A gaunt financier with an owlish face who had wintered in Cuba with his wife for three decades, Loeb was worried by the country's instability. He was also mindful of the heady international context. Revolution was sweeping Africa and Asia, and new nations were forging independence from French, British, and Belgian colonial rule. Keen to sell his Cuban investments, Loeb had even found a possible buyer—a close Batista associate named Pedro Grau. An odd man, no relation to the former president, Grau was a real estate developer with an interest in cryogenics, who wanted to build a nuclear station at Hershey that would power Havana's industrial park and supply Miami's energy needs too. But Grau lacked funding for this ambitious plan, and when Loeb began to persuade Lobo to come in, he fell away from the deal.

Lobo, once so keen to buy, now dragged his feet. Loeb insisted: "Julio, you either buy it before the end of the year or you are not going to get it." Like Loeb, Lobo was concerned by the situation. In May, a fire—suspected to have been caused by a bomb—had brought Tinguaro to a halt eight days before the end of the grinding season. Castro's 26 July movement was also extending its reach into the cities. It had even warned Lobo of a bomb that would be placed at Leonor's forthcoming wedding. As a *boda del gran mundo*, due to be held at the Cathedral, government officials would have been socially bound to come. Leonor's marriage to Jorge González, a Spaniard, was instead moved to a small chapel in Vedado and the ceremony was delayed until December, María Luisa having eloped with John Ryan, an American, and wed in London the year before.

Yet despite these warning signals—or perhaps because of them—Hershey still enticed Lobo. His motivations were complex. Lobo was now fighting his own war against the president. He had edged Batista out of the shipping firm Naviera Vacuba, one of Cuba's largest, by swapping the company's debts, which his bank controlled, for Batista's equity stake. Buying Hershey would be another step in this battle, albeit a larger one. Furthermore, this time Blanco would be unable to summon Batista's protection, as the president now spent most of his time holed up at his farm Kuquine, surrounded by barbed wire and armed guards, compulsively reading the transcripts of phone taps he had placed on his growing list of enemies. Whatever might happen next in Cuba, Lobo also calculated he

Lobo throws the first ball at an amateur baseball game on the Hershey property.
He bought the mill at midnight, New Year's Eve, 1957.

could make back his investment in three years. Such a rapid return made for an apparently safe buffer.

León signed the deal on Lobo's behalf at Loeb's New York apartment on Fifth Avenue on New Year's Eve, 1957. Lobo's option to buy the Hershey property expired at midnight, so at 11:50 p.m. one of Loeb's lawyers stood up and stopped the hands on the clock that hung on the wall. When the agreement was finally signed, the lawyer turned the clock back on and ten minutes later it rang twelve times. It was four o'clock in the morning, and all the lawyers rose from the table dressed in black tie to toast the New Year. It would be Batista's last in Cuba.

HAVANA WAS IMBUED with a kind of fairyland atmosphere the following year. The city was as beautiful as ever, despite a clampdown on many festivities and the growing rebel offensives. Castro's voice could be heard regularly on clandestine Radio Rebelde broadcasts. Yet, although bookings were down, there were still droves of tourists that winter season. Two weeks before Christmas 1958, society columnist Cholly Knickerbocker wrote in his regular Smart Set column for the *New York Herald* that his whole weekend in Havana had been "disgustingly quiet. The only real danger we faced was when our golf partner almost hit us on the head with a driver . . . and when we slipped and fell on our face trying to outlast Ambassador Porfirio Rubirosa in a bongo contest." Rubirosa— Dominican playboy, polo player, and racing driver—had been appointed ambassador to Havana the year before. El Encanto department store sold real Christmas trees at 85 cents a foot, and Christmas lights were everywhere, with hot-faced Santa Clauses ringing bells on street corners. Christmas lunch at the house of Helena Lobo was the usual family affair, full of laughter. Still, Havana was tense with rumors. "There is a mood of expectation and inevitability in the air," my mother wrote in her diary.

She had flown down from New York in early December for the holidays. New Year's Eve found her at the Isle of Pines, one hundred kilometers south of the Cuban mainland, with a group of friends for the opening of a swank hotel built by Manuel Ángel González del Valle, María Esperanza's husband. American guests had come from New York for the occasion, with two waiters borrowed from the 21 Club. My mother sat by the pool, drinking daiquiris, listening to a portable radio, and discussed the situation with her friends. "I am amazed at the irresponsibility, unawareness and frivolity which took us there," she later remembered. "I felt quite strongly that Batista had to go but I don't think for a moment I gave a serious thought to the country; I fear my main concern was to have a good time."

That night, Cubans celebrated the New Year with their usual gusto. On the radio, CMQ broadcast a special all-night program, featuring music by Machito, Orquesta Aragón, and Beny Moré, the "barbarian of rhythm." Sometime after one o'clock in the morning, an airplane rose over the roofs of Vedado, flying low. It made several slow turns overhead and banked sharply to the east and disappeared. With it went Batista. A few hours before, he had gathered with his chiefs of staff at the Camp Columbia military base and, after a short meeting, unexpectedly resigned from the presidency. As Batista boarded the plane, his incongruous last words on Cuban soil were *¡Salud! ¡Salud!*—good health and good luck. My mother, learning the surprise news on the radio, felt jubilant that Castro was victorious but, amid the luxurious setting of a foreign-owned hotel filled with American tourists at the outbreak of revolution, also in the wrong place.

No one had expected Batista to capitulate so suddenly, although he had lost nearly all his support. Immediately after the attack on the Presidential Palace eighteen months before, Batista had managed to conjure up a Who's Who of Cuban business leaders to appear on his balcony to applaud his survival—although Pepín Bosch, chairman of Bacardi, and Lobo were both notable for their absence. Now those same businessmen were demanding his resignation. The United States had also instituted an arms embargo. Meanwhile, Batista's army was demoralized and ineffective, more interested in graft than counterinsurgency. As for the 300,000 people who had once cheered Batista from the square below his balcony, soon they would be shouting *¡Viva Castro!*

Castro—only thirty-two years old, the son of a wealthy landowner in eastern Cuba—had by now spent two years in the Sierra, sustained by discipline, shrewdness, and great courage. He had also been lucky, not least in the accidental elimination of so many rivals—from the botched Palace attack and subsequent death of the Revolutionary Directorate's leader, José Antonio Echeverría, then better known than Castro, to the killing two months later of Frank País, Castro's most important rival in the 26 July movement. Batista had launched a last offensive in the Sierra that summer; after it failed, the rebels operated with impunity around Santiago. In August, Castro had dispatched Guevara west with a small column of men. By December they had reached Santa Clara, the major transport and communications hub of central Cuba. There were other rebel groups fighting at the end of 1958. But it was Castro and the 26 July movement that had captured the popular imagination.

The country changed overnight. In Havana, movie star George Raft was on floor duty at the Hotel Capri when news of Batista's departure began to spread. As the night's New Year festivities were winding down, he went up to his suite where his girlfriend, recent winner of the Miss Cuba contest, waited half-asleep.

> "*Feliz año nuevo,*" I said as I got between my silk sheets, alongside this fantastic girl. In the middle of this beautiful scene—suddenly—machine-gun fire! And what sounds like cannons! I phoned down to the desk. "This is Mr. Raft," I said. "What's going on down there?" The operator answered, but I could hardly hear her—there was so much commotion. Finally, I made out what she was saying. "Mr. Raft, the Revolution is here. Fidel Castro has taken over everything . . . Batista has left the country!"

The next day, looters appeared on Havana's streets, smashing parking meters and casinos, much as happened when Machado had fled twenty-six years before. The Sans Souci casino was torched, and a truckload of pigs was left to run through Lansky's gambling emporium, the Riviera. But the initial spasm of violence died down quickly, and when it became clear there would be no pandemonium, joyous Habaneros flooded the streets.

Castro began a slow triumphal march west from Santiago across the island, the television coverage providing many Cubans with their first glimpse of their new leader. His journey, ironically, coincided with the feast of Epiphany, the Christian celebration of the revelation of God made man.

Wearing crumpled olive fatigues and an open shirt with a medallion to the Virgen de la Caridad del Cobre around his neck, Castro arrived in Havana on January 8, riding through delirious flag-decked streets atop a tank. The bravery of the rebels, conquerors of the army of a nation, re-called a heroic era that predated even that of Martí—the conquistadores. Thus Lobo told journalists that Castro's victory could "only be compared" to the audacious conquest of Peru by the Spanish conquistador Francisco Pizarro, another "adventure undertaken by a small group of men in which few people had faith." Did Lobo think the rebels were Communist as sometimes rumored? he was asked. "I don't believe so," he replied. "With honesty, ability and progressiveness . . . Cuba will become one of the richest and best developed nations in the world." Pepín Bosch, the chairman of Bacardi, was similarly enthusiastic. Returning from exile in Mexico, he told reporters at the airport, "The triumph of the revolution makes me very happy. . . . Although it may not appear so, it had the support of almost all the Cuban people." That evening, as Castro gave his first major public address in Havana to an almost hysterically happy crowd, a white dove landed on his shoulder, an omen of peace.

In fact, few in or outside Cuba knew much about Castro. "We did not know who Fidel was," as Lobo said. "But we knew who Batista was and we were against him and for any new democratic regime." Apart from Castro's magnetism, rousing oratory, and idolization of Martí, his politics—as Eisenhower's watch-and-wait approach showed—were vague. At first Castro asked for no spoils for himself, only assuming the post of head of the army. The new government was also reassuringly stacked with middle-class and pro-business anti-Communists: the prime minister, José Miró Cardona, was even president of the Havana Bar Association. The show trials of Batistianos accused of war crimes, however, held in the sports stadium and broadcast live on television, threw a dark shadow. By May, more than five hundred had been shot. But in Washington, CIA director Allen Dulles excused the executions as a safety valve for bottled-up emotions. And in Cuba, Rufo López-Fresquet, the U.S.-educated finance minister, scolded one persistent U.S. reporter: "Instead of criticizing the executions, you ought to be doing everything you can to support our new government. We've just had the only non-Communist revolution of the 20th century."

There were other warning signs. The satirical magazine *Zig-Zag* ran a cartoon poking fun at the sycophants that surrounded Castro, who demanded an immediate apology and threatened to close the publication down. Miró Cardona, the prime minister, also resigned in February, recommending that Castro become premier instead. ("I resigned. Cuba did not protest; it accepted, it applauded," he later said.) On April 6, Lobo went to the Ministry of Finance to pay a $450,000 advance on his taxes to support the new government, as many other businessmen had done. Outside the building on O'Reilly Street in Old Havana, journalists again asked him what he thought of the new government. This time Lobo was more circumspect in his support and referred to the troubled Banco de Fomento Comercial he had bought for $500,000 the week before. "That can only be taken as a sign of confidence," he replied elliptically.

For Lobo, the new regime offered a chance for Cuba to realize a long-held vision. Since the Hershey purchase a year ago, he had continued to argue that Cuba needed to revamp its tired sugar industry, economic backbone of the country. Now he pushed for a "total but gradual" modernization. "We must modernize or die, although this must not bring joblessness," he said. His mills, Lobo added, were already looking for new ways of cultivating sugar while also searching for new nonsugar uses for cane. These new industries—such as plastics—would then be "used to provide new jobs and year-round employment." It was the Cuban Holy Grail: diversification away from sugar. Lobo pressed home the point later that month at a cocktail party at the Country Club, hosted by the Japanese ambassador. Dressed in black tie, he spent much of the evening talking intently to Humberto Sorí Marín, then minister of agriculture, who had acted as Castro's legal adviser in the Sierra. Sorí Marín would shortly quarrel with Castro and eventually be executed for treason. That, however, was still two years in the future, and if he and Lobo failed to see the direction in which Castro was steering the country, so did many others.

In late April, Castro left Cuba for a two-week victory lap around the United States, invited by the association of U.S. newspaper editors. The entourage consisted of his most conservative and pro-U.S. advisers, his more radical brother Raúl and Guevara remaining behind. Dressed in olive fatigues, Castro gave a well-received speech at the National Press Club in Washington, D.C. He spoke before the Senate Foreign Relations Committee and paid homage to the Lincoln and Jefferson memorials. Eisenhower had arranged to be out of town, so Castro met with Richard Nixon, then vice president. They talked privately for two and a half hours in the Capitol building and afterward were polite about each other, al-

Lobo talks to Humberto Sorí Marín, then minister of agriculture in the new government but executed two years later for treason. Havana, March 1959.

though the meeting had not gone well. Nixon later told Eisenhower that Castro was either a Communist or he was a dupe, "incredibly naïve." Castro continued his tour, lionized by the press wherever he went, and gave a speech to rapturous applause at Princeton. Afterward, he met with a senior CIA official, Gerry Drecher, who finished their three-hour conversation convinced that Castro was an "anti-Communist."

Still, by that summer a progressive revolution was in full swing. Castro returned to Havana on May 7, and shortly thereafter signed the Agrarian Reform into law. It was the centerpiece of the government's legislative agenda and followed a reduction in rent and utility rates in March. The bill proscribed any estate larger than 995 acres, with any excess liable to expropriation, to be repaid with long-dated bonds. A progressive tax reform followed soon after. Castro may have ominously told his finance minister after signing the tax law: "Maybe when the time comes to apply the law, there won't be any taxpayers." But at rallies Cubans of all ages chanted "With Fidel, with Fidel, always with Fidel" to the tune of "Jingle Bells," and few businessmen yet protested. Despite some private misgivings, they supported the government's plans. Even the conservative newspaper *Diario de la Marina* endorsed the land reform.

Lobo's own views at that time are unclear. His mills collectively owned 342,000 acres, and eleven of them had more land than allowed by law—Tingauro alone had 18,000 acres. Yet the land reform was aimed mostly at foreign-owned properties, and Lobo would keep the *centrales* that milled the cane, which is where his real wealth lay. "We have been going through some ugly times in Cuba," he wrote to Varvara in late June. "I don't recall more trying moments in my 40 years in business than these." Even so, Lobo added that he remained a confirmed optimist. A week later he wrote again, adopting a more Napoleonic stance, "I have just begun to fight." The following month, he returned to his usual irrepressible form. Lobo opened a new branch of Banco Financiero in Camagüey, the local paper showing him flanked by local business leaders and the Havana and Camagüey carnival queens, both looking fetching in white pillbox hats. In Havana, he hosted a birthday party for his grandchildren. In November he left for Paris to celebrate the publication of the collected correspondence between Napoleon and his finance minister, the Comte de Mollien. From there he traveled to Tangiers to sign a sugar deal, his interests there being represented by Prince Moulay Abdellah, son of King Mohammed V of Morocco. Returning to Cuba, there were the usual Galbán Lobo end-of-year lunches for employees, and the annual party at Hershey with fairground rides for the children, roast pork and dancing for the grown-ups, music provided by the Orquesta Continental and Conjunto Latino. For the moment, some traditions remained unchanged.

The atmosphere was turning sour, though. While liberals in the new government had one agenda, a parallel one was being written by Castro and Guevara in the offices of INRA, the agrarian reform institute, a fourteen-story building that overlooked the white obelisk of José Martí in the renamed Plaza de la Revolución. Indeed, by the end of 1959, the first year of the revolution, many of the moderate cabinet ministers that

Castro had chosen in January had either left government or been dismissed. President Manuel Urrutia had resigned in July, after stating his opposition to communism, and taken refuge in the Venezuelan embassy. The following day, Castro had declared to a crowd of half a million that there was no need for elections because the will of the people was supreme. "This is real democracy," Castro concluded, to wild cheers. In October, Huber Matos, Camagüey's popular military commander, had also denounced Communist encroachment in the government. Sensitive to the charge, as he was still consolidating power, Castro had Matos arrested and brought to Havana to stand trial. Raúl Castro called for his execution; Matos was sentenced to twenty years in prison instead.

In 1960, the Revolution moved up a gear. Soviet deputy premier Anastas I. Mikoyan opened an exhibit of farm machinery and Sputnik satellites at the Museo de Bellas Artes in February. He commented privately to Castro and Guevara that Cuba's revolutionary romanticism reminded him of the Bolshevik uprising of his youth. The government began to clamp down on independent media. The newspaper *Avance* was "intervened" by the authorities, followed shortly after by *El País*, then *Diario de la Marina*, and finally *Prensa Libre*. The government justified the moves by saying it needed to protect Cuba from its enemies. Indeed, Eisenhower had just issued a secret presidential order to the CIA to begin recruiting exiles to return to Cuba and wage guerrilla war.

At the start of the year, Lobo had written to Varvara inviting her to stay in Havana, even if it would not be the same city as she remembered from only a few years ago. Jean-Paul Sartre may have believed he was witnessing for the first time "happiness that had been attained by violence." But Havana's happy-go-lucky atmosphere was increasingly being replaced by a grim military barracks lifestyle with bearded sentries, barely out of their teens, patrolling the streets. In Vedado, Cuban-American writer Carlos Eire, then eight years old, noticed that his morning bus route to school had also shortened. "There were more empty seats on the bus . . . Seats vacated by kids who suddenly vanished without saying goodbye. Not many, but enough to make me aware of an emerging pattern. People were beginning to leave the country." By the spring some sixty thousand Cubans, about 1 percent of the population, had turned the locks on their front doors, pocketed the keys, and boarded the ferry or a flight abroad.

On March 17, Guevara outlined his philosophy in a televised speech:

> To win something you have to take it away from somebody . . . This something is the sovereignty of the country; it has to be taken away from that somebody who is called the monopoly, although monopolies in general have no country they have at least a common definition: all the monopolies which have been in Cuba which have made profits on Cuban land, have very close ties with the USA. In other words, our economic war will be with the great power of the North.

Lobo bent with this wind. In early 1960, he had closed his last celebrated squeeze of the sugar market, forcing his prices down the throats of U.S. refiners who had refused to buy Cuban sugar in the hope that it might weaken the revolutionary government. In March, he donated a telescope and new library to the school in Colón, the nearest town to Tinguaro. From a roughly built wooden podium, Lobo spoke of how he had always been guided by the idea of duty—to family, friends, community, and country. "All of life is duty," Lobo said, "and our duty is to help develop the future of our country." Among those duties, there was his collection of European old masters that Lobo had just entrusted to the National Museum, on permanent loan. He was finalizing plans to move his Napoleon collection into a permanent museum, a reconstruction of Josephine's Château de Malmaison to be built at the Hershey property. He had also long striven to better his workers' living conditions, certainly at Tinguaro, but at other mills too; unions had hailed the $1 million Lobo invested when he bought the mill Araújo in 1953 as a model of development.

His great wealth and talent suggest that Lobo could have done more.

Yet he was also in his sixties, in poor health, often in pain, and running the world's largest sugar-trading business and Cuba's second-largest sugar producer, if not single-handedly then in a manner more centralized than any other comparably sized organization. This was both Lobo's strength and his weakness. There were few in the family he ever delegated to. There was no one to succeed him, either. Lobo could have accomplished more, and perhaps more generously, if he had controlled less. But that was neither his style nor the way he had achieved success.

Cuba raced toward the denouement. The creation of a planning ministry was announced; Cuba would have a command economy. In May, Havana formally reestablished diplomatic relations with Moscow. The next month, Esso, Texaco, and Shell refused to refine Soviet crude oil on the island, and their assets were nationalized. In July, the U.S. Congress authorized the end of the sugar quota. Nikita Khrushchev then publicly suggested that Soviet artillery could support the Cuban people in the event of an invasion.

Lobo made a last push in September with the launch of a countrywide program to build new schools for impoverished rural children. "If we don't ensure that education reaches everywhere in our country," Lobo said at the launch party at his Vedado home, "we risk losing the civilized western ideals that we have accumulated over the centuries, for ever." He made a first payment of $10,000, tax deductible, and a list of Cuban well-to-dos pledged their contributions as well, all members of a class among whom the spirit of philanthropy had never burned bright before.

It was too little, far too late. The end was coming soon. Leonor and her husband Jorge, who was vice-president at Banco Financiero, began to use coded phrases over the phone. *Estoy encantado*, I am charmed, meant there is trouble; *el jardín está muy bonito*, the garden is beautiful, meant Lobo had to watch out. The family made preparations to leave the island. On October 11, Lobo met with Guevara. The old order was crumbling.

The rest, as they say, is history—or rather geography. A year after Castro rode into Havana, my father and mother met in New York. Six months after that they got engaged, and in September they married at her house in Havana. My mother had her elegant wedding after all, even if the militia were drilling in the streets outside. One month later, her family left Cuba, as did Lobo shortly after his midnight interview with Guevara. On the flight from Havana, the last great capitalist to leave Cuba carried with him only a regulation small suitcase and what he could fit in his pockets.

Eleven

CREPÚSCULO

A bad memory and good health, Lobo liked to say, makes for a happy life—a useful maxim during the early days of exile when bad memories and good health were all that many émigrés had. For every Cuban *hacendado* like Jesús Azqueta, who had bought a sugar mill in Venezuela, or planter family like the Falla-Gutiérrez, which transferred $40 million abroad on the eve of the Revolution, most other Cubans had kept what money they had on the island. That included Lobo. It included even Meyer Lansky. The cautious accountant-mobster had gambled everything on his hotel in Cuba, the Riviera, and lost. As Lansky said, "I crapped out."

When he arrived in New York, Lobo still owned the Olavarría trading office on Wall Street and the other Galbán Lobo offices around the world. These were valued at some $4 million, at least on paper. There was also cash and some Florida real estate held in trust for his daughters that was worth perhaps another $1 million. That totaled $5 million, a fraction of Lobo's original $200 million fortune. Furthermore, he still owed City Bank almost $7 million from the Hershey purchase, a debt he had secured against his name. That reduced his net worth to less than zero. Still, Lobo often said he was happiest when he had nothing. Although sixty-three, an age when most people think of retiring rather than starting again, he set back to work with zeal.

My aunts, uncles, and cousins meanwhile crammed into a crash pad in Miami, mattresses on the floor. Two months later, they went north to New York. Snow, flecked with dirt, seemed like unimpressive stuff. They moved into a rambling Charles Addams–style house in Jamaica, Queens. There José, my eldest cousin, shined shoes, looked after his younger siblings, and fought with hefty Irish and Polish kids who made fun of his accent and called him a spic. He took it all personally—and challenged Fidel to a duel, believing they should settle accounts, man to man.

Everyone looked for work.

"Have you come far?" a New York hostess asked my aunt one evening. She had inveigled her way into a swell drinks party, given by the Madison Avenue advertising agency where my father worked. She hoped it might produce job leads for her husband.

"Well, quite far; I live out on the island."

"Which island?"

"Jamaica," my aunt replied, dissembling about her Long Island address in Queens.

"Oh, so you arrived from the Caribbean tonight," the hostess sympathized. "The flights are horrible, aren't they?"

My aunt invented a university degree and taught Spanish at a yeshiva. My grandfather worked at Macy's on Thirty-fourth Street. Still weak from tuberculosis, he suffered frequent internal hemorrhages, often coughed blood, but never told his superiors for fear of being dismissed. My grandmother gave piano lessons and rented a cheap room in a nearby hotel so he could rest during lunch. My mother moved to a two-bedroom apartment on the higher reaches of Manhattan's Upper East Side with my father, and began a new job working at the United Nations as a guide.

She felt proud of her smartly tailored uniform. *These are the United Nations' guiding principles*, she would tell tourists in Spanish and English. *Here is an architectural mock-up of the building. These are the chambers where the Security Council sits*, and she would lift her left arm, uniformed with gold braid and a UN insignia, and open the door. *Please be quiet when you enter, there is a session in progress.*

My mother took the impartiality required of her role seriously, even after Castro spoke at the United Nations on September 26, 1960. Much had changed since Castro's rapturous visit to New York a year before. This time protesters chanted "Cuba Sí! Russia No!" outside the thirty-nine-story UN headquarters in midtown Manhattan. Castro spoke for four and a half hours, the longest speech in UN history. He had met Nikita Khrushchev six days earlier at his hotel in Harlem, the two men squeezing each other in a bear hug. That afternoon they hugged again, Khrushchev striding across the UN assembly floor to embrace Castro, the photograph subsequently running on the front pages of the world's newspapers. That day, my mother became the first UN tour guide to resign over politics, a quirky act of defiance.

Relations between Cuba and the United States had by now all but collapsed. After Washington revoked the Cuban sugar quota in July, Havana responded by nationalizing all remaining U.S. companies in Cuba in August. Washington retaliated with the trade embargo in October. Meanwhile Cuban exiles trained at secret bases across the Americas. The Normandy of their invasion was to be the Bay of Pigs.

A lanky North American approached my mother one evening. He knew her name, produced a badge from his pocket, and said what he was about to tell her was confidential. Would she like to become a spy, he asked, and be parachuted into Cuba and work as an agent behind enemy lines? Training would take place during office hours at a secret station in the Carolinas. She would travel there by helicopter in the morning, and be back home by the afternoon before her husband returned from work. No one need know, he added.

My mother's mind described an arabesque. This was her chance to join the glorious *lucha* for the *patria*—the century-long struggle that had begun with the *lucha* against the Spanish, then the *lucha* against Machado, then the *lucha* against Batista, and now the *lucha* against Castro. It was all part of the special Cuban affection—or affectation—for revolution. She imagined herself dressed as a French resistance fighter, or as Mata Hari perhaps.

Six months later, on April 17, 1961, some 1,300 armed exiles landed at Playa Girón, a glittering beach surrounded by mangrove swamps on the southern coast of Matanzas Province. My mother was not there to guide the troops ashore. Sworn to secrecy by the CIA recruitment officer, she had returned home that night and immediately told my father. He quickly dissuaded her from joining any invasion force, and she, in turn, helped to persuade Carlin, her brother, and Otto, her brother-in-law, to stay behind as well. They had been on the point of deciding who would go by drawing straws. One would fight; the other remain in the United States to act as joint breadwinner for their families.

It is hard to imagine a less likely place for a successful invasion than the Bay of Pigs. Accessible only via a single rutted road or by boat, the area crawls with crocodiles and its swamplands make it better suited to defense than attack. Lacking U.S. air cover, the exile soldiers of Brigade 2506 never got off the beach, and almost one hundred died during the sixty-five hours of fighting. The rest were captured, publicly interrogated, tried on Cuban television as war criminals, and imprisoned. Tía Angelita's husband, Don Alvaro, was chairman of the Families Committee that flew to Havana the following year to negotiate the prisoners' release in a swap for medicine and food. The former cattle rancher from Senado sat around the table at the cabinet room in Havana's Presidential Palace with Castro and James Britt Donovan, a tough Irish-American lawyer who acted for the prisoners and had been recommended to Alvaro by Bobby Kennedy as the best man for the job. Alvaro acted as Donovan's translator, and clenched his fists under the table each time he repeated Castro's words in English. Alvaro's youngest son was amid the prisoners held in the dungeon at La Cabaña fortress.

It is remarkable that the negotiations took place at all. A few days before their first meeting, a rebel group based in Miami had shelled a Havana hotel from their small boat. "Those who contribute one penny to the prisoners' negotiations shall be taking it away from the war of liberation," it said. Such opposition was an early sign of the tensions that would split the exile community for the next five decades between hard-liners and *dialogueros*, those more willing to negotiate with Havana. Then, in October 1962, the Cuban missile crisis erupted and the United States and the Soviet Union hovered on the brink of war. The prisoners' talks were canceled, and when they resumed after a two-month hiatus, Castro was more hostile. He now argued for more—cheaper medicines, more food—in return for the prisoners. Donovan snapped at Castro: "You can't shoot them. If you do, you'll go down as one of the greatest butchers in world history. . . . If you want to get rid of them, if you're going to sell them, you've got to sell them to me. There's no world market for prisoners."

On Christmas Eve 1962, twenty months after the Bay of Pigs landing, 1,113 prisoners flew from Cuba to Homestead Air Force Base in Florida. Alvaro called their departure "a rosary of miracles." He had visited the dismal Presidio jail at the Isle of Pines a month before and described to Bobby Kennedy what he saw. The prisoners, Alvaro said, looked like animals, their necks slack, their heads down, ready to die. Bring them home before Christmas, Alvaro urged. "If you wait you will be liberating corpses." The final price paid for their release was $53 million of medicine, food, and equipment, equivalent to $48,000 a head.

During the negotiations, Donovan and Castro had established a rapport of mutual respect, leavened by humor. As the last plane readied to leave Havana for Florida, Donovan turned to Castro. "Premier Castro, I've been doing a lot of thinking about this and about all the good I've done for Cuba in the last few days," Donovan said. "I've not only relieved you of a lot of liabilities, but have helped the children, the sick and the elderly. So I have decided that I'm going to come over here and run against you in the next election. Furthermore, I think I can win." Castro nodded his head. Then, shouting above the roar of the plane's engine, he replied: "Doctor Donovan, I think you may be right. So there will be no elections."

During the first years of the revolution, many Cubans who left the island had imagined only a short stay abroad. After the Bay of Pigs, Castro's hold on Cuba became stronger and more popular than ever before. For exiles, the years of no return had begun.

LOBO SET ABOUT rebuilding his fortune. He traded sugar from his office at 79 Pine Street in New York—much as he had from the Galbán Lobo office on O'Reilly Street in Havana. The motions and routines of his days remained much the same—the ringing telephones, Lobo's arms like an octopus reaching out to take the calls, the changing prices, his rapid calculations, the apartment that he lived in at the Sherry-Netherland hotel, even his courtship of famous actresses.

Lobo met Bette Davis in early 1963 at a Beverly Hills party given in his honor by a mutual friend, the Hollywood socialite Mary Rollefson, whom Lobo knew through his movie friends from Tinguaro. An enormous ice sculpture spelled out "WELCOME SUGAR KING" in the entrance hall of her house, and a Cuban combo played in the background. When Lobo kissed Davis's hand, she gave a sideways "What the hell is this all about" glance at her daughter B.D. nearby. Lesser men would have quailed. Lobo kept a firm grip on Davis's arm throughout the evening.

Lobo had long admired Davis from afar, even if she was an unlikely object of his romantic attention. In the psychological thriller *What Ever Happened to Baby Jane?* released a few months before, Davis answers the film's question by playing a vaudeville child star, now in her fifties, who lives as a recluse in an old mansion with her invalid sister. It is a chilling display of sibling rivalry and general monstrousness, with Davis running unfettered through all the stages of impending insanity. As the aged Baby Jane, Davis slouches around the house in slippers with a glass of whiskey in her hand, her face caked in chalk-white base, eyes shadowed with kohl, a cupid's bow painted over her mouth. She delivers dead birds on a silver platter to her sister for lunch, and sings to a wall-sized mirror dressed in the white frilly dress of her successful youth. Davis remembers Baby Jane as one of her favorite parts.

Lobo sent a bouquet of American Beauty roses to Davis the day after

the party with a handwritten, almost impertinent card: "To the most important woman in my life. Love Julio." A few months later, Lobo
proposed—he could not resist trying, if only to see how Davis replied.
Davis, though charmed, refused. Lobo persisted, and flowers followed
Davis wherever she stayed. She traveled to Cannes to promote *Baby Jane*,
and on the way back in Paris a handwringing concierge at the Crillon
Hotel told Davis that her suite was occupied by an ambassador who had
extended his stay. Davis was on the verge of a screaming fit when her
daughter suggested they wait a moment in the bar. B.D. telephoned Lobo,
as he had told her to call if she ever needed help. Twenty minutes later,
there was a stir in the lobby as an overwrought couple with piles of luggage
checked out. A bellboy approached Davis. "The manager's compliments,
Miss Davis, but the ambassador has been called home for consultations
and the suite you requested will be ready in half an hour." Davis later
cabled Lobo: "Flowers are magnificent and the digs are too much. I will
never know how to thank you. Bette." Even in exile, Lobo still retained
some of his old imperial pull.

It sometimes seemed as if nothing had changed. Lobo still had some
of his old lieutenants around him: Enrique León, Gerry Ascher—his
principal trader—and Gustavo Lobo, a cousin, who ran the Olavarría
office in New York. Yet everything was also different. Most of his old team
from Galbán Lobo, especially the former mill managers, was scattered
around the globe. Three key figures had also stayed behind in Cuba. Due
to her agoraphobia, Carlotta Steegers, his personal secretary, could not
countenance leaving her flat in Havana. Tomás Martínez, overall manager
of Lobo's mills, remained behind to help run the Cuban sugar industry
after the revolution. And María Teresa Freyre de Andrade, chief librarian
of his Napoleon collection, became head of Havana's National Library.
Cuban novelist Reinaldo Arenas remembered her as a "magnanimous
woman" who created a cultural aristocracy at the library, and took shelter
under her care.

Lobo had avoided the Bay of Pigs, and was only briefly involved in
the fund-raising that later led to the prisoners' release. Yet Cuban events

swirled unavoidably around him, as they did all exiles, the island often on his mind, sometimes under strange circumstances. In April 1964, Teófilo Babún Selman, a Cuban exile who operated a shipping company in Miami, contacted Lobo with a gamble no speculator could refuse: a $100,000 "bet" with the Mafia that Castro would die ninety days after the wager was made. Although Cuba was off-limits for the United States after the Bay of Pigs, this did not exclude covert assassination plans. Some of these were hatched by the CIA, bizarre efforts that included poisoned scuba-diving suits and exploding cigars. Others were cooked up by the Mafia and hawked around exile circles in Miami, like this one.

Assassination was not Lobo's style, though his curiosity was piqued. How would the "bet" work, exactly? Lobo asked. Babún suggested the funds would be put into an escrow account and then be released when the bet was closed. Lobo stalled, and told Babún it would be difficult to get a lawyer to draw up the right kind of contract. According to an interview Lobo had with the FBI, Babún told Lobo, to do the paperwork himself.

Babún had already purportedly tried to rope into the scheme Pepín Bosch, the head of the Bacardi distillery, with a $50,000 contribution. Bosch subsequently told the FBI he would never get involved in a death contract, and that while he knew Lobo, he would never ask him for anything, under any circumstances. When Babún telephoned Lobo a month later, Lobo replied that he did not want to go through with the "bet" either. Babún grew angry and called Lobo a "welcher," although he later told the FBI that he had never talked to Lobo about any assassination plan, and if Lobo had suggested anything else "he was a liar."

Such plans and bets, accusations and counteraccusations, and the malice and misunderstandings that followed were part of the hothouse of exile life, the desperate plans of sometimes desperate people. They believed they were fulfilling their patriotic duty, just as so many Cubans on the island did. Yet their stories lead nowhere and leave only doubts. Just as the Bay of Pigs failed, so did all these assassination plans, and when John F. Kennedy was shot in Dallas in 1963, all the doubts and frustrating traces the United States had wanted to sow within Cuba blew backward.

Who had killed Kennedy? Was it the KGB, Fidel Castro, the Mob, the CIA, or an extreme Cuban exile group still smarting over JFK's betrayed promise to provide air cover at the Bay of Pigs?

Lobo, the lone wolf of high finance, remained largely aloof from all this, just as he had from political life on the island, although he was openly pleased when anti-Castro rebels burned down one of his mills, Niquero, in May 1964. "I want all the mills to be destroyed if it will help," he told a reporter from the *New York World Telegram and Sun*. Lobo said he was happiest, though, about what he hoped would happen next. "Later on, I will undertake to have them all rebuilt, mine and others." This was in character. In exile, as on the island, Lobo was a creator rather than a destroyer, and finance rather than pistols were his tools. Yet even then, at the moment of this boast, Lobo was suffering from the backwash of his own past, by traces of his empire he had left behind in Havana and that now flooded into his present. The personal debts he had taken on to close the Hershey deal returned to haunt him, and by the summer of 1964 Lobo was hardly in a position to pay either his phone bill or expenses at the Sherry-Netherland hotel, let alone fund the reconstruction of a country.

It had all looked so different only a year before. Lobo had boasted then that he would soon be wealthier abroad than he had ever been in Havana. "I left Cuba on October 14, 1960, without even a toothbrush," he told a British journalist during a visit to London. "In three years I have recovered what was taken from me. I am doing the same volume of business as I was then. And when I return to Cuba and my property is restored to me I shall be much better off than before." The revolution had robbed Lobo of his sugar mills, but he still had his contacts, his prestige, and his trader's instincts. The year 1963 was the wildest in the sugar market in four decades. Lobo's New York office still handled a fifth of all foreign sugar that entered the United States. Lobo's speculations had gone exceptionally well.

At the start of the year the sugar price had stood at 2.5 cents a pound. By late March it had more than doubled. When North American candy companies, soft-drink firms, and jelly and jam makers also started buying, the sugar price rose further: to 7 cents a pound in April, then 13 cents by the end of May. Some people talked about a "one-way street" for the sugar price. Stories circulated on Wall Street of a dentist who had made $500,000 speculating on the market. In the early summer, the U.S. government started to buy as well. Prices rose by another two cents in a week. Lobo told his son-in-law John Ryan that he was "$25m ahead of the game."

"We are witnessing history," Lobo told an interviewer from *Fortune* magazine in March, perhaps thinking back to his own past—the Dance of the Millions, those years of easy money he had witnessed when he first joined the Galbán Lobo office in 1920. Indeed, Cuba was again partly responsible for the rising sugar price. Cuban production had collapsed. Since 1959, some two million tons, about a tenth of world exports, had fallen out of the market. Prices soared.

The sugar price cooled toward the end of year and Lobo stepped back into the market. He bought 100,000 tons at 11 cents per pound, a position worth $22 million. Prices began to rise again in early 1964. León and Gustavo Lobo urged him to sell. "The market could still absorb his position. He could sell, declare a fat profit and give everyone a handsome bonus," León remembers telling Lobo. But Lobo, ever willing to take the big risk, wanted to let his bet ride. "This market is going higher," he told León.

Lobo could have played it safe and hedged his position. That would have provided a floor if prices fell. Yet, once hedged, Lobo would also have locked in his gains at a lower margin. The big profit, he knew, only comes when you go all out. Lobo could not resist the siren call of great opportunity, the possibility of doing better than merely well. With a big win, Lobo could pay off his old Hershey debts. He could even start to rebuild his empire. "Every gain made by an individual is almost instantly taken for granted," as Aldous Huxley once wrote. "The luminous ceiling toward which we raise our longing eyes becomes, when we have climbed to the next floor, a stretch of disregarded linoleum beneath our feet." Lobo planted his feet on the linoleum and steadied himself for the ride.

"The trouble was it was really tough to fight the decision of a man who had such a record of good decisions," remembered León. Gerry

Ascher expressed Lobo's overconfidence in another way. He sent a satirical verse to Lobo one Christmas, referring to his boss with the old cablegram code, SUG.

> I know what I'm doing
> And you don't, you see.
> I am SUG, *comprende*
> And you are not me.

The sugar price edged ahead by half a cent and it seemed that Lobo, sixty-six years old, still had his magic touch. But all men make mistakes and, as Karl Popper said, "great men make great mistakes." The sugar price began to fall. When the descent accelerated, Lobo could not wriggle out of his position. Nor could he count on the physical sugar that he once commanded, all those hundreds of thousands of tons that his mills produced which allowed him to drive the price higher when need be, hanging short-sellers out to dry like so many bagasse husks. In the early summer of 1964, the sugar price dropped to 4.5 cents. Lobo had bought at a price more than twice as high. He had lost $6 million.

Now "that damned Hershey deal" returned to haunt him. On July 1, squeezed for cash due to his trading losses, Lobo missed a $500,000 payment on the $6 million he still owed to City Bank for the Hershey purchase. When he skipped the payment, the total of Lobo's Hershey debt immediately came due. Learning of this, sugar traders demanded immediate payment of the $6 million that Lobo separately owed them. His business collapsed like a house of cards. On July 23 Lobo declared bankruptcy and sought Chapter 11 protection.

Lobo made brave promises at first. He said he would roll up his sleeves, keep working, and trade his way out of the losses. "I will take the consequences . . . as I always have in 45 years of world sugar trade," he said. "I'll pay everyone," he added confidently.

"But he was crazy," León remembered. "There was no way he could pay. Our lawyer said Julio should be taken to see a psychiatrist. This was a man who had always kept his word with the world, and now he just didn't understand that he couldn't."

It was the same ending as befell so many other famous speculators through history—including Lobo's erstwhile business partner from Cuba, the real estate magnate William Zeckendorf, who filed for bankruptcy on the same day. Like Zeckendorf, Lobo had stretched himself too thin. He had been rash, and his luck had run out. This time there was no telegram from the French government waiting for Lobo back at the hotel, as there had been in 1939 when a failed speculation had almost bankrupted *la casa*. Lobo no longer had the properties he had once owned in Cuba which he could have used to pay his creditors or to post as collateral; all that was gone. He was still known as the King of Sugar, the Cuban merchant who controlled the world market. Only Lobo was now operating solely from Wall Street, not Havana, and Cuba—three years after the Bay of Pigs, eight months after the assassination of JFK—was a dirty word in the United States. The *New York Herald Tribune* headlined its coverage of his bankruptcy "BIGGEST SUGAR SACK SPLITS SEAMS."

Lobo left New York for Spain in 1965, pursued by creditors, lawyers, those who still believed he was rich, and the Internal Revenue Service, which said he owed $20 million in back taxes. The federal inspectors wanted to examine Lobo's accounts from 1957, two years before Castro's arrival in Havana, one year before the Hershey deal, and another world. By the time he left New York for Franco's Spain, Lobo had arranged for the sale of his seat on the New York sugar exchange, the company apartment on the eighteenth floor of the Sherry-Netherland, and his share in the new "Tinguaro" sugar mill that he had built in the Louisiana bayou, where he had invited Bette Davis to stay. Lawyers meanwhile picked over the carcass of the New York trading business. It was eventually taken over by Czarnikow-Rionda, the merchant business of Manuel Rionda's Cuban enterprise which had collapsed in 1930 under the weight of its own debts. The spokes on the wheel had turned again.

"Lobo had such huge prestige. That's why the bankruptcy was so tragic," said León. Over forty-five years, Lobo had built the world's largest sugar business. He lost the greater part to the revolution, and the remainder to the markets. He had nobody else to blame. The final dissolution of his empire marked the end of an era, almost a death. Even the messages that Lobo's friends sent to him read like letters of condolence.

I ALSO LEFT NEW YORK for Europe the following autumn, only for England and due to my family's politics rather than because of a sudden change in fortune. My father's father had been a member of Parliament during the Second World War, and his wife, my paternal grandmother, had assumed his parliamentary seat after he was shot down during a bombing raid over Belgium. My father's great-aunt, Eleanor Rathbone, had also been a formidable social reformer, in the mold of her Quaker forebears from Liverpool who had campaigned against slavery in the eighteenth century. My father felt these family traditions as a call to duty and a political career of his own.

I was not quite three years old at the time, and our departure for London—my father, my mother, my ten-month-old sister, a prim norland nanny called Sally, and I—is my first memory. I knelt on a red plastic banquette, pressed my stomach against the wall of the ship's cabin, and looked out of a brass porthole at New York. I remember seeing sailboats keeling in the breeze on the bay, pennons fluttering, and the jagged silhouette of the New York skyline receding into the haze. Our ship slipped out onto the Gulf Stream, the twisting snake of warm water that Hemingway called the "great blue river" and that circles up from the Gulf of Mexico, past Havana, through the Florida straits, and north along the eastern seaboard of the United States. It is the strongest ocean current in the world, and as it circles north and then east toward the British Isles, water evaporates, the current cools, and by the time the Gulf Stream passes Scotland it is more briny too. In sugar-toothed but gray London, life for my mother would also feel less sweet.

In England, she got lost in the usual transatlantic linguistic confusions: a bend in the road versus a curve, private versus public schools, pants

versus trousers, losing more than words (but developing a fondness for
English humor) when searching for the ladies' room/loo on the first floor/
ground floor of a store—or rather a shop. More than strange vocabulary,
though, England for her was a triple exile: from her new home in New
York, from her family that had settled there, and, because of that, a final
farewell to the last shreds of her former life in Havana as well. Gabriel
García Márquez had visited London eight years before and described
what he saw with a Caribbean eye that could have been my mother's. He
wrote of the "people that left work with the same trudge as they went to
it, and on the small step outside the houses, always the same, always silent,
always closed, stand half a dozen bottles of milk."

My father rented a house on a street of red-brick terraced houses, with
black drainpipes trellised like vines around the back. I went to school in
the basement of a nearby church, stuttered in Spanish and English, and
learned to "Do the Hokey Cokey" in a gloomy stone crypt, holding hands
in a circle with the other children. The nanny wheeled my younger sister
to the park in a perambulator. My mother gave birth to my younger
brother, and my father was elected a member of Parliament in 1974, a
conservative of the lightest blue.

As the wife of an MP, my mother posed for campaign photographs,
thumbs-up next to my father. At the Houses of Parliament, police guards
ushered her inside past the queue of tourists that trailed from the Strang-
ers' Entrance, around the block and past a bronze statue of Oliver Crom-
well. She was now more part of the Establishment than she had even been
in Havana. Yet she also felt more estranged. The Englishwomen she knew
wore lumpy tweed jackets and skirts, rough hair pinned back with garish
silk scarves, and had voices that sounded as though spoken through a
mouth full of potatoes. In New York or Miami, by contrast, even a friend
of my mother's dressed in a gray office suit somehow managed to look
luscious, like a mango wrapped in protective foam. She missed what she
remembered of Latin gaiety and was awed by the English reserve.

Cuba and Castro were frequent topics of conversation in London, and
her hot outbursts about the island were often followed by a distrustful look

and then a patting of her hand, like the "there, there" spoken to a distressed child. She planned her revenge on this condescension at a parliamentary reception, and I picture the scene now, my mother fixing her hosts first with her arrogant look, then her charming look, then her insouciant look, her "hair done up, long dangling earrings, a lot of make-up—and nothing else." Sadly she never acted out this provocative fantasy, as she was sure her hosts would fix their gaze on her face, smile politely, and say *Margarita, how good of you to come* (so eliciting her disappointed look, and lately there had been too much of that).

Self-protectively, she resolved these cultural differences into prejudices, a very Manichean scheme, buttressed by the part-truths of Latin versus Anglo-Saxon racial stereotypes, and the weather. In England the clouds hugged the ground like wigs. In Cuba they paraded in orderly rows of puffy dirigibles over feathery palm trees. My mother could not always contain the contrast.

One afternoon, when very young, my brother, sister, and I had wailed from the backseat of her car after a burst of intense sunlight punctured the English gloom, blinding us. "Argh, the sun!" we had screeched. She was trolling gently down the high street, on the way to the supermarket, and swerved suddenly to the side of the road. She rarely drove with such alacrity, except sometimes at the approach to an amber traffic light. Then her knuckles whitened on the steering wheel of her red Renault 5 as she accelerated and shouted "Fangio!" after the Argentine racing car driver who had mesmerized Havana in 1957. Those who had seen drivers like Juan Manuel Fangio, Stirling Moss, and the gifted amateur Alfonso Gómez Mena tear around the Havana circuit that year still remembered the way Fangio negotiated the ninety-degree corner into Calzada with his Ferrari in a beautiful four-wheel drift. Who could resist, or forget, such élan? In London, drawing on such memories, my mother stopped the hatchback in a screech of brakes, turned around in her seat, and in a grim voice, not quite shouting but fluted by high notes, said to my brother, my sister, and me: "Don't you *ever* complain about the sun again." Chastened, we squinted into the glare as she put the car back into gear and set off again.

· · ·

ARRIVING IN MADRID, Lobo took a small apartment on Hermanos Bécquer, a street that lies off the central Paseo de la Castellana. Taking no
chances, he practically hugged the United States this time: from his
fourth-floor apartment, the fortress of the U.S. embassy was only ninety
feet across the street. In Havana, the United States had been ninety miles
away. Franco's daughter also lived nearby, yet Franco's Spain rarely figured
in Lobo's Madrid life, hardly even as backdrop, even when Admiral Luis
Carrero Blanco, Franco's prime minister, was killed by a car bomb on
Hermanos Bécquer on December 19, 1973. To a worldly businessman
from Havana—or any other Latin American from Venezuela, Colombia,
or even Panama—Madrid was then an unsophisticated town, with sheep
grazing by what is now the M30 ring road, cut off from Europe by fascism.
Rather than look to Spain, Lobo gazed outward and backward to Cuba.

He helped Cubans that he knew when he could, sending his former
secretary, Carlotta, shoes after she mailed him a paper cutout of her foot
size. He set up a Cuban center in Madrid, modeled on the Spanish re-
gional centers that had once flourished in Havana. It was a place, Lobo
said at the inauguration in 1966, "where Cubans of all races and creeds
can meet; not a Country, Yacht or Tennis Club, but not a poor house
either." Lobo applied himself with his usual tenacity. He raised funds,
organized talks and seminars on Cuban themes, and ate in the club restaurant under a huge photograph of the Malecón that spread across a
whole wall. He always wore a black tie in mourning for Cuba's fate, and
once suffered to sit next to Batista, a distasteful experience.

Journalists still beat a path to Lobo's apartment on Hermanos Bécquer, curious to know the fate of the Napoleon of Sugar, who, like Napoleon himself, had ended his days in exile. All of these newspaper stories
noted the entrance hall of Lobo's apartment, hung with the Cuban coat
of arms; a view of palm trees and a bay at sunset, framed on a triangular
shield topped with a red Phrygian cap and an oak branch and laurel
wreath on either side. They described the cluttered desk in Lobo's otherwise sparse office, where he sat under another Cuban coat of arms, em-

blazoned with Philip II's famous phrase, "He who holds the island of Cuba also has the key to the New World." Yet at home or at the center, as in Cuba, Lobo remained a controversial figure. José R. Fernández, a founding member of the center, recalls that Lobo's detractors outnumbered his fans. Critics found him stingy, crafty, and severe with employees and subordinates. All, though, agreed he was intelligent and cultivated, and, as Fernández wrote, the center in Madrid enjoyed its best years when he was in charge.

Lobo lived modestly. The days were long gone when he could afford to misplace six officers' uniforms from Napoleon's Grand Army, as he had on TWA flight 703 from London to New York in 1965, and then breezily claim a fraction of their value from the insurers. Simple living did not seem to bother him. "What is more absurd than avarice in old age," he wrote in 1972, quoting Cicero to Alexander Herman, an old friend. "It is like a traveler loading up with provisions when he is getting near the end of the road." He had no pension. He no longer bought art except, as he joked, green U.S. engravings that depicted "the heads of Washington, Franklin, and Monroe." He attempted to set up a sugar mill in the Caribbean, but it never got off the ground. He established a small business in Madrid, importing Scotch whiskey. Yet the Commerce Ministry gave Lobo the necessary import permits out of charity as much as anything else, and the business faded after a while. He sometimes itched to trade sugar, yet stuck to his promise made after the New York bankruptcy that he would never dabble in the markets again. "As you know, since leaving New York, I've not touched a grain of sugar," he wrote to Maurice Varsano, a former competitor who had founded the giant French sugar group Sucre et Denrées and now called himself the "King of Sugar," Lobo's old crown. "Sometimes I feel like a fool when I can see the market as clearly as I used to," Lobo added. "But I don't want to break my promise to myself." Anyway, Lobo had no capital to trade with. Any funds the family did have were tied up in the Moorings, the Florida property company owned by Leonor and María Luisa, and this was burdened with the last $3.7 million of Hershey debt, a point of frequent acrimony among Lobo and his daughters. Money was tight, everywhere. Leonor lived in Vero Beach, Florida, with her husband, struggling with the Moorings. María Luisa lived in London, at Thurloe Square, a smart residential address in the center of town, but took in lodgers to pay her bills.

By the early 1970s, Lobo had resigned himself to a life of contemplation—those meditative years he had often promised himself when he had been rich. "I am completely retired from business," he wrote to Lillian Fontaine in 1972. "My creative years are over." Lobo, a man who had once moved markets with a nod of his head, who had expected subordinates to snap to attention when he came into the office, and had turfed out ambassadors from Parisian hotels with a single telephone call, now lived off the monthly payments that his daughters sent him, and the sale of the last of his Napoleon papers that Leonor had managed to smuggle out of Cuba two decades before. "It's painful to be selling the remains [of my Napoleon collection]," Lobo wrote from Madrid to his Parisian auctioneer, Dominique Vincent. "Unfortunately . . . that is the only solution."

Lobo had one final Cuban encounter, suffered one last kick in the teeth. In addition to two crates of Napoleon papers that Leonor had got out of Cuba, in a brave dawn dash around Havana a few days before Lobo's meeting with Guevara, she had also stashed a further two crates at the French embassy in Havana, where they had since remained. The idea that Lobo might retrieve them grew out of a trip that María Luisa made to Havana in 1975, her first return visit. It was a controversial trip, and in the hothouse of exile politics, many émigré Cubans felt that the journey marked her as a traitor to her class, and that María Luisa had simply swapped allegiances from one Big Daddy to another. But María Luisa was living in London then, and in the cold gray English weather her love for things Cuban, the romance of her past, and her father's name had flared anew.

In Havana, María Luisa toured former haunts and met old friends, such as Lobo's former secretary, Carlotta, and also Celia Sánchez, María Luisa's former workmate from Pilón and still Castro's closest confidante. In Havana they renewed their friendship, discussed the Napoleon documents, and when María Luisa left, Celia cabled Madrid to tell Lobo that he could take the two crates of Napoleon documents kept in the French embassy.

María Luisa returned to Havana on February 15, 1978, with Julio Enrile, Lobo's Spanish lawyer. Their trip was never going to be routine. It turned into a disaster. The French behaved questionably, the Cubans criminally, and Lobo emerged poorer than he had begun.

First, the French ambassador told María Luisa that she owed $15,000 in storage fees. When she blanched, he suggested the payment could be offset by some of the documents themselves. A Napoleon expert from Paris had inventoried the collection in the intervening years, he said, and some of the documents were of particular interest to Paris, especially Napoleon's letters to Talleyrand and a rare doctor's report written on St. Helena about the emperor's health. Suspicious of the offer, María Luisa declined. Carlos Rafael Rodríguez, the vice president, spoke to the French diplomat, while María Luisa negotiated with Celia. Because it was effectively impossible to find $15,000 in Havana to pay the storage fee, the apparent impasse was only broken after the Cubans offered to lend María Luisa the money instead. The terms were for thirty days, with the loan secured against the 178 packets of Napoleon documents stored in the French embassy, worth an estimated $600,000 out of a total collection that Lobo had valued in 1959 at $3 million. On March 23, after María Luisa paid the storage fee, the French released the documents, and the sacks were taken away in a flatbed truck to the National Museum, where they would be stored while shipping arrangements were made. María Luisa never saw them again.

At the National Museum, one of Celia's aides said she wanted to keep back certain documents of particular Cuban interest—letters that Napoleon had written about the Russian campaign and also to Simon Bolívar. Then Marta Arjona, director of the National Museum, said the collection was incomplete. The French, she told María Luisa, had failed to release all the documents. Because of that, the terms of the loan were broken. Cuba would therefore have to keep everything until the French returned the missing papers. Starting to panic, María Luisa offered to pay off the loan in cash. Arjona refused. María Luisa returned to the French embassy. After a heated conversation, the ambassador asked her to leave. Shortly after, María Luisa returned to Europe empty-handed. Lobo was furious. Letters that he wrote subsequently to Celia Sánchez in Havana went unanswered. The French Foreign Ministry in Paris meanwhile brushed him off.

Lobo called it "the most crooked deal I have ever been into," although he had had a similar experience twelve years before. That time it had been over his more valuable art collection. In 1966, the brother of the former head of the Galbán Lobo office in London wrote to Lobo in Madrid saying he had noticed some of his old paintings listed for sale at an art auction in Toronto. Until then, Lobo believed these artworks—three Diego Riveras, a Dalí, a Dufy, and a Murillo—had been lost for good. Carlotta, his secretary, had left them for safekeeping at the Venezuelan embassy after the revolution. When Caracas broke off relations with Havana in 1961, Mexico took over the embassy building and in the confusion Lobo's paintings had disappeared.

Lobo's private art collection was not the largest in Havana, but it included some notable works, including a Rembrandt landscape, two Renoir nudes, a Tintoretto, and dozens of sketches and watercolors by pre- and postimpressionist masters. It did not hold the same meaning for Lobo as his Napoleon collection, nor had he bought the paintings with the same connoisseur's eye. But it was still worth a fortune by any standard, and in Havana Lobo had loaned three dozen of the best works to the National Art Gallery to hang on its walls. Indeed, the pictures now up for auction in Toronto formed part of that very collection he had loaned to Cuba's National Gallery eight years before. They included an oil portrait of a woman by George Romney, an oceanscape by Alfred Sisley, and an oil of ships in a storm by the seventeenth-century Dutch painter Willem van de Velde.

That summer, Lobo met in Paris and London with two members of the Canadian syndicate, Irving Hennick and a man called "General" Starkman. He presented them with copies of the act of custody, signed by the then directors of Havana's National Museum, which had pledged to

look after the paintings on Lobo's behalf. Other catalogues established
the paintings were his beyond doubt. Starkman told Lobo that his group
traveled frequently to Cuba, that it could retrieve any of his artworks
which he might miss, and that they had obtained his pictures in Havana
quite legally, they thought. He suggested that Lobo could buy back his
pictures up for sale at the auction. Because their ownership was disputed,
Lobo would pay a pittance. Having established ownership, he could then
resell them for more. Lobo told Starkman he had "no intention whatsoever of dealing with thieves who have wrecked my country, stolen my
worldly possessions, and those of my family and friends." And there the
matter rested, and with it a portion of Lobo's lost wealth.

LOBO'S HEALTH WITHERED SLOWLY with the usual imprecations of age.
He caught pneumonia in 1970. He broke two ribs when he tripped outside his sister's apartment block on New Year's Eve two years later and
fell into a four-day coma after banging his head on the stone steps. Blood
was leached from his skull, and the doctor's report noted that shrapnel
was still lodged at the base of Lobo's skull. He struggled to keep his spirits up. "When you lose your wealth you lose nothing; he who loses his
health loses something," Lobo wrote to Herman after the operation. "But
he who loses his dreams is really licked. I've lost the first, part of the second, and am trying damned hard not to lose the third."

He still retained a lust for life. From Madrid, he wrote frequently
to old flames and friends: Joan Fontaine; Varvara Hasselbalch; Hedda
Hopper, the gossip columnist; and his second wife, Hilda Krueger—now
married to a wealthy Russian-born industrialist. He found new female
companionship, almost marrying for a third time to a Spaniard, María
Dolores Vila-Coro. Businessmen still sometimes sought his advice. Carlos de la Cruz, a successful Miami-based Cuban entrepreneur then living
in Madrid, remembered Lobo's great "acuity, even though he was only
making do." Lobo no longer multitasked during these meetings as he had
years before, answering questions while executing sugar trades at the same
time. Lobo's phones had stopped ringing with calls from brokers many

years before, and his old team had long disbanded. He remained lucid, perceptive about the world, and up to date—but also diminished, and apparently immune to nostalgia. The end was growing near, each moment was valuable, and there was little time to waste over recollections. "Of Cuba I know little. I have left all that behind," he told one Mexican journalist in 1975.

"Wouldn't you like to go back?" the interviewer insisted.

"I think that my return is unlikely: I am seventy-seven, I am broken, I can hardly walk, and, besides, who wants a bag of old bones?"

Lobo admitted that he would like to see his things again, "to see if they have been looked after." But, he added, "if they gave them back to me, I would rather they gave them to the people of Cuba instead."

Lobo's shrinking made a sad sight. His life had largely revolved around business, that business he had treated like a game, and now the game was over. He still traveled, around Europe, to Madeira, even to St. Helena with a group of Napoleon experts, and tried to write his memoirs, as Napoleon had done. But the attempt never got off the ground. Lobo knew his Shakespeare well: "I can call spirits from the vasty deep," boasted Glendower in *Henry IV*. "Why, so can I, or so can any man; But will they come when you do call for them?" as Hotspur replied. After the fall, Lobo could no longer summon his once prodigious memory. Only fragments of the past filtered back in unexpected moments, often from his distant youth, such as *thé dansant* at the Country Club in the 1920s when he had held a woman in his arms during a *danzón*. "Ah, they were quite a thing those afternoons," he told Leonor, who often visited her ailing father in Madrid.

Some of his most vivid recollections came after he suffered a stroke in 1981 and was plagued by hallucinatory dreams. "Strange things happened," Lobo recalled. "I went out into Havana at night, with no money, traveling on a tram or a bus to places I hardly knew. On one trip I went to an old bathing hut on the bay. On another, I went to a clothes store, asking for provisions for the poor and spent the night on a bunk left for those that needed somewhere to sleep. I also went to the Yacht Club once, and threw myself into the water. A strange bug bit me as I swam. I woke up crying, inconsolable at the thought of the death of my mother, my father, my brother and sisters, Leonor, Jacobo and Helena."

Lobo suffered another stroke later that year. It was remarkable that he had lasted this long. Only his stubbornness had kept death at bay—that and the spur of constant physical pain. Most of his peers had already died, including his younger sister Helena and his brother-in-law Mario Montoro, although María Esperanza, who also lived in Madrid, visited daily. Despite everything, they had remained friends. Lobo's health slid rapidly, his spark only sometimes reemerging. Frustrated one day because he wanted to go outside but nobody would take him as he had a cold, he called the police. "Hello, this is Julio Lobo. I am a very important man from Havana and I have been kidnapped by my daughters," he said. Lobo must have been convincing because a policeman came around to the apartment shortly after. When Leonor explained to the bemused official what had happened, Lobo burst out laughing.

Varvara found a more depressing scene when she visited her old friend in Madrid in 1982. The plants in his room were half dead, the paintings crooked, and Lobo was coughing, half-conscious in bed. He was attended by a priest, Varvara remembered, who looked as though he "might have been painted by El Greco; tall, slim with a long, narrow face, an aristo-cratic nose and attenuated fingers, one eye pointing up, the other pointing down, as if he was glancing at God and the Devil at the same time." When the priest left the room, someone whispered, "He has been looking for sinners—and money." "No, he's bankrupt," someone murmured.

The year before his death, Lobo wrote to Carlotta in Havana, sensing the end. "I want to go back to Cuba, to die there and be buried alongside my mother and father," he said. "My history and my love of this country are calling me. . . . So I'm asking you, as an old employee and almost family, to find out what I have to do to go to Cuba as soon as possible— perhaps by the middle of this year." He copied the letter to the Cuban ambassador in Madrid. Vain hope: he never saw the country again.

Lobo died on January 30, 1983, a Sunday. He was buried two days later in the crypt of the Almudena Cathedral in Madrid, a building then still unfinished, although Lobo had donated some funds toward its completion. His body was dressed in a guayabera, as he wished, and wrapped in a Cuban flag. He had collected more enemies than friends during his life, most of them were dead or abroad, and only a handful of mourners attended.

Around him lay the mortal remains of several princes and princesses of the Spanish royal family, distant relatives of the same monarchs that had exiled Lobo's forebears from Spain almost five centuries before, when Columbus had sailed to the Americas and first introduced sugarcane to the New World. Ten generations of Lobos had since successively transplanted themselves around the world. Expelled from the Madrid of Spain's Golden Age, they had traveled to the Amsterdam of Rembrandt; expelled from the Caracas of Cipriano Castro, they had arrived in the newly founded Republic of Cuba; and expelled from the Havana of Fidel Castro, Lobo had returned to Madrid, the city of his earliest forebears. Julio Lobo Olavarría died thousands of miles from the city he considered home, yet his final resting place represented a circling return, of sorts, for the last of Cuba's great Sugar Kings.

EPILOGUE

※

No evil lasts a hundred years, because nobody exists
that could survive it.

—Cuban proverb

would like to bring this story to a valedictory close. It has been such a
long journey that I cannot say for sure when I actually set off. Perhaps
it was when my mother spoke to me as a young child and seeded me
with recollections that left me with a strange nostalgia for a place that
I had never seen. Or perhaps it was later, when I first opened her photo
albums, and I was captivated by the glamour of the images that fell loose
from their bindings and spilled onto my lap. Or maybe it was in Miami,
when I first began to understand the weight of words such as *revolución*
and *exilio* and Cuba became more than the fairyland pirate island that it
could seem in London. That was when I first wondered seriously about
the island's past, and its present and future—preoccupations for which
there can never be a tidy, final farewell. I felt sometimes that I might
have been less concerned by such ideas if I had grown up in the United
States, surrounded by Cuban stories which would then have become so
familiar that I would have taken them for granted and then left them
behind. But almost everything about the pairing of England and Cuba

seemed to me like a contradiction requiring my own personal, internal reconciliation. And then there was the reconciliation that Cuba itself so obviously lacked.

By the late 1970s, many of my cousins lived on New York's Upper West Side, on streets in the low hundreds. In the summer, loosed fire hydrants sprayed water over the pavements to cool off the heat. Other relations lived in Miami, in homes that ranged from my grandparents' two-room apartment by the airport to the art-crammed space of my sister's godmother, an astonishingly generous and statuesque woman named Dolores, who held court in great style fourteen floors above the Miami bay. Not everyone—indeed, very few—had prospered in exile, although some did.

We went to Miami most summers. My mother ran a toy shop in London and saved through the year for the cost of the flights and the rented bungalow. At home, we spoke English. In Miami, the language switched to Spanish as soon as the plane landed and stayed there. Lobo, in his way, had foreseen this. "Soon we, as Cubans, will probably have annexed Miami as our own and Florida will soon become a Spanish American or Latin American state again," he had written in the 1970s from Madrid. It was a perceptive comment that reversed the usual idea of the United States as a towering colossus that dictates all Cuban events, an attractive David versus Goliath setup, long supported by North American bully-boy tactics, which boosted Cuban self-esteem and earned Cuba sympathy around the world. It was also a true comment, and by the 1970s one with which few Anglo-Americans then living in Miami would disagree. Cuba's exiles did seem to have captured the city, especially after the 1980 Mariel boatlift, when Cubans really *did* invade Miami after Castro said that anyone who wanted to leave the island could, and more than 100,000 did. During the Reagan years, Cuban exile politics also often captured Washington's agenda.

I remember one Miami evening in particular. My grandfather, fragile from the tuberculosis from which he never fully recovered, raised himself from a deep chair after a family dinner, typically boisterous with the usual reminiscences of Havana life: the time Tía X had done *this*, the moment

Don Y had done *that*, the party when my mother had leapt from a high wall into a crowd, shouting with glee, "Catch me!" and broken her leg. All these stories were told with a feeling that they illustrated certain family traits, however eccentric, and so formed part of a tradition that was worthy of respect. Silence fell as my grandfather stood up. First he toasted his assembled descendants, eighteen of us then, later rising to thirty-eight cousins, uncles, and aunts. Then he declared, no shouted, that the best way to accelerate Castro's downfall would be to sell Levi's jeans in Havana's Plaza de la Revolución. No—tighten the embargo! No—loosen it! Castro and his *barbudos*, as I learned each year, were always *about* to fall; as the perennial joke went, probably by Christmas.

In the popular imagination, Cuba's exiles have spent the past fifty years furiously plotting and scheming about the day they can reclaim their supposedly ill-gotten gains and turn back the clock in Cuba to more wretched, prerevolutionary days. Growing up in phlegmatic England—going to English schools and eating English food—I sometimes thought of Miami exiles in a similar way. I certainly recognized anger in the high emotion of family conversations that went on in rapid Spanish long into the night; in the often hysterical denunciations of Castro I heard on exile radio shows in Miami; and in the bomb threats against those who believed in the possibilities of rapprochement, as well as the rival governments-in-waiting with their self-appointed ministers of this and ministers of that which I read about in the local newspapers. The violent traditions of the *bonche* days continued, on both sides of the Florida straits.

My mother's propertied background made my family, like the Lobos, a member of Cuba's exiled moneyed class. Yet I always struggled to reconcile the image of revanchist exiles with my grandmother, who spent the last twelve years of her life bedridden in a room whose blinds were drawn against the light that bothered her eyes. Her darkened apartment was the first port of call for any grandchild who came to town. Sometimes, she would pull herself up in bed to pencil X's on rough maps of her Havana home that she drew on the back of old telephone bills. She claimed that treasure was buried there, and urged us to find it. No one believed that real gold lay under the roots of the mango tree in her old patio in Vedado, though. Rather, the task of reclaiming lost emotional treasure, and the burden that that implies, was the crux of the issue, it seemed to me—the real heart of the matter.

MARÍA LUISA LEFT LONDON shortly after her father died and made Miami her home. She had been traveling frequently to Cuba, which made her a suspicious figure in England, even though London generally maintained good relations with Havana. After one such trip, she came to my mother's home, and a lanky man dressed in a blue suit jumped over the wall and approached our house through the garden. All elbows and knees, this Wormold-type character from MI6 sat in the kitchen to drink a mug of tea while María Luisa told my mother of her latest visit to Havana. On another occasion, the Cuban consul came around for supper. The strained conversation took a surreal turn when my mother brought out her photo albums and opened the pages to show pictures of a party held at the Country Club decades before. María Luisa recalled she had been there too, and then the consul exclaimed, "So was I!"—although, he added, he had watched the festivities hidden among the high branches of a tree.

Leonor, meanwhile, lived in Vero Beach, 150 miles north of Miami. The two sisters were barely on speaking terms, their characters as opposed as they had always been, and they argued, latterly through lawyers. After Lobo's death, a complex case sprang up over claims to one of his confiscated properties in Cuba, the old Hershey mill. As this might one day be theoretically worth millions, or more likely nothing at all, to outsiders the fight often seemed to be less about money than over a lost past, perhaps the "emotional treasure" of my grandmother's pot of gold. But then Cuba as a bitter family feud is an apt metaphor for the revolution. Indeed, its legacy is much like the jagged emotional hinterland of a bad divorce that, like all such divorces, has generated terrible enmities that can be hard for outsiders or even its children to understand. The most dramatic example of this is the tragic tale of Elián González, the five-year-old boy fished out of the waters between Cuba and Florida in 1998 after his mother and her boyfriend perished on a raft in the straits. When the boy's father, divorced from his mother and living in Cuba, demanded Elián's return, so was launched the most intense passion play between Miami and Havana since the revolution first began. Elián was subsequently returned to Cuba, and the government erected a statue of José Martí to celebrate this "victory." Cast in bronze, it stands on the Malecón opposite the U.S. Interests Section, Martí pointing with one hand at its blank windows while with the other he clasps a boy protectively to his chest. It is supposed to be his own son rather than Elián, which is a lie that points to a bigger truth, because Martí, of course, chose revolution over his son.

Living in the United States, Leonor rooted herself in the present and looked to the future. Her father had been proud when she first became head of the English department at St. Edward's, a large local school in Vero Beach. Subsequently, she helped set up the Vero Beach Museum of Art, which grew to become an important arts center, and worked with her husband to make a success of the Moorings real estate development, eventually working off the old Hershey debts. María Luisa looked more to the past. She continued to travel to Cuba, following the trail of her father's life, and began researching the life of the Condesa de Merlin. She eventually produced a beautiful book about Havana's architecture, and visitors to Cuba's National Library reported seeing her bent over a reading desk for hours as she searched for *temps perdu*. Back in Florida, María Luisa became an important figure in Miami's secret life, and she turned her beachfront house on Key Biscayne into one of the few places where Cubans in exile and from the island could talk freely, whatever their political beliefs. Like her ancestor the Condesa de Merlin, María Luisa presided over a salon of artists and intellectuals.

Such exile nostalgia might seem self-indulgent, or simply irrelevant given the time that has passed and the decrepit condition of much of the island today—so different from that remembered. Yet I came to realize that many Cubans who live on the island suffer from a similar nostalgia. When María Luisa died of cancer in 1998, her four children traveled to the island and, after a funeral held in Havana's cathedral, arranged to scatter her ashes at Tinguaro. When they arrived at Lobo's old mill, the workers seemed to have fallen under a melancholy spell. They told Lobo's grandchildren that they missed the 1950s, when the harvest was double what it had shrunk to and the mill had worked at full tilt under Lobo's direction. They remembered that Lobo gave scholarships to promising students, and recalled María Luisa as a young woman, following her father on his rounds, supervising the schools and clinics on his plantations. That evening, as dusk settled over Tinguaro's waving fields of cane, María Luisa's children spooned some of her cremated remains into the giant rollers of a cane-crushing mill. They asked the manager if he would like to do the same. He said he would, placed the box of ashes nearer the slow-grinding mechanism, and then, to everyone's amazement, plunged his hands into the box and—quickly, furiously—smeared María Luisa's ashes over his face and chest and white shirt.

"I never asked him why he did that," Victoria Ryan, María Luisa's eldest daughter, told me. "I was too shocked. But I always regret not asking. Was it because he wanted to try and imbibe some of Lobo's old power, in a voodoo sense? Did he want to turn back the clock? I imagine all these things, but I'll never know for sure."

CUBA'S GREAT AGE OF SUGAR has passed. Two thirds of the island's mills have closed, their parts cannibalized as spares for the mills that remain. Production has dropped to a fraction of what it once was, and Cuba's rickety sugar industry can no longer compete with more efficient producers elsewhere. Fidel Castro's retirement from the leadership, his replacement by his brother Raúl, both brothers' inevitable death, and the eventual unpicking of the U.S. embargo may well downsize the history of Cuba further, and maybe the island itself. The charisma of the Castro brothers' revolution has been unique, but then so too have been its material failures. Castro may have summoned a small part of the future that he promised Cubans in 1959—the island's independence, or "dignity," as he called it. But not, as journalist Ann Louise Bardach has put it, breakfast, lunch, or dinner.

Havana, meanwhile, for all its splendor, looks like a city under siege, scarred by the traces of constant attack. Yet it is the "projectiles of mis-management and the bullets of a centralized economy that have shaped its landscape." Yoani Sánchez, who wrote that phrase, is the best known of a growing number of Cuban bloggers who record daily Havana life in all its inadequacies and, despite Internet access restrictions, manage to post their thoughts on the Web. Awarded the Ortega y Gasset prize for journalism in 2008, Sánchez's thoughts range from the domestic—how, whenever she approaches her Soviet-era apartment block, she hugs the wall to avoid walking under the balconies because of the kids who kill their boredom by throwing condoms filled with urine onto passersby below—to the gently political. One of her commonest refrains is a weary com-plaint against an official political rhetoric that still embraces words such as *conflict* and *struggle*, instead of "prosperity, reconciliation, harmony and coexistence."

Such seemingly mild objections—for which, on November 6, 2009, Sánchez was forced into an unmarked car, beaten, threatened, and dumped in the street—point to a deep and enduring problem of the Cuban revo-lution. Because for all the talk of sovereignty, almost one in ten Cubans lives *outside* the island today. When anyone in Europe seems to take that for granted, and somehow views exile as a necessary corollary to what was, *surely*, a just revolution, a righteous poke in the eye of the Yankee impe-rialists, I point out that it is as strange and absurd a situation as if six million British people lived in exile in Calais, eighty miles from London, and Harold Macmillan—dead for more than twenty years—was still prime minister, as he was when Castro and the other *barbudos* came down from the hills. If "Who am *I*?" is the primary question of philosophy, "Who are *We*?" is the primary question of politics, and it is one that Ha-vana has been unable to answer.

"Ahhh, everything was so beautiful in those days," Angela, the daugh-ter of María la Gorda, Fat Mary, remarked to me. I was visiting the family of my mother's old nanny in Havana. Now in her late nineties, María la Gorda lives in a three-room house on a street with tiny porches out front in a respectable working-class neighborhood behind the Tropicana night-club, cared for by her daughter, an energetic seventy-five-year-old. Angela was proudly reminiscing about her own father, who before the revolution had worked in Matanzas as a *colono*, a small-time sugar farmer, near the *central* Álava, one of Rionda's former mills, while María worked with my mother's family in Havana, six days a week, every Sunday off, for twenty-five years.

Our families have never lost touch. Fifty years ago, María used to sneak food to my mother because she suffered from allergies and my grandmother's cure was to starve them out. Now it was my turn to sneak her food, or rather money, as I handed Angela a small envelope that my mother had asked me to take to Havana. "I hope it helps," I said. Angela's mouth then settled into a caricature of a sad clown's upside-down smile. She never went out, she said. The last time she had made a day excursion was three years ago. Besides, where would she go? Everything was so expensive. Transport was a huge problem. Even if she had to go to the doctor herself, she could never be sure when she would get back, and she couldn't leave María alone. So they stayed indoors and scraped by on their ration cards and a monthly pension of 150 pesos a month, worth about $7. Other than weekend visits by Angela's children—an engineer; a soldier; a daughter, although she had just emigrated to the United States, having won a visa in the lottery; and another son, a doctor, although he had been sent to work in Caracas—that was it. Such isolation made Angela and María extreme examples of *insulados*, in-isles, people who have turned their back on a Cuba they find ugly or threatening, and stay indoors, a mirror image of *exiliados*, the ex-isles of abroad.

THE LEGACY OF CASTRO'S REVOLUTION will be disputed for decades. For every argument advanced in its favor—the health care that had enabled María la Gorda to have a pacemaker, the education that had allowed one of Angela's sons to become a doctor—there is an equal riposte: the lack of medicine, classroom books, jobs, pretty much everything. Such discussions only circle back on each other. What is inarguable, though, is that the island has lost its capital. In many ways, this is a historical repeat of Cuba's legacy from the struggle for independence against Spain, when the country was left half-free and also half-ruined, as Bernabé Sanchez recorded from his fallen-down mill in Camagüey more than a century ago.

Luis Machado, a prominent Cuban businessman in the 1930s, reflected on that struggle in words that are still relevant today. "Three generations of Cubans have fought and died for the freedom, sovereignty and independence of our people," he wrote. "Our generation's challenge is economic and social. If our parents forged an independent Cuba, we have to make our country not only wealthy, but Cuban."

Lobo was one of those to heed Luis Machado's call. He sought to make the country "great through wealth." He had an impressive ability to compete with and beat American capitalists on their own terms. He turned the U.S. sugar quota, "the yoke," as Che Guevara called it, to Cuba's advantage in 1934 by squeezing the market and driving sugar prices higher. He was at the forefront of those Cubans, and there were many others, who bought back foreign-owned mills after the Second World War. While Castro stood on the steps of the University of Havana in 1948 and denounced the foreign ownership of Cuba, it was Lobo who did something about it, launching a hostile corporate raid on one of the biggest of those American enterprises, the railroad firm Cuba Company, a move that eventually delivered it into Cuban hands.

Many Cubans still hold themselves and their country in high regard. The island may look small compared with the United States. But next to its Caribbean neighbors, with a landmass the size of England and Wales, Cuba is rather large. Few countries—perhaps none—waged three successful African campaigns in the second half of the last century, as Cuba did. The country has as much a tradition of empire as it does of victimhood, and, for better or worse, Cubans have often been more in control of their own destiny than is frequently presumed. There is little reason why it should be less so in the future.

Lobo was rootless and cosmopolitan in ways that harked back to the great sugar kings of Cuban history, such as Francisco Arango y Parreño, the first person to refer to Cuba as "a country" at the Spanish court in 1788. Like such men, Lobo was intellectually restless; the global nature of sugar required them to be so. Yet for all his globe-trotting, his strange obsession with Napoleon, and his international love affairs, Lobo felt resolutely Cuban and always returned to the island. He was proud of the scholarships, the schools, and the hospitals that he built on his mills, and was withering in his criticism of those who established sugar companies abroad, which then competed with Cuba. "I always felt this was wrong," Lobo once wrote, even as he realized how rash it was to have concentrated so much of his own wealth in one place.

The period when Lobo's empire was at its peak coincided with that moment when the old Cuba that he in many ways represented was also about to fall—the glorious if corrupt Havana of the Batista years. Yet Lobo saw the country's failings and vanities for what they were, and like many others wanted to change them. He was apolitical to the extent that this was possible under Batista during the 1950s. When their business interests clashed, Lobo was as relentless with the president as he was with any other business foe. Does that sound too good to be true? The apolitical businessman is a familiar figure in Anglo-Saxon countries; less so in the Latin world.

Lobo's attempts to transform the Cuban sugar industry—last truly liberal in the 1920s, and by the 1950s almost state-controlled—were genuinely revolutionary. Because of that, his efforts were also unpopular. The final irony is that many of the innovations that Lobo wanted to introduce—such as mechanization and land tenure reform—were introduced by the revolutionary government itself. "That bunch of robbers have managed to do what Batista, Mañas and Barroso didn't allow, for their own reasons," Lobo wrote to one of his old lieutenants in 1974. Yet economics if not politics would have eventually forced those same changes—just as Batista would also have fallen even without Castro and all his madness.

Lobo died in Madrid, deposed from the country he loved, his legacy all but obliterated and, if not in poverty, down to his last two hundred thousand dollars—a five hundred and sixtieth part of the fortune he had once had. To some, that may seem like a fitting end for Cuba's richest man and one of the world's greatest speculators. Yet his drive and financial genius ensure that he would have made a success of himself anywhere.

Cuba's struggles have meanwhile left the island a sad curio, patronized by visitors from abroad who want to see the country before "everything changes." Yet does the end of something—a life, a period of history— always tell the full truth about it, or about what might happen next?

IF THIS STORY was a piece of theater, the curtain would now fall, only to rise again shortly after to show an empty stage onto which all the characters involved would appear to take a bow. First would come the chorus: foreigners in business suits, tourists wearing flowery shirts, swarthy-looking types with trilby hats and machine guns under their arms, bearded men dressed in olive fatigues, showgirls in tasseled sequins, plump Spanish shopkeepers, and thin but muscled cane workers, mostly black. A corpulent president and his family—the children wearing patent leather shoes, the wife a pencil skirt, jacket, and hat, and he in white linen—would take a bow, perhaps to boos, and so too an instantly recognizable figure carrying a telescopic rifle, with a large but soft and well-tended beard, the son of a well-to-do Spanish sugarcane farmer who appeared in the first scenes. Last to step up to the footlights, with a slight limp, would be a short man, wearing white trousers, a guayabera, and a black bow tie. Then the curtain would fall for the last time, the lights would come up, and everyone would go home. But Cuba is not a piece of entertainment with a neat ending, and the story goes on.

Lobo's obituaries dwelt on his fame as the onetime King of Sugar, his vast former properties in Cuba, his remarkable Napoleon collection, his business acumen, his exile, and his reputed wealth—although that was all gone. He sometimes seemed to prefer it that way. "I am happier now with nothing than when I had the largest fortune in Cuba," Lobo had written to Hilda Krueger ten years before he died. "Money is a diabolical invention that separates parents from children, brothers from each other, and friends from friends."

I once thought that might be a fitting epitaph, and for so many reasons: for Lobo's own turbulent and bloodied life before Castro came down from the hills, for the years of division that followed after, and for the endless possibilities for forgiveness that the revolution's eventual and welcome end will finally hold. Yet while Lobo, a stoic, lived happily with little at the end of his life, he always relished the memories of when he had had it all and reigned over a global empire from an office in Old Havana. Lobo made Cuba not only wealthy but more Cuban. So let there be more Lobos, as Tinguaro's workers once declared. The King is dead! Long live the King!—and Cuba's future Queens, Emperors, Empresses, *princesas*, *distinguidos*, and *caballeros* too.

ACKNOWLEDGMENTS

While this is not an authorized biography, it would have been impossible to write without the help of Julio Lobo's family. So I would especially like to thank Leonor Lobo Montalvo de González for the many hours that she spent talking to me about her father's life; I deeply appreciated her trust and candor. I also owe a hefty thanks to the Ryan Lobos—Victoria, John, Carolina, and Alin—who opened their grandfather's archive to me. To others, I would like to make clear—because the question was sometimes asked, especially in Havana—that I received no favor or promise of any kind from the Lobo family to fund this project.

I am, however, extremely grateful to the J. M. Kaplan Fund for its generous financial support during the early stages of research and to Carl Van Ness at the University of Florida's George A. Smathers Library, who found me an academic berth from which to do it. The book might never have gotten off the ground without their help.

It has been said that the only debts that leave one richer are debts of gratitude. In which case I became a very wealthy man during the course of this nearly five-year project. Almost everyone I spoke to helped in some way. In particular, though, I would like to thank, by geography and in roughly alphabetical order:

In the United Kingdom: Flavia Campilli, the staff at Canning House library, Frank Canosa, Malcom Deas—for the perch at St Antony's College; Isabel Fonseca, William Fiennes; Eleo Gordon—for showing me her family's memoirs; David Herbert, Rurik Ingram—Julio Lobo's godson,

not least for introducing me to his extraordinary mother, Varvara; Mario
Lobo, Sophie Molins, Julio Nuñez, and Bella Thomas. At the *Financial
Times*, Kripa Pancholi and Graham Lever helped with the artwork. At
Breakingviews, I am grateful to my then editors Hugo Dixon and Jona-
than Ford, who gave me leave to write.

In Madrid: Juan Arenas, Víctor Batista, Victoria Fernández; and
Laura Galbán and Eugenio Suarez-Galbán for sharing Luis Suarez-Galbán's *Memorias*.

In Paris: Richard O'Connell.

In the United States: Pedro Arellano Lamar, Julieta Cadenas, Bruce
Chappell at the University of Florida, Carlos de la Cruz, Enrique Fernández, all the de Córdoba clan—especially Macky and José, who again scooped
history's first draft; Wendy Gimbel, Enrique León for his patience and help,
Carlos Alberto Montaner, the staff at the New York Public Library, Angela
Sanchez—who buttressed the work on Bernabé Sanchez's letters with
enthusiasm and expertise; Francisco Sanchez, Juan C. Santamarina—for an
early draft of his forthcoming book *The Cuba Company*; Rachel Schneider-
man, Judith Thurman, Jennifer Ulrico at the Columbia University Alumni
Association, Magda del Valle, and Antonio Zamora. I am saddened that
Muriel McAvoy, who took such care to forward me rare Lobo material that
she uncovered from her research on Manuel Rionda, did not live to see the
finished book.

In Cuba: Many people helped with the project, even if they may not
have agreed with where I was coming from or perhaps where I arrived. I
therefore want to underline that this work is solely the author's responsibility. With that in mind, I would like to extend my deepest thanks for their
hospitality, time, and conversation; to Natalia Bolívar Arostegui, Argel
Calcines, Monsignor Carlos Manuel de Céspedes, Roland Ely, Guillermo
Jiménez Soler, Zoila Lapique Becali, Reny Martínez, Roberto Méndez
Martínez, Natalia Revuelta Clews, Sulema Rodríguez Roche, Ileana Sánchez, and Joel Jover. Manuel Alfonso Gil helped with research.

My agents, Deborah Rogers and Melanie Jackson, gave the kind of
support most authors probably wish for. At The Penguin Press, I want to
thank my publisher, Ann Godoff, and my editors Vanessa Mobley, who

helped me first run with the ball, and Laura Stickney, who helped me carry it across the line—magicians both.

I owe particular debts of gratitude to Hugh Thomas, who encouraged the project from start to finish; G. B. Hagelberg, my sounding board on all matters to do with Cuban sugar and the most punctilious of readers; and William Hobson, who helped me see my pages more clearly. Any remaining errors or shortcomings are the author's own.

Finally, thanks to Serenella Cazac, *beija-flor*; Ruby and Mo, for their sustaining good cheer; Margarita, my beloved mother, the source from whence it all sprang; and Tim, dearly missed father and best friend.

NOTE ON SOURCES

This book is based on two collections of previously unresearched documents. The largest is the Lobo family archive. While the record is far from complete, lost or presumably destroyed in Cuba many years ago, Lobo—the great administrator—was a thorough filer and stored originals of many important documents, or copies of them, abroad. His archive, therefore, consists of some four dozen boxes of personal papers, letters, and newspaper clippings that date mostly from after the revolution but contain many earlier documents too. Of particular interest is the correspondence with his father; also the memoir that Lobo began to write toward the end of his life, even if its disjointed fragments sometimes left this researcher feeling like an archaeologist, trying to reassemble whole skeletons from fragments of bone. I enjoyed partial access to the Lobo archive in Miami (Lobo Archive Miami: LAM). A near-replica of the collection exists in Vero Beach, Florida; occasional documents were sourced from there (Lobo Archive Vero Beach: LAVB). Other papers are kept in Geneva (Lobo Archive Geneva: LAG). In Copenhagen, Varvara Hasselbalch kindly made available to me her correspondence with Lobo. In Havana, sadly, neither I nor any other researcher has yet found a trace of any Galbán Lobo document—not even an income statement or balance sheet lying in a deep cellar of the national library.

The second collection of documents on which this book is based is the five hundred letters that Bernabé Sanchez wrote from Camagüey between 1898 and 1900. I fortuitously happened upon them during a trip to Cuba in 2004 and extricated them from the undergrowth—both literal and metaphorical. They are now kept in the Department of Special Collections at the University of Florida's George A. Smathers Library in Gainesville, pending their eventual return to Camagüey, a condition of the deed of gift. Copies of the originals and a typed transcript can be viewed at http://www.uflib.ufl.edu/lac/introduction.html.

Research in public archives was carried out at the University of Florida's Braga Brothers Collection; the UK's Public Records Office in Kew; the Franklin D. Roosevelt Presidential Library at Hyde Park; and classified CIA and FBI documents released under the Freedom of Information Act.

Throughout the book, descriptions of events have been double sourced, following normal journalistic practice. Press clippings are detailed in the endnotes. Quoted dialogue is drawn from letters, reported conversation, and author interviews: Leonor Lobo Montalvo de González, Vero Beach, FL, Aug. 3–4 and Nov. 11–12, 2005; Enrique León, Miami, FL, Dec. 11, 2004; April 4, April 11, and Aug. 22, 2005; Roland Ely, Havana, Sept. 27, 2005; Varvara Hasselbalch, Copenhagen, Jan. 20–21, 2006; Fichu Menocal, Havana, April 29, 2006; Eusebio Leal, April 2007; Joan Fontaine, phone interview, May 13, 2007; Carlos de la Cruz, Miami, Aug. 2007; Ana María Brule, phone interview, June 10, 2008; Victoria Fernández, June 26, 2008. Other interview subjects did not wish to be mentioned by name.

NOTES

INTRODUCTION

5   **Some writers believed Lobo was Dutch:** José Pardo Llada, "¿Quién recuerda a Julio Lobo?," *El Nuevo Herald*, Aug. 30, 1990, 13A; Enrique León, "Respuesta a José Pardo Llada: mis memorias de Julio Lobo," *El Nuevo Herald*, Oct. 8, 1990, 11A.

6   **more [cinemas] than New York:** Havana had 135. Bertrand de la Grange and Maite Rico, "La Habana: ruinas y revolución," *Letras Libres*, Mexico, January 2009.

7   **"I am enchanted":** Condesa de Merlin, 1842, *Viaje a la Habana* (Editorial de Arte y Literatura: La Habana, 1974), 77.

7   **a significant symmetry:** G. B. Hagelberg, "Reversal of roles in US and Cuba," *Financial Times*, Jan. 7, 2009.

8   **"with its flickering lamp":** cited by Hugh Thomas, prologue to María Luisa Lobo Montalvo, *La Habana: Historia y Arquitectura de una Ciudad Romántica* (New York: Monacelli Press, 2000), 15.

CHAPTER I: A TRISTE TROPICAL TRYST

11   **Ernesto "Che" Guevara summoned:** The principal source describing their meeting is Lobo's memoir of the event. Further details were corroborated by Enrique León. See also Hugh Thomas, *Cuba: or The Pursuit of Freedom* (Updated edition, London: Da Capo Press, 1998), 1298–99, which draws from a 1968 interview with Lobo, and Jon Lee Anderson, *Che Guevara: A Revolutionary Life* (London: Bantam Press, 1997), 483–84.

12   **"We are going through very difficult times":** Letter to Varvara Hasselbalch, June 23, 1959.

12   **"I often feel like":** Letter to Varvara Hasselbalch, July 1, 1959.

12   **controlled fourteen sugar mills:** Lobo did not own all his mills outright; he often had coinvestors, although he always operated with a controlling interest. In chronological order of purchase: Agabama, also known as Escambray (1926); Pilón, also known as Cabo Cruz (1943); San Cristóbal (1944); Tinguaro (1944); Unión (bought 1945; interest sold 1953); Caracas (bought 1946, sold 1953); Niquero (1948); La Francia (bought 1950); Perseverancia (1950); El Parque Alto (1951); Tánamo (1951); El Pilar (1951); Araújo (1953); San Antonio (1958); Hershey (1958); Rosario (1958).

13   **Lobo "doesn't sense a trend":** Dana Thomas, *The Money Crowd* (New York: G. P. Putnam's Sons, 1972), 147.

13   **Lorenzo Montalvo, the Julio Lobo of his day:** Roland Ely, *Cuando Reinaba Su Majestad el Azúcar* (Buenos Aires: Editorial Sudamericana, 1963), 93.

13   **"We didn't care":** Thomas, *Cuba*, 1019.

14   **"The long city":** Greene, *Our Man in Havana*, 53.

14   **"In Batista's day, I liked the idea":** Quoted in Anderson, *Che Guevara*, 377.

15   **"Gracious living":** letter to Varvara Hasselbalch, Jan. 25, 1960.

16   **"less gaiety, less freedom":** Simone de Beauvoir, *Force of Circumstance* (London: Penguin Books, 1965), 569.

16   **My mother's family, Sanchez y Sanchez:** Which, by tradition, did not use an accent, unlike the normal Sánchez spelling used elsewhere in the book.

19   **In another paean to sugar:** Lobo Montalvo, *La Habana*, 26.

20   **"For the shit we're going to be guarding":** Anderson, *Che Guevara*, 453–55.

20   **"Señor Lobo, it is good of you to come":** Lobo memoir, LAM.

21   **"a dovecot":** Thomas, *Cuba*, 936, n.12.

21   **"I lost hope":** Anderson, *Che Guevara*, 213.

22   **His bedroom had once been a reconstruction:** Varvara Hasselbalch, *Varvara's Verden* (Copenhagen: Ascheoug Publishers, 1997), 107.

23   **"Not a stain, or a blemish":** Lobo memoir, LAM; corroborated by León to author.

23   **"One of the most human of all desires":** Letter to Varvara Hasselbalch, July 1, 1959.

25   **Acosta's poem is an emotive portrait:** Antonio Benítez-Rojo, *The Repeating Island* (Durham, NC: Duke University Press, 1992), 115–21.

26   **"All that talent":** Anderson, *Che Guevara*, 484.

26   **he cornered the global sugar market:** Thomas, *The Money Crowd*, 147–48.

29   **Sicily—an important sugar producer:** The invention of the first vertical three-roller sugar mill, an important technological innovation, is sometimes attributed to Pietro Speciale, prefect of Sicily, in 1449. Either way, Sicily had one of the world's earliest sugarcane industries, with a record of export from around A.D. 900. Sidney W. Mintz, *Sweetness and Power: The Place of Sugar in Modern History* (London: Penguin, 1985), 27.

29   **"Uncle, you're looking wonderful":** Giuseppe Tomasi di Lampedusa, *The Leopard*, trans. Archibald Colquhon (London: Collins Harvill, 1986), 165–83.

30   **Leonor banged on his door:** González to author, Aug. 3, 2005.

31   **The powerful Falla Guttiérez family had moved $40 million abroad:** Thomas, *Cuba*, 1150, n.60.

31   **Conversations Lobo said he had had with Allen Dulles:** León to author.

32   **"*Chico*, I was born naked":** Lobo memoir, LAM.

CHAPTER 2: THE BETRAYAL OF JOSÉ MARTÍ

36   **Bernabé's mill was also among the first:** Spanish law provided for a *patronato*, a transition period that amounted to eight years of indentured servitude. Hence 1888, rather than 1880, is often given as the date of the abolition of slavery in Cuba, although the *patronato* officially ended in 1886, two years earlier than decreed, by general agreement.

38   **"So many feats they did to admiration":** Robert Graves, "Ogres and Pygmies," in *The Complete Poems*, edited by Beryl Graves and Dunstan Ward (Manchester, UK: Carcanet Press, 2000).

40   **Martí also had a wonderful sense of humor:** Alfredo José Estrada, *Havana: Autobiography of a City* (New York: Palgrave Macmillan, 2007), 114.

40   **"Without Camagüey":** Luis Álvarez Álvarez and Gustavo Sed Nieves, *El Camagüey en Martí* (Havana: Editorial José Martí, 1997), 74.

41   **To the west, closer to Havana, planters were wont:** Edwin F. Atkins, *Sixty Years in Cuba* (Cambridge, MA: Riverside Press, 1926), 76.

41   **a "special, freedom loving mentality":** Manuel Moreno Fraginals, *El Ingenio* (Havana: Editorial de Ciencias Sociales, 1978), Vol. I, 146.

41   **"as if just one body":** Guillermo Cabrera Infante, *View of Dawn in the Tropics* (London: Faber & Faber, 1988), 20–28.

42   **In the twenty-eight volumes of his collected works:** Álvarez Álvarez and Sed Nieves, *El Camagüey en Martí*, 17.

42   **"my mind is not here with me":** Ibid., 16.

43   **"I love my duty more than my son":** Cited in Rafael Rojas, *Motivos de Anteo* (Madrid: Editorial Colibrí, 2008), 124.

44   **Their unsigned letter:** Álvarez Álvarez and Sed Nieves, *El Camagüey en Martí*, 69–71.

44   **"in a rough line, like a squadron of rebels":** Enrique Loynaz del Castillo, *Memorias de la Guerra* (Havana: Editorial de Ciencias Sociales, 1989), 58–59.

45   **"No well-established person in Camagüey":** *La Tribuna*, May 30, 1895.

45   **Loynaz wrote to the revolutionary junta's:** Loynaz del Castillo, *Memorias de la Guerra*, 80–82.

45   **"The main reason for the setback":** Álvarez Álvarez and Sed Nieves, *El Camagüey en Martí*, 108.

45   **"Martí was very clear about that":** Ibid., 134, for the text of the letter; Thomas, *Cuba*, 303, comments on it.

46   **"Climbing hills together":** José Martí, *Selected Writings*, trans. Esther Allen (New York: Penguin Books, 2002), 380–412.

46   **Francisco Vicente Aguilera:** Former president of the Republic Under Arms, had an estimated personal fortune of $3 million when the Ten Years' War broke out in 1868; also owned three mills—the Jucaibana, Santa Isabel, and Santa Gerturdis; 10,000 *caballerías* of land (332,000 acres), 35,000 head of cattle, 4,000 horses, 500 slaves (subsequently freed), coffee estates, retail and warehouse interests, all inherited from his

father, who had Camagüey roots. Travels in Europe as a young man exposed him to progressive ideals. A freemason, he built Bayamo's local theater at a cost of $80,000. Died penniless in New York in February 1877, aged fifty-six. Guillermo Jiménez, *Los Propietarios de Cuba, 1958* (Havana: Editorial de Ciencias Sociales, 2006), 7.

47   **the culmination of an impulse that had been building:** Joshua Jelly-Shapiro provides a historical synthesis in "An Empire of Vice," *The Nation*, June 10, 2009.

48   **a "country wrapped in the stillness of death":** Louis A. Pérez, *On Becoming Cuban* (Chapel Hill: University of North Carolina Press, 1999), 101.

50   **"enemy of the revolution":** Loynaz del Castillo, *Memorias de la Guerra*, 84.

50   **At the very least, autonomy would have preserved:** Hugh Thomas suggests that in the long term autonomy might even "have been the solution to guarantee a permanent political and economic structure better designed than independence to secure a consistently rising standard of living, accompanied by cultural and social homogeneity." Thomas, *Cuba*, 380.

50   **"You know that abandoning my interests and family":** Pérez, *On Becoming Cuban*, 103.

Chapter 3: A Sense of Home

51   **the women wearing white muslin, the men dressed in frock coats:** Merlin, *Viaje a la Habana*, 101.

51   **Habaneros looked on with bemusement:** The atmosphere is evoked by Tom Gjelten, *Bacardi and the Long Fight for Cuba* (New York: Viking, 2008), 81.

51   **"desolation, starvation and anarchy":** Cited in Estrada, *Havana*, 145.

52   **"Neither a colony nor a free state":** Cited in Marta Bizcarrondo and Antonio Elorza, *Cuba/España: El dilema autonomista, 1878–1898* (Madrid: Editorial Colibrí, 2008), 408.

52   *Les charmes de l'âge d'or:* Merlin, *Viaje a la Habana*, 97.

53   **"a veritable Klondike of wealth":** Pérez, *On Becoming Cuban*, 107.

55   **"whistling, happy, clean dressed, as if for a party":** Nemecio Parada, *Vísperas y comienzos de la revolución de Cipriano Castro* (Caracas: Monte Ávila Editores, 1973), 34. The *cubanos* were probably surplus rifles that filtered into Latin America over the course of Cuba's struggle for independence.

55   **"ruin the bank":** Heriberto recalled his meeting with Castro and subsequent departure from Venezuela in a speech he gave four decades later in Havana, *Apuntes Autobiographicos de Heriberto Lobo* (mimeo, 1937), LAM.

55   **an American banker read an interview:** *New York Herald*, May 5, 1900, with subsequent coverage in the *New York Tribune*, May 6–7.

56   **"Come in, don't worry":** Virgilio Pérez Veiga, *Heriberto Lobo: un gran carácter que supo sonreír* (mimeo, 1951), LAM.

57   **a small Venezuelan earthquake:** The October 29, 1900, earthquake did little damage to Caracas. Nevertheless, perhaps thinking of the devastating 1812 earthquake, Castro was so unnerved by the tremors that he jumped from the first-floor balcony of the Palace and broke a leg on the flagstones of the Plaza Bolívar below.

57   **He sped through customs:** *New York Times*, Feb. 27, 1913.

57   **When Castro appeared, she rushed him:** Letter to Carmen Cecilia González, Nov. 10, 1978.

58   **"Do you see any change in me?":** Pérez Veiga, *Heriberto Lobo*.

63   **They eventually found the hoard:** José de Córdoba, "Cuba through the eyes of an exile," *Wall Street Journal*, Sept. 9, 1987.

64   **"I was here first":** "A Woman in Her Garden: An Appreciation of the Life and Work of Dulce María Loynaz," by Judith Kerman, has recordings of interviews with people in Havana who remembered her. http://www.loynazenglish.org/.

Chapter 4: Sugar Rush

66   *Domina tus pasiones:* Letter to Julio Lobo, 1919, LAM.

67   **When the games ended:** González to author.

67   **He also showed an unusual interest in Napoleon:** "El Museo Julio Lobo de la Habana," *Vida Universitaria*, Vol. IX, May 1958.

67   **in 1910, just before his twelfth birthday:** Lobo recalled the moment in a rare interview with Juan Emilio Friguls, his semiofficial public relations agent, *Diario de la Marina*, Sept. 11, 1958. Friguls is still alive in Havana at time of writing, but not talking much. Tate Cabré and Argel Calcines, "Juan Emilio Friguls: el decano se despide," *Opus Habana*, March 20, 2008. http://www.opushabana.cu/index.php?option=com_content&task=view&id=1079&Itemid=45.

67   **one of the six youngest boys:** Columbia University Alumni Register, 1932.

67   **Cubans still settled their differences with swords:** Although duels were illegal, notices invariably

appeared in the newspapers the next day, detailing seconds, the reason for the fight, and the loser, always wounded while "examining his weapons." Ruby Hart Phillips, *Cuba: Island of Paradox* (New York: McDowell, Obolensky, 1958), 209.

67   **"I decided to become a sugar expert":** *"Hacerme fuerte en el azúcar,"* Lobo memoir, LAM.

68   **A patrician Spaniard with dark hair:** Muriel McAvoy, *Sugar Baron: The Life and Times of Manuel Rionda and the Fortunes of Pre-Castro Cuba* (Gainesville: University Press of Florida, 2003).

69   **On both sides of the Gulf of Mexico:** Rebecca Jarvis Scott, *Degrees of Freedom: Louisiana and Cuba After Slavery* (Cambridge, MA: Harvard University Press, 2005), 1–5.

69   **"Once that perfume":** Lobo memoir, LAM.

70   **Less innocently, he made hand copies of the refineries' balance sheets:** Ibid.

70   **"Your average mark in October":** Letter to Julio Lobo, 1917, LAM.

71   **One Easter, Lobo canoed:** Lobo memoir, LAM.

71   **"full of fire":** Ibid.

71   **an "individualist, who does not spare himself":** José Tiglao, *Sugarland* (Bacolod City, Philippines: Sugarland Publications, Sept. 1964).

72   **Lobo imagined an improved model that would explode:** Lobo memoir, LAM.

74   **"Why unhappy *mi corazón?*":** Letters to Julio Lobo from Virginia, April 24, 1919; Oct. 5, 1922; Oct. 16, 1925.

74   **"Do not concern yourself":** Letter to Julio Lobo from Heriberto, dated only 1919, LAM.

74   **it was called the "Dance of the Millions":** The name was taken from a 1916 musical production that played at the Teatro Nacional and then the Alhambra. Ned Soublette, *Cuba and Its Music: From the First Drums to the Mambo* (Chicago: Chicago Review Press, 2004), 347.

74   **Small-time sugarcane farmers . . . shopped:** John H. Parker's wonderful book, *We Remember Cuba*, 2nd ed. (Sarasota, FL: Golden Quill, 1993), 25.

75   **¿Qué sucederá si no deja Ud. un testamento?:** Cited in Wendy Gimbel, *Havana Dreams: A Story of Cuba* (London: Virago, 1999), 75.

75   **in the pages of *Social*:** María Luisa Lobo Montalvo and Zoila Lapique Becali, "The Years of *Social*," *The Journal of Decorative and Propaganda Arts*, Vol. 22, 1996.

75   **no child, as the saying went, lacked for shoes:** Nicolas de Rivero, editor and publisher of the *Diario de la Marina*, described life in Senado after one visit at the time as the "greatest happiness one can find, or very close," a compliment that went beyond the usual courtesies of the age. Nicolas de Rivero, "Nuestro director en el central Senado," *Diario de la Marina*, undated article c. 1916, author's collection.

75   **"If things go on at this rate":** *El Mundo*, April 30, 1916, cited in Thomas, *Cuba*, 539.

76   **At night the fragrant aroma:** Teresa Casuso, *Cuba and Castro* (New York: Random House, 1961), 9.

76   **Lobo, just twenty-two years old, named his terms:** Lobo memoir, LAM.

76   **"stimulate the country to extreme prosperity":** Quoted in Thomas, *Cuba*, 543.

76   **National City had opened:** Harold Van B. Cleveland and Thomas F. Huertas, *Citibank, 1812–1970* (Cambridge, MA: Harvard University Press, 1985), 106.

77   **As much as 80 percent of National City:** Ibid.,106

77   **José ("Poté") López Rodríguez, the wealthiest man in Cuba:** Leland Hamilton Jenks, *Our Cuban Colony: A Study in Sugar* (New York: Vanguard Press, 1928), gives a lively discussion of the fates of this and other Cuban speculators in the bust, 244.

77   **Before the crash, Cuban-owned mills:** Cesar Ayala, "Social and Economic Aspects of Sugar Production in Cuba, 1880–1930," *Latin American Research Review*, Vol. 30, No. 1 (1995), 95–124.

78   **The firm had sold the three mills it owned:** Guillermo Jiménez, *Las Empresas de Cuba, 1958* (Havana: Editorial de Ciencias Sociales, 2004), 56.

78   **"consequently the greatest one to blame":** McAvoy, *Sugar Baron*, 186.

78   **"paradox of artificial limitation in Cuba":** John Maynard Keynes, *Stocks of Staple Commodities* (London & Cambridge Economic Service, August 1929). See also the collected writings, Vol. XII, *Economic Articles and Correspondence: Investment and Editorial* (London: Macmillan Press), 551; and J. W. F. Rowe, *Studies in the Artificial Control of Raw Material Supplies: Sugar* (London & Cambridge Economic Service, Special Memorandum 31, September 1930).

79   **"the bankruptcy of Cuba was inevitable":** Letters to Julio Lobo from New York, June 29, July 1, July 5, 1927, LAM.

79   **On Waldorf-Astoria Hotel–headed paper, Heriberto wrote:** Letters to Julio Lobo sent by Heriberto from Paris on July 13, July 21, Aug. 2, Aug. 11, Sept. 14, Oct. 4, 1927, LAM.

79   **In 1921, showing early promise:** Letter from Julio Lobo to Maurice Varsano, Jan. 14, 1977. Lobo added that in 1933 he also had "the distinction, if you can call it that" of making the lowest ever priced sale of sugar, at less than 0.5 cent per pound.

80 "an Anglo-Saxon frame of mind": *El Camagüeyano*, Sept. 27, 1926.

80 The news came as a thunderclap to *El Viejo*: McAvoy, *Sugar Baron*, 197.

81 "The sale was solely due to your skill and hard work": Letter to Julio Lobo, Oct. 31, 1927, LAM.

81 "He sees advantage in getting down from his high horse": Letter to Julio Lobo, Oct. 2, 1928, LAM.

81 "This is a very delicate time": Ibid.

81 "Mr Tarafa . . . did not think it advisable": Braga Brothers Collection, University of Florida, Series 1, Box 40, letter from Domingo A. Gáldos to James M. Gruber, April 2, 1923; cited in Juan C. Santamarina's forthcoming book *The Cuba Company*, 155.

82 Heriberto drily suggested: Letter to Julio Lobo, Nov. 2, 1928, LAM.

82 "In civilized countries, they create occupation": Julio Lobo y Olavarría, *El Plan Chadbourne: nuestro cancer social* (Havana: Maza Cabo Impresores, 1933).

83 "dark night of the soul": Lobo memoir, LAM.

83 "the disastrous results suffered by the house": Lobo letter of resignation, April 25, 1932, LAM.

Chapter 5: Death in the Morning

84 *"Morris of Lykes Brothers"*: Phillips, *Cuba: Island of Paradox*, 97.

85 "All our misfortunes in Cuba": Letter to Varvara Hasselbalch, May 2, 1962.

86 The sugar price fell and unemployment grew: For more on the depressed Cuban economy in 1933, and the strikes and rebellions that it fomented, see: Brian H. Pollitt, "The Cuban Sugar Economy and the Great Depression," *Bulletin of Latin American Research*, Vol. 3, No. 2 (1984), 3–28; Barry Carr, "Mill Occupations and Soviets: The Mobilisation of Sugar Workers in Cuba, 1917–1933," *Journal of Latin American Studies*, No. 28 (1996), 129–56; Barry Carr, "Identity, Class, and Nation: Black Immigrant Workers, Cuban Communism, and the Sugar Insurgency, 1925–1934," *The Hispanic American Historical Review*, Vol. 78, No. 1 (1998), 83–116.

86 literally feeding his opponents to the sharks: Frank Argot-Freyre, *Fulgencio Batista: From Revolutionary to Strongman* (New Brunswick, NJ: Rutgers University Press, 2006), 38.

86 ". . . good looking young fellows, wore good clothes": Ernest Hemingway, *To Have and Have Not* (London: Arrow Books), 3–5.

87 "not one minute more, not one minute less": Argot-Freyre, *Fulgencio Batista*, 44.

87 "Outwardly Havana was a tomb": Carleton Beales, *The Crime of Cuba* (Philadelphia and London: J. B. Lippincott Co., 1933), 445.

87 "As he crossed the street": Ruby Hart Phillips, *Cuban Sideshow* (Havana: Manzana de Gomez, 1935), 67.

88 "Who is ruling Cuba?": Cited in Luis E. Aguilar, *Cuba 1933: Prologue to Revolution* (Ithaca, NY: Cornell University Press, 1972), 167.

89 The first confrontation: Argot-Freyre, *Fulgencio Batista*, 94.

89 "one of the soundest, if not the soundest": Lobo was meanwhile judged "almost as able as his father," although Welles was cautioned against confidential conversations because of Lobo's youth. "Memorandum for Ambasador Welles," August 1933; Folder: Cuba—State, legal communications; Box 37, papers of Charles W. Taussig; Franklin D. Roosevelt Library, Hyde Park, New York.

90 "unless Cuba was able to sell more sugar": Lobo recalled the moment during a speech on June 10, 1964; also reported in the trade journal *Sugarnews*, July 1964. LAM.

90 "the sea pounding against the rocks outside": Lobo memoir, LAM.

90 "It is so comforting to hear an English voice": *Daily Express*, London, Sept. 21, 1933; *The Western Mail* followed up the story on Sept. 22–23.

91 Julio, who knew Churchill: Winston Churchill wrote to Julio from his house at Westerham in Kent on August 7, 1946, responding to a note that Julio had sent. Churchill, then leader of the opposition, thanked him for his message, "which brought back many happy memories of the times we spent together in Havana and Miami Beach." I am grateful to Pedro Arellano Lamar for showing me the letter. I hope he eventually finds the Churchill photograph taken on Senado's tennis court too.

92 "When the situation in the country is sorted out": Efraín Morciego, *El Crimen de Cortaderas* (La Habana: Union de Escritores y Artistas de Cuba, 1982), 132–33.

92 He had also instituted an eight-hour day: Ibid., 114.

93 sugar workers elsewhere were then lucky to be employed for seventy days: The sugar output restrictions had shrunk the average length of the *zafra* to 66 days in 1933, from 250 days or more during the boom years. Carr, "Mill Occupations and Soviets," 131.

93 "Although we know the capitalist class is always antagonistic": Gjelten, *Bacardi and the Long Fight for Cuba*, 125.

93 "a harmonious end to the conflict is expected": *Diario de la Marina*, Nov. 5, 1933.

93 The final death toll ranged between two and five hundred: Argot-Freyre, *Fulgencio Batista*, 120.

95   **In the most folkloric version of the story:** The description probably stems from another event, equally folkloric, that took place during La Chambelona rebellion in 1918. Private information to author. See also Morciego, *El Crimen de Cortaderas*, 156.

96   **Eyewitness accounts gathered by a Cuban researcher:** Morciego, *El Crimen de Cortaderas*.

97   **"the Giant from Senado":** Roberto González Echevarría, *The Pride of Havana: A History of Cuban Baseball* (New York: Oxford University Press, 2001), 282–83.

99   **"There must have been three thousand of them":** Gabriel García Márquez, *One Hundred Years of Solitude*, trans. Gregory Rabassa (London: Pan Books, 1981), 251.

99   **Senado "always had a good reputation":** Dispatches by Grant Watson, Dec. 13, 1933, and March 1, 1934 (Public Records Office, London, FO 371/17518).

100 **"Eyes still young today":** Rubén Martínez Villena, "The Rise of the Revolutionary Movement in Cuba," *The Communist*, XII, 1933. Cited in Aguilar, *Cuba 1933*, 231.

CHAPTER 6: A TALENT FOR SPECULATION

104 **"The new sugar magus":** *Cuba Importadora e Industrial*, March 1937. "Nuevo mago azucarero, convierte su ciencia en oro, y en resumen es un toro, para entrar en el dinero."

104 **"the Sephardic millionaire":** Alejo Carpentier, *La consagración de la primavera* (Havana: Editorial Letras Cubanas, 1978), 41. "El millonario sefardita, famoso por su milagrosa vivencia en cuanto a alzas y bajas de valores."

105 **Then it was an almost dingy place:** Xavier Galmiche et al., *Havana: Districts of Light* (Paris: Vilo, Telleri, 2001), 182.

105 **"Es anticuado vivir en la ciudad":** Ibid., 25.

106 **"The only other trader":** Freeman Lincoln, "Julio Lobo, Colossus of Sugar," *Fortune*, Sept. 1958.

106 **"G[albán-Lobo] with his organization":** Braga Brothers Collection, BBC III 61, Box 3. See cables from Braga to Sharples and Rook 3/28/1941, and from Rook to Rionda 1/3/40.

106 **"in white pantaloons and thin shoes":** Dana, *To Cuba and Back*, 44.

106 **Cuba's first plantations were named after saints:** Moreno Fraginals, *El Ingenio*, Vol. 1, 112.

107 **From the second floor of *la casa* he could see:** Lobo Montalvo, *La Habana*, 28.

107 **There were also smells:** Guillermo Jiménez, *La Habana que va conmigo* (Havana: Editorial Letras Cubanas, 2002), 28.

108 **The plain-looking dowager was a *su altesa*:** Parker, *We Remember Cuba*, 138.

108 **"a master or a slave":** Merlin, *Viaje a la Habana*, 112.

108 **Even Havana's beggars:** Parker, *We Remember Cuba*, 131.

108 **"I am the *King of This World*":** Luis Calzadilla Fierro, *Yo soy el Caballero de París* (Badajoz, Spain: Gráficas Diputación de Badajoz, 2000), 21.

110 **"lively and passionate, even to excess":** Merlin, *Viaje a la Habana*, 12.

111 **Lobo never commented:** It is possible, though, to piece together roughly what happened from available evidence. Lobo commented briefly on the deal to Lincoln, in *Fortune*, 1958. There was also nearly daily coverage by the *New York Times* from Dec. 15, 1934, to Jan. 18, 1935. The names of the main shorts and longs are in an unpublished letter that Lobo wrote to Margarita González in 1979 (LAM). That said, it is not clear why Douglas, Hayden, et al. were shorting Cuban sugar. It may have been as a legitimate hedge for their own production. It may have been with the aim of making a quick trading profit. Conceivably, it may even have been to try to drive weaker Cuban-owned milling companies out of business.

112 **the quota was used more often to subsidize and protect:** Julio Lobo, speech to annual convention of U.S. confectioners, June 10, 1964, LAM; also reported in *Sugar News*, July 1964.

113 **they netted an estimated profit of some $150,000:** The calculation assumes that the cost of sugar for the Cuban longs was 2.18 cents per pound—the same as that charged to the U.S. sugar refiners in October's prearranged sale. However, if Cuban holders of physical sugar such as Lobo and García had paid less for their original stakes, then their subsequent profits would also have been more.

114 **Plans had even been submitted:** Galmiche et al., *Havana: Districts of Light*, 182.

114 **a Potemkin village for foreign visitors:** James C. McKinley Jr., "Old Havana gets a lift, but Cubans don't benefit," *New York Times*, Dec. 6, 2007.

115 **a parasitical vine that strangles Cuba's noble ceiba tree:** Rev. Abiel Abbot, *Letters Written in the Interior of Cuba* (Boston: Bowles and Dearborn, 1829), 59; cited in Roland Ely, *Cuando reinaba su majestad el azúcar* (Buenos Aires: Editorial Sudamericana, 1963), 318.

115 **"the exorbitant interest doubles the debt":** Merlin, *Viaje a la Habana*, 113.

115 **"those persons [who] have a peso sign in the head":** Fidel Castro Ruz, speech, Sept. 28, 1966, http://www.cuba.cu/gobierno/discursos/1966/esp/f280966e.html.

115 **"Jews of the Caribbean":** Ann Louise Bardach, *Cuba Confidential* (New York: Penguin, 2002), 101.

115 "seeking, prying and executing on information": Letter to Gerry Ascher, April 22, 1967, LAM.

116 the first submarine telephone cable: Heriberto Lobo was invited to join the project as an early investor, but turned it down because he thought the investment too risky. Heriberto's relatively low appetite for risk—born of his experiences in Venezuela, as well as the Cuban bust of the 1920s—is a marker of how the father differed from the son.

116 When President Harding finished a brief call to his Cuban counterpart: Diario de la Marina, April 12, 1921.

116 "an astonishing aptitude": Leland Jenks, Our Cuban Colony (New York: Vanguard Press, 1928), 207.

117 "carnivals of speculation": For more on this fascinating subject, see Edward Chancellor, Devil Take the Hindmost: A History of Financial Speculation (New York: Farrar, Straus & Giroux, 1999).

119 "A fat blond man is summoned": "Perfil financiera: Julio Lobo," Cuba Importadora e Industrial, March 1937.

120 "The difficulty," Lobo confided to one competitor: Letter to Maurice Varsano, Jan. 14, 1977.

120 the speculator "is not so much a prophet": Keynes, Collected Writings, Vol. XII, 260.

120 "not due to clairvoyance": LAM.

121 "In that way, I gained a huge advantage": Lobo memoir, LAM.

121 "No man can control a commodity": Lincoln, "Julio Lobo, Colossus of Sugar."

122 "The sugar b[usines]s has mostly been handled by gentlemen": Cable from George Braga to Sharples and Rook, March 28, 1941, Braga Brothers Collection, to author from McAvoy. See also McAvoy, Sugar Baron, 284.

122 "I generally believe the worst about lobos": Luis Conte Agüero, Eduardo Chibás, el adalid de Cuba (Mexico: Editorial Jus, 1955), 392.

122 "Papa always told me": Lobo memoir, LAM.

123 León, a shrewd man, meanwhile provided Lobo with political advice and legal counsel: He had been a schoolmate of other Cuban liberals such as Felipe Pazos, who later became president of the National Bank, and Aureliano Sánchez Arango, a respected education minister.

123 León never regretted: León to author.

123 He rarely stopped for an elaborate lunch: Letter to Mercedes Formica, Feb. 18, 1971, LAM.

124 "When a Cuban mill owner needs money to pay bills": Lincoln, "Julio Lobo, Colossus of Sugar."

124 He fenced, boxed: Cuba Importadora e Industrial, March 1937.

124 "She was the most beautiful woman in Cuba": Undated letter to John Ryan, LAM.

125 "Please explain to Madame Reine": Letter to Margarita González, Dec. 21, 1941, LAM.

125 One of Lobo's worst moments: Lobo memoir, LAM.

126 Batista frequently denied that he was either a socialist: Argot-Freyre, Fulgencio Batista, 231.

126 "Re yr wire of this morning": Franklin Delano Roosevelt Presidential Library, Hyde Park, NY; papers of Charles Taussig; Lobo file; Aug. 9, 1940, cable #52.

128 Lion, incidentally, had recently married the singer and dancer Josephine Baker: Lion's marriage also showed that Paris was then more open to black culture than Havana. When Baker visited Havana in 1950, she was feted by journalists and her shows were sold out, but the Nacional barred her from entering.

CHAPTER 7: THE EMERALD WAY

130 Heinz Lüning, known as the "Canary": Phillips, Cuba: Island of Paradise, 215.

131 Britain—Cuba's largest market for tobacco—banned Cuban cigar imports: Ibid., 193.

131 The 1944 crop hit 4.3 million tons: Anuario Azucarero de Cuba, Vol. XXIII (Havana: Cuba Económica y Financiera, 1959).

132 Pilón, a midsize mill: Also known as Cabo Cruz.

134 the kerosene lamps inside the countryside's thatched bohíos: "Problems of the New Cuba," Report of the Commission on Foreign Affairs (New York: Foreign Policy Association, 1935), 73–74.

134 "How much does Rionda pay you?": LAM. The Cuban peso was pegged to the U.S. dollar, at an exchange rate of 1:1.

134 "with his wife and smart friends": Esteban Montejo, The Diary of a Runaway Slave, ed. Miguel Barnet (London: Bodley Head, 1968), 19.

134 "One of the things I learnt": Lobo memoir, LAM.

134 Lobo tromped through the batey: The description is by Lincoln in Fortune, but just one reference among many that corroborate Lobo's engagement with his mills.

135 women of good breeding passed their time: Cited in Thomas, Cuba, 147.

135 "travel on the bus": González to author.

136 "This evening light is so difficult": Lobo Montalvo, La Habana, 21.

137 Lobo gave the girls simple instructions: Ibid., 20.

137 **tobogganed down steep hills of sugar:** Ibid., 18.

138 **"Julio, business is not always this good, you know":** León to author. Alfredito Fernández owned the exclusive Funeraria Fernández in Vedado, on the corner of Paseo and Second streets.

139 **Carlos Manuel de Céspedes:** Interim president of Cuba's rebel forces during the Ten Years' War, was deposed and sent into exile by the revolutionary House of Representatives. He traveled without escort and was killed by Spanish troops at San Lorenzo in Oriente Province in March 1874.

139 **Celia remained close to the Lobos:** For an official version of Celia Sánchez's childhood and subsequent role in the revolutionary government, see Pedro Álvarez Tabío, *Celia; ensayo para una biografía* (Havana: Oficina de Publicaciones del Consejo de Estado, 2004).

140 **arrangements had to be made to transfer his salary to Celia instead:** León to author.

140 **"Julio, it is not safe here for you and your daughters":** González to author.

142 **Leonor went on to write a version:** Leonor Lobo Montalvo González, *Mi Ascensión al Pico de Turquino* (Havana, 1946); *Diario de la Marina* also carries an interview, Aug. 10, 1946, 2.

142 **"my father called her a quitter":** José de Córdoba, "Tilting at Mills," *Wall Street Journal*, March 11, 1999.

142 **"They are two characters, wholly opposed":** Letter to Virginia Lobo, Nov. 1, 1948, LAM.

CHAPTER 8: SUN, SEA, AND SHOOTINGS

143 **twenty-four gold dinner plates from Tiffany's:** *Diario de la Marina*, Aug. 2, 1946.

144 ***Caracas* would be Lobo's largest mill:** *Farr's Manual of Sugar Companies* (New York: Farr & Co., 1959).

144 **Lobo meanwhile returned to his office with Carlotta:** Lobo's memories of the subsequent phone call and the events that followed are contained in his unpublished memoir and in a long letter he sent to Carmen Cecilia González on July 2, 1976. Lobo hoped at one point that González, a Venezuela-based historian, would write his biography. LAM.

144 **"killing each other over ideologies more obscure":** Guillermo Cabrera Infante, *Mea Cuba* (London: Faber & Faber, 1994), 140.

145 **"Anonymously":** A typically skillful reply. A senator further commented that the diamond looked different from the original. "In that case," Grau responded, "if it is not the same diamond, please give this one to me because it is mine." Humberto Vázquez García, *El Gobierno de la Kubanidad* (Santiago de Cuba: Editorial Oriente, 2005), 325–32.

148 **"Justice comes late, but it comes":** *La justicia tarda, pero llega.* Desiderio Ferreira was Machado's second-in-command of police.

148 **"more dangerous than all the time I fought against Batista":** Cited in Charles Ameringer, *The Cuban Democratic Experience: The Auténtico Years* (Gainesville: University Press of Florida, 2000), 29. The university was a revolutionary training ground for Castro. While there, he also joined the failed filibustering expedition against the Trujillo dictatorship in the Dominican Republic in 1947. The following year he traveled to Bogotá and was active in the mass riots that convulsed the Colombian capital after the killing of the liberal Colombian politician Jorge Eliécer Gaitán.

150 **"To say the name Lobo is to speak of money-changing":** *Prensa Libre*, Aug. 9, 1946. *Bohemia*'s coverage is collected in Enrique de la Osa's *Sangre y Pillaje* (La Habana: Editorial Pablo de la Torriente, 1990), 53–63.

150 **three other businessmen who had fled to New York, fearing for their own lives:** *Diario de la Marina*, Aug. 11, 1946.

150 **"I feared such terrible conditions would come":** Cable to Lobo, Aug. 14, 1946, LAM. Berenson was well known in Cuba for having tried to negotiate the landing in Havana of almost a thousand refugee Jews who had sailed from Germany on board the freighter *St. Louis* at the start of the Second World War. He failed to raise enough money to pay for the refugees' residency visas. A film was later made of their plight, *Voyage of the Damned*.

151 **"We are not hoodlums":** De la Osa, *Sangre y Pillaje*, 53–62.

151 **"Mr. Lobo may not be an angel":** *Prensa Libre* and *Diario de la Marina*, Aug. 13, 1946. "El señor Lobo no será un arcángel, no tiene halos, ni cacarea la honestidad . . . El central está restaurándose como nunca lo hizo antes una poderosa compañía norteamericano, nunca este central ha tenido un fomento agrícola tan intenso, y este central pertenece a ese señor lobo, tan 'lobo' . . . ¿Podría decir el Sr. Piñango qué ha hecho él por Cuba? . . . Nada le conocemos . . . Cuba se sentiría muchísimo mejor con mucho más Julio Lobos y muchísimos menos Piñangos."

152 **The saga's complexities are worthy of a radio soap opera:** *Bohemia*, Sept. 22, 1946.

153 **Lobo quarreled with the Cuban doctors over their fees:** *Bohemia*, Nov. 10, 1946.

154 **"very disagreeable years":** Letter to Carmen Cecilia González, July 14, 1976, LAM.
154 **his biggest fight of all:** a corporate raid: Santamarina, *The Cuba Company*, chapter 3.
155 **But it was a "betrayed revolution":** Tad Szulc, *Fidel: A Critical Portrait* (New York: William Morrow & Co., 1986), 165–67.
155 **"Some people have made the country great":** Enrique León, "Respuesta a José Pardo Llada: mis memorias de Julio Lobo," *El Nuevo Herald*, Oct. 8, 1990, 11A.
155 **He wrote from New York to his mother in Havana:** Letters to Virginia Lobo, April 29, June 15, July 1, and Nov. 1, 1948, LAM.
156 **During one trip to Haiti:** Lobo memoir, LAM.
156 **he traveled home from the airport in a bulletproof car:** *El Crisol*, Jan. 12, 1948.
159 **"¿Qué pasa?" he asked:** Pérez Veiga, LAM.
159 **the single shot woke Lobo:** González to author.
160 **"The truth is I have been unlucky":** Letter to María Luisa, Jan. 19, 1950, LAM.
162 **"They say that I was a terrible President":** Arthur M. Schlesinger Jr., *A Thousand Days* (Boston: Houghton Mifflin, 1965), 216.
162 **Prío was cordial until the last:** Carlos Alberto Montaner, *Viaje al corazón de Cuba* (Barcelona: Plaza & Janés Editorial, 1999), 61.
162 **"My life alone is no pleasure":** Letter to María Luisa, Nov. 4, 1950, LAM.

CHAPTER 9: IMPERIAL AFFAIRS
166 **"Opulence, the adulation of money-makers":** Cited in Chancellor, *Devil Take the Hindmost*, 235–36.
166 **"Money not only does not bring happiness":** Letter to María Luisa, April 15, 1950, LAM.
167 **"My fame lacked only one thing—misfortune":** Jean Paul Kauffmann, *The Dark Room at Longwood* (London: The Harvill Press, 1999), 28.
168 **Thus there have been Napoleons:** The "Napoleon of Crime" has a curious Cuban connection. Adam Worth, the Victorian master thief that Arthur Conan Doyle took as his model for the evil Professor Moriarty—Sherlock Holmes's greatest criminal adversary—had two illegitimate daughters with Kitty Flynn, a New York hostess. In 1881, Flynn, an attractive adventurer and opportunist, married Pedro Terry, the favored son of Cuban planter Tomás Terry. Young Terry took Flynn's two daughters under his wing, and when the elder of these girls married the eminently respectable figure of Charles Trippe, their son Juan inherited some of the Terry sugar fortune. Juan Trippe, grandson of a career criminal and heir to one of Cuba's largest fortunes, went on to establish an airline operating out of Havana, soon transforming it into one of the world's biggest—Pan American. Trippe was no Napoleon of the Air, however. Gore Vidal called him the "robber baron of the airways." Ben Macintyre, *The Napoleon of Crime: The Life and Times of Adam Worth, Master Thief* (Farrar, Straus & Giroux, 1997), 129–36 and 293.
168 **Orestes Ferrara:** A respected historian of figures such as Machiavelli and the Borgias, Ferrara was also a skillful duelist. He once fenced with General Enrique Loynaz de Castillo, the war of independence hero who had clashed with Bernabé Sanchez, beating Loynaz with a wound to the head. Affronted by the defeat, Loynaz rushed after Ferrara with his usual impulsiveness, shouting, "What no Spaniard ever did in combat, that damned Italian did," and had to be restrained by spectators.
168 **"so that she never forgot the taste":** Lobo memoir, LAM.
168 **"An infinite capacity for taking pains":** Alistair Horne, *The Age of Napoleon* (London: Weidenfeld & Nicolson, 2004).
168 **"had an extraordinary ability to create":** Rosario Rexach, "El Recuerdo de Julio Lobo," *Diario las Americas*, June 12, 1983.
169 **"an unusual man, whose most memorable quality":** J. L. Loeb, *All in a Lifetime: A Personal Memoir* (New York: John L. Loeb, 1996), 168.
169 **"In addition to his abilities as a soldier":** Julio Lobo y Olavarría, *La Mascarilla de Napoleón Bonaparte* (La Habana: Ucar García, 1957), 1.
169 **Lobo dispatched his assistants to France:** Author interview, Ana María Brules, June 10, 2008.
170 **"It was a sacred place for Julio":** Cited in Sulema Rodríguez Roche, "Un prodigioso legado; la biblioteca Napoleónica de Julio Lobo," University of Havana, Master's Thesis, 2006.
170 **"this priceless contribution":** *Lettres au Comte de Mollien*, Museo Julio Lobo, Département des Manuscrits à La Havane (Paris: Editions Charles Gay, 1959). The full text of de Gaulle's letter runs: "Paris, 24 Mai 1960. Monsieur: En réunissant et en publiant ce très intéressant choix de lettres de Napoléon 1er au Comte Mollien, vous avez apporté à l'historie de l'époque impériale une inappréciable contribution. Je vous en félicite et je vous remercie de m'avoir mis à même d'en profiter, en me raisant

homage del ouvrage consacré à cette correspondance. Veuillez croire, Monsieur, à mes sentiments les plus distingués et les meilleurs. Le Général de Gaulle."

171 **imperial dignitaries were known to suspend a piece of sugar:** Horne, *Age of Napoleon*, 100.

171 **found a complete ten-volume edition of rare Egyptian drawings:** "Biblioteca Nacional Cubana expone libro Bonapartista sobre Egipto," *World Data Service*, Aug. 22, 2006.

171 **One of Lobo's few surviving extended disquisitions:** Julio Lobo y Olavarría, *La Mascarilla de Napoleón Bonaparte*. See also Francesco C. Antommarchi, *The Last Days of the Emperor Napoleon*, 2 vols. (London: Henry Colburn, 1825).

172 **At 5:51 p.m., the thirty-two-year-old Corsican-born doctor:** Frank McLynn, *Napoleon: A Biography* (London: Jonathan Cape, 1997), 655.

172 **Burton smashed it on the floor:** Julia Blackburn, *The Emperor's Last Island* (New York: Vintage, 1997), 172.

174 **"in gratitude for the operation on his mother's eyes":** Emilio Bacardí y Moreau, *El Dr. Francisco Antommarchi: sus días en Cuba* (Madrid: Playor, 1972), 161–81.

175 **"I really loved her":** Kauffmann, *Dark Room at Longwood*, 74.

176 **(Mademoiselle George later observed):** Horne, *Age of Napoleon*, 45.

176 **"like a pain under the heart continually":** Cited by Sally Beauman, afterword to *Rebecca*, by Daphne du Maurier (London: Virago Press, 2003).

177 **"majestic stride and presence":** *Herald Tribune*, Oct. 16, 1979.

178 **("I am certain both will become part"):** Letter to Lillian Fontaine, dated only Thursday, 1954, LAM.

178 **("rather unusual; I trust you will like it"):** Letter to Lillian Fontaine, March 5, 1954, LAM.

178 **"So beware!":** Letter to Lillian Fontaine, Nov. 20, 1953, LAM.

179 **a person among his "first row":** Letter to Joan Fontaine, March 31, 1977, LAM.

179 **"As you know, early in the 1950s":** Letter to Joan Fontaine, Feb. 1, 1982, LAM.

179 **"Like you, I am a loner":** Letter to Julio Lobo, March 5, 1981, LAM.

179 **"I am so glad you were touched":** Letter to Julio Lobo, Feb. 11, 1982, LAM.

179 **"The sadness which envelopes my heart":** Letter to Joan Fontaine, May 31, 1977, LAM.

180 **"Years ago, when I was still at MGM":** Esther Williams, *The Million Dollar Mermaid* (New York: Simon & Schuster, 1999), 291.

180 **Lobo's hospitality grew out of the traditional generosity:** Ely, *Cuando reinaba su majestad el azúcar*, 691.

181 **"You know I am modest in my habits":** Letter to María Luisa, Oct. 4, 1950, LAM.

182 **"When Hollywood stars visit":** Hipólito Caviedes, from an otherwise undated 1959 article published in *ABC*, LAM.

182 **Lobo was always at work:** See, for example, interview by Roberto Bourbakis, "El Museo Julio Lobo," in *Cubazúcar*, Feb. 1958, 8–10.

182 **"land was bad, the cane was bad, the mill was bad":** León to author.

183 **"A sugar factory should be as clean":** Julio Lobo y Olvarría, "Tinguaro," *Compendio anual de la revista Cubazúcar*, Año IV, Diciembre 1958, No. 1.

183 **"We spent a lovely weekend at Tinguaro":** Letter to María Luisa, May 4, 1950, LAM.

184 **"Was it possible for the spirits of the young people":** Cirilo Villaverde, *Cecilia Valdés*, trans. Helen Lane (New York: Oxford University Press, 2005), 142.

185 **"The Cuban people should not accept":** Raúl Cepero Bonilla, *Escritos históricos* (Havana: Editorial de Ciencias Sociales, 1989), 244.

185 **Lobo knew that to achieve his ideas:** Lincoln, "Julio Lobo, Colossus of Sugar."

185 **when he imported an experimental cane-cutting machine:** Thomas, *Cuba*, 1144.

186 **"One has to modernize or disappear":** Lobo, "Tinguaro."

187 **How interesting, *Bohemia* pointed out:** Cited in Thomas, *Cuba*, 800.

187 **"nothing surprises me because he was a crook":** Lobo memoir, LAM.

187 **Blanco faced a large margin call:** Lobo comments in *Diario de la Marina*, Jan. 11, 1953. See also Cepero Bonilla, *Escritos históricos*, 225–29.

187 **with two officials from the Sugar Institute:** León to author.

187 **That had been the "good Batista":** Mark Falcoff, *Cuba, The Morning After* (Washington, DC: AEI Press, 2003), 22–24.

188 **Batista played canasta, watched horror films:** Thomas, *Cuba*, 791.

188 **In his private office:** Szulc, *Fidel*, 212; and *Bohemia*, "La Mansion Campestre del Despota," Jan. 1959.

188 **"master of the world market":** Cited in Thomas, *Cuba*, 1272.

188 **Lobo offered three cents a pound:** Cepero Bonilla, *Escritos históricos*, 242–43.

189 **schoolchildren emptied their piggy banks:** "Sweet rationing ends in Britain," *On This Day: 1950–2005*, BBC News, http://news.bbc.co.uk/onthisday/hi/dates/stories/february/5/newsid_2737000/2737731.stm/.

189 **Baron Paul Kronacher, a Belgian producer and occasional visitor at Tinguaro:** Letter from Lobo to Varvara Hasselbalch, Nov. 9, 1954. Kronacher's Cuban involvement is also mentioned in the Braga Brothers' files, Record Group III, Series 50, Box 7.

189 **Jesus Azqueta, developed a mill in Venezuela:** Lobo memoir, LAM.

189 **believed it "undignified":** Ibid.

189 **Prices continued to fall, as did the Cuban crop:** By 1955, world production had risen to 38 million tons from 36 million in 1952; Cuban production meanwhile fell from 7.2 million to 4.5 million. Food and Agriculture Organisation, *The World Sugar Economy in Figures, 1880–1959* (Rome: FAO, 1960).

189 **he founded a new enterprise, Banco Financiero:** Domestic banks were required by the government to finance Cuban planters for any sugar production in excess of their domestic quotas, but the banks could then repo these loans at a higher rate back to the National Bank. As a result, there was an automatic profit to be had. Lobo was quick to take it. León to author.

190 **"I know now the time has come":** Letter to Lillian Fontaine, July 19, 1953, LAM.

191 **"The idea might seem fantastic":** "¿Se retira Julio Lobo?" *Semanario de la Actualidad*, Sept. 9, 1954.

191 **"The life I had been living":** Letter to Varvara Hasselbalch, Oct. 15, 1953.

191 **"I've been in pain for so long now":** Letter to Lillian Fontaine, Nov. 4, 1953, LAM.

192 **"As Jonah said to the whale":** Letter to Varvara Hasselbalch, Oct. 16, 1953.

192 **She had met Lobo two years before:** Hasselbalch, *Varvara's Verden*, 105–16.

195 **A self-made millionaire:** James Grant, *Bernard Baruch: The Adventures of a Wall Street Legend* (New York: Simon & Schuster, 1983).

198 **The clipping that Lobo sent:** "A home town is born," *National Municipal Review*, November 1954, LAM.

199 **This was probably Cuba's first commercially successful steam-powered mill:** Ely, *Cuando reinaba su majestad el azúcar*, 93 and 512–14.

199 **"If only current generations of hacendados":** Lobo, "Tinguaro."

200 **"a Phoenix, rising from its ashes":** Telegram to Varvara Hasselbalch, May 5, 1954.

CHAPTER 10: AT THE ALTAR

201 *"The Americans invented wash and wear":* Eladio Secades, *Las Mejores Estampas de Secades: estampas costumbristas cubanas de ayer y de hoy* (Miami: Ediciones Universal, 1983), 17.

202 **At night a line was trailed out to sea:** Johnson Family history, 1860–2006, mimeo, 73.

203 **"the fashion of impudent dressing":** *Time*, Jan. 24, 1949.

203 **Lansky had revamped the Nacional's casino:** Lansky properly arrived in Cuba after Senator Estes Kefauver's hearings on Mob-related activities busted his Florida operations in 1953. Lansky served a two-month sentence and then moved south to Cuba, invited by Batista, who had seen the professionalism of Lansky's operations firsthand in Florida. Batista put him on the government payroll as his tourism and gambling adviser.

203 **Carmen maintains she is the inspiration for Eloise:** Cristina Rathbone, "Cuban at Last," *Tropic Magazine; The Miami Herald*, Oct. 31, 1993, 8–11.

204 **"first great patriotic, democratic and socialist revolution":** *Verde Olivio*, July 30, 1961, cited in Falcoff, *Cuba, The Morning After*, 29.

205 **more doctors per capita than France:** According to one writer broadly sympathetic to the revolution, Richard Gott, *Cuba: A New History* (New Haven, CT: Yale University Press, 2004), 165.

205 **the "Paris of the Caribbean," the "Monte Carlo of the Americas":** T. J. English, *Havana Nocturne: How the Mob Owned Cuba* (New York: William Morrow, 2007), and Robert Lacey, *Little Man: Meyer Lansky and the Gangster Life* (London: Century, 1991).

207 **The second volume was released on June 2, 2007, at a launch party:** Ciro Bianchi Ross, "Los Propietarios," *Juventud Rebelde*, June 10, 2007.

209 **"Not bad for someone who did not know how to read":** Lobo memoir, LAM.

210 **tourism was then Cuba's fastest-growing industry:** Tourist revenues in 1947 were only $17 million. Over the following decade, they rose at an annual 14 percent rate. Sugar and tobacco, by contrast, were broadly stagnant, although there was impressive growth in Cuban light industry, such as textiles, as well as mining. *Anuario Azucarero de Cuba*, 1959; and *Estudio Sobre Cuba* (Coral Gables, FL: University of Miami Press, 1963), 1126.

210 **The number of hotel rooms in Havana doubled:** A fantastic rate of growth, but to put it into perspective, Las Vegas has 124,000 hotel rooms, twenty-five times as many as Havana did.

210 **Pan American Airways made it easier to travel:** English, *Havana Nocturne*, 153.
210 **Banco Financiero helped finance the construction of the Riviera and the Capri:** The attraction of such loans to Lobo was that the Bandes guarantee essentially made them risk-free. Hence, when a New York swell named Julio Rosengard one day presented himself to the board with impeccable references, including a seat on the board of trustees of a private university outside Boston, Suffolk, Lobo's bank agreed to the loan. León to author.
210 **it did count among its shareholders Amadeo Barletta:** Enrique Cirules, *The Mafia in Havana* (New York: Ocean Press, 2004), 184–86.
210 **A successful businessman, Barletta:** English, *Havana Nocturne*, 100.
210 **Their association ended in 1957:** Jiménez, *Las Empresas*, 112.
210 **He paid a further $25,000 to Castro's rebels:** León to author. Lobo also mentions it in his memoir. León confirmed the first payment; LAM contains a receipt for the second.
211 **Both Castros later singled out the Bacardís:** Jiménez, *Las Empresas*, 528.
211 **often boasted to Spanish officials:** Private information to the author.
212 **Hershey spent most of his later years living on the estate:** Joël Glenn Brenner, *The Emperors of Chocolate* (New York: Random House, 1999), 137–38.
212 **a classic Lobo market squeeze:** *BusinessWeek*, April 1959, explores the possible sequence of events.
213 **Lobo backed out, sold his stake to Loeb:** For a recap, see *Wall Street Journal*, March 7 and April 6, 1956; *Miami Herald*, March 4; also Raúl Cepero Bonilla, *Prensa Libre*, Dec. 7, 1956.
213 **Krueger had first met Lobo in Havana:** "Propone Grau a la escritora Hilda Krueger el plan que su gobierno piensa desarollar," *Diario de la Marina*, Dec. 26, 1945. Three years later, Krueger published *La Malinche, or Farewell to Myths* (New York: Storm Publishers, 1948).
214 **In Berlin, Krueger also knew Jean Paul Getty:** Robert Lenzer, *Getty: The Richest Man in the World* (London: Grafton Books, 1985), 111–28.
215 **a large real estate deal with the U.S. real estate tycoon Bill Zeckendorf:** Lobo and Zeckendorf planned to buy Cuba's oldest mill, the Toledo, which abutted Havana and was ripe for real estate development. Zeckendorf had already agreed to the terms of Toledo's purchase for $7.5 million with its owner Manuel Aspuru, Lobo's old friend, but had called in Lobo as a partner. The failure to buy Hershey still fresh in his mind, Lobo counseled Zeckendorf to bring Batista into the deal as well. Zeckendorf traveled to Havana, drove through the gates of the Presidential Palace "under the muzzles of sub-machine guns on the roof," and listened politely while Batista talked about the need for a large-scale housing development in Havana. "You have a fine prospect here in Havana," Batista said at the end of the meeting, according to Zeckendorf. Aspuru traveled to New York to close the deal a few days later, but it unraveled unexpectedly at the last minute. Zeckendorf happened to sit next to Aspuru's two daughters on the plane to Havana; they were aghast when he complimented them on the pending sale, which they knew nothing about, and on landing in Cuba phoned their father in New York and convinced him to cancel the deal, the sale of their "inheritance." The old allure of being an *hacendado* still exerted its pull. *The Autobiography of William Zeckendorf* (New York: Holt, Rinehart and Winston, 1970), 254–60. Zeckendorf's book is riddled with small errors, but León confirmed the broad outline of the story.
215 **"My emotional life with my two wives":** Letter to Mercedes Formica, July 13, 1971, LAM.
216 **"Most people do the wrong thing at the right time":** Letter to Varvara Hasselbalch, July 1, 1958.
217 **Grau lacked funding for this ambitious plan:** *BusinessWeek*, April 1958.
217 **"Julio, you either buy it":** Loeb, *All in a Lifetime*, 168.
217 **In May, a fire:** *Cubazucar*, June 1957.
217 **a bomb that would be placed at Leonor's forthcoming wedding:** González to author.
217 **He had edged Batista out of the shipping firm Naviera Vacuba:** Jiménez, *Empresas*, 491.
218 **Loeb's lawyers stood up and stopped the hands on the clock:** León to author; see also Oscar A. Echevarría, *Captains of Industry: Miguel Angel Falla; the Cuban Sugar Industry* (Miami: New House Publishers, 2002), 27.
219 **"disgustingly quiet. The only real danger we faced":** Cited in Shawn Levy, *The Last Playboy: The High Life of Porfirio Rubirosa* (New York: HarperCollins, 2005), 227.
219 **Sometime after one o'clock in the morning, an airplane rose:** Rosa Lowinger and Ofelia Fox, *Tropicana Nights: The Life and Times of the Legendary Cuban Nightclub* (New York: Harcourt, 2005), 1–4.
220 **As Batista boarded the plane, his incongruous last words:** Cited in Georgie Anne Geyer, *Guerilla Prince* (Little, Brown and Company, 1991), 197.
220 **Batista had managed to conjure up a Who's Who of Cuban business leaders:** See Pedro Manuel Rodríguez, *El Segundo Asalto al Palacio Presidencial* (Havana: Delegación del Gobierno, 1960).
220 **Batista's army was demoralized and ineffective:** Lobo knew this firsthand. The government troops dispatched to hunt down Castro and his rebels in the Sierra had first stationed themselves at Lobo's mill,

Pilón. Led by a cruel braggart, Alberto del Rio Chaviano, brother-in-law of the army chief of staff General Francisco Tabernilla, and infamous for killing and torturing prisoners captured after Castro's attack on the Moncada Barracks in Santiago three years before, the soldiers had helped themselves freely to Pilón's supplies. The army only reimbursed Lobo later when he filed three invoices: one for Chaviano, another for Tabernilla, and a final one for himself. "That is the way things were then," Lobo recalled ruefully. LAM.

221 *"Feliz año nuevo,'* I said as I got between my silk sheets": Lewis Yablonsky, *George Raft* (New York: McGraw-Hill, 1974), 221–22.

221 Lobo told journalists that Castro's victory could "only be compared": *Chicago Daily Tribune,* Jan. 8, 1959.

222 "The triumph of the revolution makes me very happy": Gjelten, *Bacardi and the Long Fight for Cuba,* 208.

222 "Instead of criticizing the executions": Ibid., 212.

222 The satirical magazine *Zig-Zag:* Estrada, *Havana,* 235.

222 ("I resigned. Cuba did not protest"): *Diario de la Marina,* Nov. 12, 1960.

222 Lobo went to the Ministry of Finance to pay a $450,000 advance on his taxes: The fact that the Bacardi payment was the same size suggests these two businesses were of a similar scale—and profitability. Gjelten, *Bacardi and the Long Fight for Cuba,* 208.

223 "That can only be taken as a sign of confidence": This, and Lobo's other comments at the time, are gathered in *Bohemia,* May 5, 1959.

223 "We must modernize or die": *Herald Tribune,* March 21, 1959.

224 "Maybe when the time comes to apply the law": Cited in Gjelten, *Bacardi and the Long Fight for Cuba,* 226.

225 "We have been going through some ugly times" and "I have just begun to fight": Letters to Varvara Hasselbalch, June 23 and July 1, 1959.

225 From there he traveled to Tangiers: Cable between Czarnikow Rionda's Havana and London offices; to author from McAvoy, sourced Braga Brothers Collection, Nov. 23, 1959.

226 "There were more empty seats on the bus": Carlos Eire, *Waiting for Snow in Havana* (New York: The Free Press; Simon & Schuster, 2002), 237.

CHAPTER II: *CREPÚSCULO*

230 most other Cubans had kept what money they had on the island: There was much capital flight during the last months of Batista, yet Cuba ended 1959 with some $350 million in gold reserves, among the highest in Latin America, which suggests the amount of money withdrawn was not particularly high. Many Cubans also owned real estate in New York and Florida—most famously José Manuel Alemán, a spectacularly corrupt minister under Grau and then Prío. Some Cubans had also invested in Canada, Europe, and parts of Latin America, especially Venezuela. Even so, Cuban wealth invested abroad was then estimated at around $400 million—a fraction of the $10 billion Latin Americans as a whole were thought to keep abroad. Thomas, *Cuba,* 1182–187.

230 "I crapped out": Lacey, *Little Man,* 258.

230 These were valued at some $4 million: Memo by John H. Groh, Feb. 20, 1980, LAVB.

233 Alvaro acted as Donovan's translator: Pablo Pérez-Cisneros, John B. Donovan, and Jeff Koenreich, *After the Bay of Pigs* (Miami, FL: Alexandria Library Inc., 2007), 93.

234 "Premier Castro, I've been doing a lot of thinking": Ibid., 182.

235 "What the hell is this all about": B. D. Hyman, *My Mother's Keeper* (London: Michael Joseph, 1985), 84–88.

236 "Flowers are magnificent": Cable to Lobo, May 20, 1963. LAM.

237 According to an interview Lobo had with the FBI: Federal Bureau of Investigation DBA 80042, 14 July 1964; FBI, DBA 77673, 15 July 1964; and *Plans of Cuban Exiles to Assassinate Selected Cuban Government Leaders,* memorandum, Central Intelligence Agency, DD/P 4-2944, 10 June 1964.

238 "I want all the mills to be destroyed": *New York World Telegram and Sun,* May 15, 1964.

238 "I left Cuba on October 14": Undated 1963 newspaper clipping, LAM.

239 "$25m ahead of the game": Groh memo, LAVB.

239 "We are witnessing history": Investment column, *Fortune,* March 1963.

240 "I know what I'm doing": LAM.

240 Now "that damned Hershey deal" returned to haunt him: To upack the deal-math somewhat: Lobo bought Hershey for $24.5 million, of which $15 million was in cash and $9.5 million in debt. These debts were paid down at a fast rate, thanks to forward sales of Hershey sugar and other quick assets, so that at the end of 1959 total debt had fallen to $6.75 million. In the United States, after leaving Cuba, Lobo

arranged a moratorium with City Bank on Dec. 29, 1961. The bank agreed to the moratorium on the conditions that: a) Lobo would trade his way to success and eventually pay down the debt; and/or, b) Castro might fall, in which case Lobo would regain his property and also be able to pay off the debt. On October 28, 1963, City Bank agreed to restructure the debts again. This time the Moorings, the Florida real estate company owned by his daughters, would assume $3.7 million, payable in five annual installments of $740,000, a cost that would be assumed by Galbán Lobo. Galbán Lobo Nassau would meanwhile assume the balance of the debt. After allowing for an immediate payment by Lobo of $1 million, this left $2 million, payable in five annual installments of $400,000. Combine that with the $3.7 million held by the Moorings, but paid by Lobo, and his total City Bank debt was $5.7 million. Groh memo, LAVB.

240 **On July 23 Lobo declared bankruptcy:** The most comprehensive round-up of events is in *BusinessWeek*, "The Bet That Failed," July 23, 1964, although all major papers—including the *Financial Times*, the *Wall Street Journal*, and the *New York Times*—covered the story.

241 **William Zeckendorf, who filed for bankruptcy on the same day:** *New York World-Telegram*, July 23, 1964.

243 **"people that left work with the same trudge":** Gabriel García Márquez, 1958, "Un Sábado en Londres," in *Obra periodística. Vol. 4. De Europa y America: 1955–60*, ed. Jacques Gilard (Barcelona: Bruguera, 1983).

245 **"where Cubans of all races and creeds can meet":** *Diario de las Americas*, Oct. 28, 1966.

246 **José R. Fernández, a founding member of the center, recalls:** In a memoir of the Cuban center at http://www.asociacioncaliope.org/historiacc.htm.

246 **The days were long gone when he could afford to misplace six officers' uniforms:** Correspondence between Lobo and TWA, March 28–April 28, 1965, LAM.

246 **"What is more absurd than avarice in old age":** Letter to Alexander Herman, Nov. 11, 1972.

246 **the Commerce Ministry gave Lobo the necessary import permits out of charity:** Private information to author.

246 **"since leaving New York, I've not touched a grain of sugar":** Letter to Maurice Varsano, Jan. 14, 1977, LAM.

246 **Maurice Varsano:** See Jacques Lamalle, *Le Roi du Sucre* (Paris: Lattés, 1979), 77–88.

247 **took in lodgers to pay her bills:** José de Córdoba, "Tilting at Mills," *Wall Street Journal*, March 11, 1999.

247 **"I am completely retired from business":** Letter to Lillian Fontaine, April 14, 1972, LAM.

247 **"It's painful to be selling the remains":** Letter to Dominique Vincent, May 21, 1980, LAM.

247 **In addition to two crates of Napoleon papers that Leonor had got out of Cuba:** Leonor and Jorge, her husband, had piled assorted Napoleon documents and accoutrements, such as Josephine's tiara, into four roughly built wooden crates. They had then driven around Havana at dawn, the boxes sticking out the back of their Renault. Leonor left two of the crates with Norberto, the resourceful butler of the Bacardi family, who later smuggled them out of the country. The other two they left for safekeeping at the French embassy after the British ambassador, disturbed from his sleep, had refused them help while standing on the steps of his residence in his dressing gown.

247 **María Luisa was living in London then:** She had set up base in London in 1973, after moving from Peru.

248 **Their trip was never going to be routine. It turned into a disaster:** Deposition by Julio Enrile, Lobo memorandum, 1978; and letters from Lobo to Celia Sánchez, April 24, 1978, and June 12, 1978, LAM.

250 **there the matter rested, and with it a portion of Lobo's lost wealth:** Lobo memoranda Aug. 1, Aug. 23, and Dec. 10, 1966, LAM. Others took the matter further. See Timothy O'Brien, "The Castro Collection," *New York Times*, Nov. 21, 2004; Sunday Business, Section 3.

250 **"When you lose your wealth you lose nothing":** Letter to Alexander Herman, Oct. 27, 1972, LAM.

250 **"acuity, even though he was only making do":** To the author.

251 **"Of Cuba I know little":** *Vision*, March 15, 1975.

251 **"Strange things happened":** Lobo memorandum, 1981, LAM.

252 **"He has been looking for sinners—and money":** Hasselbalch, *Varvara's Verden*, 114.

252 **"I want to go back to Cuba, to die there":** Letter to Carlotta Steegers, Jan. 15, 1982, LAM.

EPILOGUE

256 **"Soon we, as Cubans, will probably have annexed Miami":** Lobo memoir, LAM.

259 **When they arrived at Lobo's old mill, the workers seemed to have fallen under a melancholy spell:** Linda Robinson, "The Final Homecoming of Cuba's Sugar Queen," *U.S. News and World Report*, March 22, 1999.

263 **"Three generations of Cubans have fought and died":** Luis Machado was also head of Cuba's Chamber

of Commerce at the time. Cited in Marifeli Pérez-Stable, *The Cuban Revolution: Origins, Course, Legacy* (New York: Oxford University Press, 1993), 19.

263 **Cuba is rather large:** The point is made by G. B. Hagelberg and José Alvarez in "Cuba's Economic Culture and Reform Process," Association for the Study of the Cuban Economy, proceedings, August 2008, http://lanic.utexas.edu/project/asce/pdfs/volume18/pdfs/hagelbergalvarez.pdf.

263 **Few countries—perhaps none—waged three successful African campaigns:** Jorge I. Domínguez, "Hello from Havana," *Harvard Magazine* 111, no. 6 (July–August 2009), 24–27.

263 **the first person to refer to Cuba as "a country":** Gustavo Pittaluga, *Diálogos sobre el destino* (Miami, FL: Mnemosyne Publishing, 1954 [1963]), 120.

264 **down to his last two hundred thousand dollars:** Last will and testament of Julio Lobo Olavarría, LAM.

265 **"I am happier now with nothing":** Letter to Hilda Krueger, Aug. 1974, LAVB.

BIBLIOGRAPHY

Aguilar, Luis E. 1974. *Cuba 1933: Prologue to Revolution*. Ithaca, NY: Cornell University Press.

Álvarez Álvarez, Luis, and Sed Nieves, Gustavo. 1997. *El Camagüey en Martí*. Havana: Editorial José Martí.

Alvarez Díaz, José R. 1963. *Estudio Sobre Cuba: Colonia, República, Experimento Socialista: estructura económica, desarollo institutional*. Coral Gables, FL: University of Miami Press.

Alvarez Tabío, Pedro. 2004. *Celia; ensayo para una biografía*. Havana: Oficina de Publicaciones del Consejo de Estado.

Ameringer, Charles. 2000. *The Cuban Democratic Experience: The Auténtico Years*. Gainesville: University Press of Florida.

Anderson, Jon Lee. 1997. *Che Guevara: A Revolutionary Life*. London: Bantam Press.

Antommarchi, C. Francesco. 1825. *The Last Days of the Emperor Napoleon*. 2 vols. London: Henry Colburn.

Anuario Azucarero de Cuba. 1960. Havana: Cuba Económica y Financiera.

Arenas, Reinaldo. 1993. *Before Night Falls*. London: Viking.

Argote-Freyre, Frank. 2006. *Fulgencio Batista: From Revolutionary to Strongman*. New Brunswick, NJ: Rutgers University Press.

Atkins, Edwin F. 1926. *Sixty Years in Cuba*. Cambridge, MA: Riverside Press.

Ayer, Pico. 1995. *Cuba and the Night*. London: Quartet.

Bacardí y Moreau, Emilio. 1972. *El Dr. Francisco Antommarchi: sus días en Cuba*. Madrid.

Bardach, Ann Louise. 2002. *Cuba Confidential*. New York: Penguin.

Beales, Carleton. 1933. *The Crime of Cuba*. Philadelphia and London.

Beauvoir, Simone de. 1965. *Force of Circumstance*. London: Penguin Books.

Beauman, Sally. 2003. Afterword in *Rebecca* by Daphne du Maurier. London: Virago Press.

Benítez-Rojo, Antonio. 1992. *The Repeating Island*. Durham, NC: Duke University Press.

Blackburn, Julia. 1997. *The Emperor's Last Island*. London: Vintage.

Brenner, Joël Glenn. 1999. *The Emperors of Chocolate*. New York: Random House.

Cabrera Infante, Guillermo. 1971. *Three Trapped Tigers*. New York: Harper & Row.

Cabrera Infante, Guillermo. 1988. *View of Dawn in the Tropics*. London: Faber & Faber.

Cabrera Infante, Guillermo. 1994. *Mea Cuba*. London: Faber & Faber.

Calzadilla Fierro, Luis. 2000. *Yo soy el Cabellero de Paris*. Badajoz, Spain: Graficas Diputación de Badajoz.

Carpentier, Alejo. 1978. *La Consagración de la Primavera*. Havana: Editorial Letras Cubanas.

Carr, Barry. "Mill Occupations and Soviets: The Mobilisation of Sugar Workers in Cuba, 1917–1933," *Journal of Latin American Studies*, No. 28, 1996, 129–56.

Carr, Barry. "Identity, Class, and Nation: Black Immigrant Workers, Cuban Communism, and the Sugar Insurgency, 1925–1934," *The Hispanic American Historical Review*, Vol. 78, No. 1, 1998, 83–116.

Casuso, Teresa. 1961. *Cuba and Castro*. New York: Random House.

Cepero Bonilla, Raúl. 1989. *Escritos históricos*. Havana: Editorial de Ciencias Sociales.

Chancellor, Edward. 1999. *Devil Take the Hindmost: A History of Financial Speculation*. New York: Farrar, Straus & Giroux.

Cirules, Enrique. 2004. *The Mafia in Havana*. New York: Ocean Press.

Cleveland, Harold Van B., and Thomas F. Huertas. 1985. *Citibank, 1812–1970.* Cambridge, MA: Harvard University Press.

Conte Agüero, Luis. 1955. *Eduardo Chibás, el adalid de Cuba.* Mexico: Editorial Jus.

Dana, Richard Henry. 1859. *To Cuba and Back.* London: Smith, Elder & Co..

Davis, Bette. 1987. *This 'n That.* New York: G. P. Putnam's Sons.

de Córdoba, José. "Cuba Through the Eyes of an Exile," *Wall Street Journal,* Sept. 9, 1987.

de Córdoba, José. "Tilting at Mills," *Wall Street Journal,* March 11, 1999.

Del Toro, Carlos. 2003. *La alta burguesía cubana, 1920–58.* Havana: Editorial Ciencias Sociales.

Didion, Joan. 1987. *Miami.* London: Weidenfeld & Nicolson Ltd.

Dominguez, Jorge. 1998. "The Batista Regime in Cuba," in *Sultanistic Regimes,* edited by H. E. Chehabi and Juan J. Linz. Baltimore: Johns Hopkins University Press.

Dominguez, Jorge. 1978. *Order and Revolution.* Cambridge, MA: Harvard University Press.

Echevarría, Oscar A., ed. 2002. *Captains of Industry: Miguel Angel Falla; the Cuban Sugar Industry.* Miami: New House Publishers.

Ely, Roland. 1963. *Cuando Reinaba Su Majestad El Azúcar.* Buenos Aires: Editorial Sudamericana.

Ely, Roland. 2005. "Las migraciones de los comerciantes sefarditas en el Gran Caribe: el caso de los Lobos Cubanos," *Asociación de Historiadores del Caribe,* XXXVII annual conference, Cartagena.

English, T. J. 2007. *Havana Nocturne: How the Mob Owned Cuba.* New York: William Morrow.

Estrada, Alfredo José. 2007. *Havana: Autobiography of a City.* New York: Palgrave.

Falcoff, Mark. 2003. *Cuba, the Morning After.* Washington, DC: AEI Press.

Farr's Manual of Sugar Companies. 1959. New York: Farr & Co.

Fontaine, Joan. 1978. *No Bed of Roses: An Autobiography.* New York: William Morrow.

Foreign Policy Association. 1935. *Problems of the New Cuba: Report of the Commission on Foreign Affairs.* New York.

Galmiche, Xavier, et al. 2001. *Havana: Districts of Light.* Paris: Vilo, Telleri.

García, Fe Iglesias. 2005. *Economía del Fin del Siglo.* Santiago: Instituto Cubano del Libro, Editorial Oriente.

García Márquez, Gabriel. 1981. *One Hundred Years of Solitude,* translated by Gregory Rabassa. London: Pan Books.

García Márquez, Gabriel. 1958. *Un Sábado en Londres.* In *Obra periodística. Vol 4. De Europa y America: 1955–60.* Edited by Jacques Gilard. Barcelona: Bruguera, 1983.

Geyer, Georgie Anne. 1991. *Guerilla Prince.* New York: Little, Brown and Company.

Gimbel, Wendy. 1999. *Havana Dreams: A Story of Cuba.* London: Virago.

Gjelten, Tom. 2008. *Bacardi and the Long Fight for Cuba.* New York: Viking.

González Echevarría, Roberto. 2001. *The Pride of Havana: A History of Cuban Baseball.* New York: Oxford University Press.

Gott, Richard. 2004. *Cuba: A New History.* New Haven, CT: Yale University Press.

Grant, James. 1983. *Bernard Baruch: The Adventures of a Wall Street Legend.* New York: Simon & Schuster.

Greene, Graham. 1958. *Our Man in Havana.* London: Penguin.

Greene, Graham. 1980. *Ways of Escape.* London: Bodley Head.

Guerra Alemán, José. 2007. *Cuba Infinita.* Vol. III—Los Tristes 30s y los Dinamicos 40s; Vol. IV— Los Fabulosas 50s. Miami, FL: Editorial Véritas.

Guillermoprieto, Alma. 2004. *Dancing with Cuba.* New York: Pantheon.

Hasselbalch, Varvara. 1997. *Varvara's Verden.* Copenhagen: Ascheoug Publishers.

Horne, Alistair. 2004. *The Age of Napoleon.* London: Weidenfeld & Nicolson.

Hyman. B. D. 1985. *My Mother's Keeper.* London: Michael Joseph.

Jenks, Leland Hamilton. 1928. *Our Cuban Colony: A Study in Sugar.* New York: Vanguard Press.

Jiménez, Guillermo. 2002. In Coyula, Mario (ed.), *La Habana que va conmigo.* Havana: Editorial Letras Cubanas.

Jiménez, Guillermo. 2004. *Las Empresas de Cuba, 1958.* Havana: Editorial de Ciencias Sociales.

Jiménez, Guillermo. 2006. *Los Propietarios de Cuba, 1958.* Havana: Editorial de Ciencias Sociales.

Jelly-Shapiro, Joshua. "An Empire of Vice," *The Nation,* June 10, 2009.

Kauffmann, Jean-Paul. 1999. *The Dark Room at Longwood.* London: The Harvill Press.

Keynes, John Maynard. 1983. *Collected Writings. Vol. XII. Economic Articles and Correspondence: Investment and Editorial.* London: Macmillan Press.

Krueger, Hilde. 1948. *La Malinche, or farewell to myths.* New York: Storm Publishers.

Lacey, Robert. 1991. *Little Man: Meyer Lansky and the Gangster Life.* London: Century.

Lamalle, Jacques. 1979. *Le Roi du Sucre.* Paris: Lattés.

Lampedusa, Giuseppe Tomasi di. 1986. *The Leopard,* translated by Archibald Colquhon. London: Collins Harvill.

Lenzer, Robert. 1985. *Getty: The Richest Man in the World.* London: Grafton Books.

León, Enrique. "Respuesta a José Pardo Llada: mis memorias de Julio Lobo," *El Nuevo Herald*, Oct. 8, 1990, 11A.

Levy, Shawn. 2005. *The Last Playboy: The High Life of Porfirio Rubirosa*. New York: HarperCollins.

Lincoln, Freeman. "Julio Lobo, Colossus of Sugar," *Fortune Magazine*, Vol. 58, No. 3, September 1958.

Lobo, Heriberto. 1937. "Apuntes Autobiográficos de Heriberto Lobo," LAM, mimeo.

Lobo Montalvo de González, Leonor. 1946. *Mi Ascensión al Pico de Turquino*. Havana.

Lobo Montalvo, María Luisa. 2000. *La Habana: Historia y Arquitectura de una Ciudad Romántica*. New York: Monacelli Press.

Lobo y Olvarría, Julio. 1933. *El Plan Chadbourne: nuestro cancer social*. Havana: Maza Cabo Impresores.

Lobo y Olvarría, Julio. 1957. *La Mascarilla de Napoleón Bonaparte*. Havana: Ucar García.

Lobo y Olvarría, Julio. 1959. *Lettres au Comte de Mollien: Département des Manuscrits à La Havane, Museo Julio Lobo*. Paris: Editions Charles Gay.

Lobo y Olvarría, Julio. "Tinguaro," *Compendio anual de la revista Cubazúcar*, Año IV, Diciembre 1958, No. 1.

Loeb, J. L. *All in a Life Time: A Personal Memoir*. New York: John L. Loeb.

Lowinger, Rosa, and Ofelia Fox. 2005. *Tropicana Nights: The Life and Times of the Legendary Cuban Nightclub*. Harcourt.

Loynaz del Castillo, Enrique. 1989. *Memorias de la Guerra*. Havana: Editorial de Ciencias Sociales.

Macintyre, Ben. 1997. *The Napoleon of Crime: The Life and Times of Adam Worth, Master Thief*. New York: Farrar, Straus & Giroux.

Martí, José. 2002. *Selected Writings*, translated by Esther Allen. London: Penguin Books.

McAvoy, Muriel. 2003. *Sugar Baron: The Life and Times of Manuel Rionda and the Fortunes of Pre-Castro Cuba*. Gainesville: University Press of Florida.

McLynn, Frank. 1997. *Napoleon: A Biography*. London: Jonathan Cape.

Merlin, Condesa de. 1842. *Viaje a la Habana*. Havana: Editorial de Arte y Literatura, 1974.

Montaner, Carlos Alberto. 1999. *Viaje al corazón de Cuba*. Barcelona: Plaza & Janés Editorial.

Montejo, Esteban. 1968. *The Diary of a Runaway Slave*, edited by Miguel Barnet. London: Bodley Head.

Morciego, Efrain. 1982. *El Crimen de Cortaderas*. Havana: Union de Escritores y Artistas de Cuba.

Moreno Fraginals, Manuel. 1978. *El Ingenio*. Vols. I, II, III. Havana: Editorial de Ciencias Sociales.

Ortiz, Fernando. 1947. *Cuban Counterpoint*, translated by Harriet de Onís. New York: Knopf.

Osa, Enrique de la. 1990. *Sangre y Pillaje*. Havana: Editorial Pablo de la Torriente.

Parada, Nemecio. 1973. *Vísperas y comienzos de la revolución de Cipriano Castro*. Caracas: Monte Ávila Editores.

Pardo Llada, José. "¿Quién recuerda a Julio Lobo?," *El Nuevo Herald*, Aug. 30, 1990, 13A.

Parker, John H. 1993. *We Remember Cuba*. 2nd ed. Sarasota, FL: Golden Quill.

Pederson, Susan. 2004. *Eleanor Rathbone and the Politics of Conscience*. New Haven, CT: Yale University Press.

Pérez, Louis A. 1988. *Cuba: Between Reform and Revolution*. New York: Oxford University Press.

Pérez, Louis A. 1999. *On Becoming Cuban*. Chapel Hill: University of North Carolina Press.

Perez-Cisneros, Pablo, John B. Donovan, and Jeff Koenreich. 2007. *After the Bay of Pigs*. Miami, FL: Alexandria Library Inc.

Pérez-Stable, Marifeli. 1993. *The Cuban Revolution: Origins, Course, Legacy*. New York: Oxford University Press.

Pérez Veiga, Virgilio. 1951. "Heriberto Lobo: un gran carácter que supo sonreír," LAM, mimeo.

Phillips, Ruby Hart. 1935. *Cuban Sideshow*. Havana: Manzana de Gomez.

Phillips, Ruby Hart. 1959. *Cuba: Island of Paradox*. New York: McDowell, Obolensky.

Picón-Salas, Mariano. 1953. *Los Días de Cipriano Castro*. Caracas: Ediciones Garrido.

Pittaluga, Gustavo. 1969 [1954]. *Diálogos sobre el destino*. 2nd ed. Miami, FL: Mnemosyne Publishing.

Pollitt, Brian H. "The Cuban Sugar Economy and the Great Depression," *Bulletin of Latin American Research*, Vol. 3, No. 2, 1984, 3–28.

Portell-Vilá, Herminio. 1986 [1996]. *Nueva historia de la Republica de Cuba*. 2nd ed. Miami, FL: La Moderna Poesía.

Rathbone, Cristina. "Cuban at Last," *Tropic Magazine; Miami Herald*, Oct. 31, 1993, 8–11.

Rexach, Rosario. "El Recuerdo de Julio Lobo," *Diario las Americas*, June 12, 1983.

Rodríguez L., Pedro Manuel. 1960. *El Segundo asalto al Palacio Presidencial*. Havana: Delegación del Gobierno.

Rojas, Rafael. 2006. *Tumbas sin Sosiego*. Barcelona: Editorial Anagrama.

Rojas, Rafael. 2008. *Motivos de Anteo*. Madrid: Editorial Colibrí.

Santamarina, Juan C. Forthcoming. *Cuba Company*. Chapter 3: "From Maturity to Dissolution, 1932–1959."

Schlesinger, Arthur M., Jr. 1965. *A Thousand Days*. Boston: Houghton Mifflin.

Schwartz, Rosalie. 1997. *Pleasure Island: Tourism and Temptation in Cuba*. Lincoln: University of Nebraska Press.

Scott, Rebecca Jarvis. 2005. *Degrees of Freedom: Louisiana and Cuba After Slavery*. New York: Harvard University Press.

Secades, Eladio. 1983. *Las Mejores Estampas de Secades: estampas costumbristas cubanas de ayer y de hoy*. Miami, FL: Ediciones Universal.

Soublette, Ned. 2004. *Cuba and Its Music: From the First Drums to the Mambo.* Chicago: Chicago Review Press.

Suarez Galbán, Luis. "Memorias de Luis Suarez Galbán," mimeo, Dec. 1914.

Symmes, Patrick. 2007. *The Boys from Dolores.* London: Constable & Robinson.

Szulc, Tad. 1986. *Fidel: A Critical Portrait.* London: William Morrow & Co.

Thomas, Dana. 1972. *The Money Crowd.* New York: G. P. Putnam & Sons.

Thomas, Hugh. 1998 [1971]. *Cuba: or the Pursuit of Freedom.* London: Da Capo Press.

Thomas, Hugh. 2000. Prologue to *La Habana: Historia y Architectura de una Ciudad Romántica,* by María Luisa Lobo Montalvo. New York: Monacelli Press.

Vázquez García, Humberto. 2005. *El Gobierno de la Kubanidad.* Santiago de Cuba: Editorial Oriente.

Villaverde, Cirilio. 2005. *Cecilia Valdés,* translated by Helen Lane. New York: Oxford University Press.

Voss, Ursula L. 2006. *Los Bacardí.* Random House, Mondadori.

Wallich, Henry Christopher. 1950. *Monetary Problems of an Export Economy: The Cuban Experience, 1914–47.* Boston: Harvard University Press.

Wilkinson, Alex. 1990. *Big Sugar.* New York: Vintage.

Williams, Esther. 1999. *The Million Dollar Mermaid.* New York: Simon & Schuster.

World Bank. 1950. *Report on Cuba.* Baltimore: Johns Hopkins University Press.

Yablonsky, Lewis. 1974. *George Raft.* New York: McGraw-Hill.

Zanetti, Oscar, and Alejandro García. 1998. *Sugar and Railroads: A Cuban History, 1837–1959.* Chapel Hill: University of North Carolina Press.

Zeckendorf, William. 1970. *The Autobiography of William Zeckendorf.* New York: Holt, Rinehart and Winston.

LIST OF ILLUSTRATIONS

1. My mother, Havana, 1955. Author's collection.
2. Julio Lobo portrait, with woman wearing dark glasses. LAM.
3. Julio Lobo in the trading room. LAM.
4. Wedding of John Rathbone and Margarita Sanchez, Havana, 1960. Author's collection.
5. Galbán Lobo mural, Old Havana. Author's collection.
6. Havana graffito. Author's collection.
7. Bernabé Sanchez at Senado. Author's collection.
8. Senado's *batey*. Author's collection.
9. Papa Né. Author's collection.
10. Heriberto and Virginia Lobo, Caracas, 1899. LAM.
11. Cipriano Castro in 1913. U.S. Library of Congress.
12. Leonor, Julio, Jacobo, and Helena Lobo. LAM.
13. Julio Lobo's old home. Author's collection.
14. Manuel Rionda, Tuinucú. Braga Brothers Collection, University of Florida.
15. "El Veneno," Louisiana, 1917. LAM.
16. Julio Lobo portrait. LAM.
17. Caribbean landscape, by Emilio Sanchez. Emilio Sanchez Foundation, New York.
18. Three soldiers at Senado. Author's collection.
19. María Esperanza Montalvo on her wedding day, 1932. LAM.
20. Galbán Lobo mural, Old Havana. Author's collection.
21. María Esperanza Lobo Montalvo portrait, c. 1945. LAM.
22. Leonor, María Esperanza, and María Luisa Lobo Montalvo portrait. LAM.
23. Cuban landscape, by Esteban Chartrand. LAM.
24. Bandaged Lobo, after 1946 shooting. LAM.
25. Carlos and Caridad Sanchez, Lake Placid. Author's collection.
26. Three generations of the Lobo family. LAM.
27. Lobo cartoon by Conrad Massaguer, courtesy of Guillermo Jiménez.
28. Julio Lobo's Napoleon room. LAM.
29. Napoelon's death mask. Hutton Collection of Life and Death Masks, Princeton University Library.
30. Lobo's ex libris. LAM.
31. An afternoon at Tinguaro, by Hipólito Caviedes. LAM.
32. Tinguaro's swimming pool. Author's collection.
33. Banco Financiero, Havana. LAM.
34. Varvara's photograph of Tinguaro's *batey*, copyright Varvara Hasselbalch.
35. María Luisa and Julio Lobo. LAM.
36. Havana Country Club, New Year's Eve. Author's collection.
37. Leonor and Julio Lobo. LAVB.
38. Lobo throws the first ball at Hershey. LAM.
39. Lobo talks to Humberto Sorí Marín, Havana, March 1959. LAVB.

INDEX